Felon for Peace

The Memoir of a Vietnam-Era Draft Resister

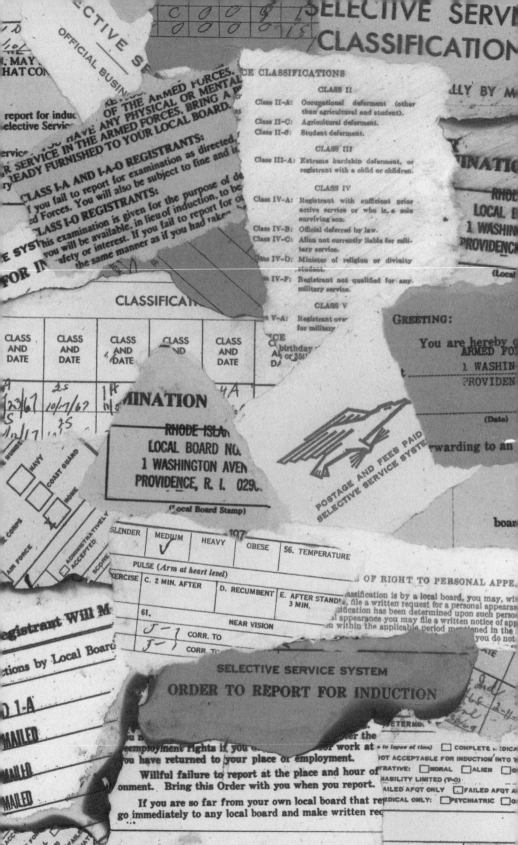

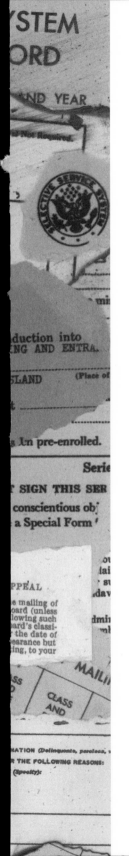

Felon for Peace

The Memoir of a

Vietnam-Era Draft Resister

Jerry Elmer

Vanderbilt University Press

NASHVILLE

10 09 08 07 06 05   1 2 3 4 5
Printed on acid-free paper
Manufactured in the United States of America

Frontispiece: Shredded draft files from the June 1970 raid
on the Providence draft boards. Collage by Peg Duthie.
Design by Dariel Mayer.

Library of Congress Cataloging-in-Publication Data

Elmer, Jerry, 1951–
Felon for peace : the memoir of a Vietnam-era
draft resister / Jerry Elmer.—1st ed.
    p. cm.
    Includes index.
ISBN 0-8265-1494-4 (cloth : alk. paper)
ISBN 0-8265-1495-2 (pbk. : alk. paper)
    1. Vietnamese Conflict, 1961–1975—Draft resisters—
United States. 2. Elmer, Jerry, 1951–
I. Title.
DS559.8.D7E46 2005
959.704'31—dc22

2005005031

To earlier generations of war resisters,
for having shown the way,
and to future generations of war resisters,
for continuing the struggle.

Contents

Illustrations

Acknowledgments

I AM GRATEFUL TO Dr. Scott Bennett, Dr. Joseph Gerson, Ms. Elizabeth Kaplan and Ms. Joan Webb for helpful comments on drafts of the manuscript. Dr. Bennett was also kind enough to point out and correct several factual inaccuracies.

I thank Michael Ames of Vanderbilt University Press for having the perception, when he received an oddball manuscript, to see what it might eventually become, and for having the patience to help me get it there. I thank Peg Duthie for the wisdom and humor she brought to copyediting.

Finally, I thank my wife, Anita Kestin, for love, patience, and encouragement.

Author's note: I have adopted a convention in this book with reference to names. People whom I know personally are generally referred to by their first names. People I do not know personally are usually referred to by their last names. Thus, for example, Phil Berrigan is "Phil," but President Nixon is not "Dick."

Introduction

ON MY EIGHTEENTH BIRTHDAY in 1969, at the height of the Vietnam War, I publicly refused to register for the draft, a felony punishable by five years' imprisonment (then and now). The statement I presented to what would have been "my" draft board began:

> I am a pacifist. That is, my opposition to the draft stems not merely from an opposition to the current war in Vietnam, but rather from an opposition to *all* wars. I could not cooperate with the Selective Service System even in "peacetime." The war in Vietnam could end tomorrow, but the basic nature and direction of American foreign policy would remain unchanged. Vietnam is not an isolated blemish tarnishing an otherwise noble record of American foreign policy. Vietnam is, rather, just another sore of the same disease that led us into Guatemala in 1954, and into the Dominican Republic in 1965.

That is, at the core of my political beliefs is a commitment to active nonviolence. It was this commitment that led me to decide not to go to college after high school, but to work for the War Resisters League (WRL) instead. During the first eighteen months after I graduated from high school, I burglarized fourteen draft boards in three cities on the East Coast, destroying the files of men eligible to be drafted and rendering those draft boards inoperable. I went on to work full-time in the nonviolent peace movement for almost twenty years. (When I later attended law school, I was the only convicted felon in Harvard Law School's class of 1990.)

My commitment to nonviolence is both an ethical or philosophical one *and* a practical or tactical one.

Pacifism is, first, a moral commitment. It is the violence against and the killing of human beings that make war wrong. Many wars in history have been fought for noble goals; the opposition in World War II of the Allied powers to Hitler and the Axis is just one contemporary example. But the means to achieve those goals have been horrific. In the case of World War II, for example, the Allied fire-bombings of Dresden and Tokyo and the American atomic bombings of Hiroshima and Nagasaki come to mind. To a pacifist, the bloody calculus that the end justifies the means is never acceptable.

In 1946, the United States and the other victorious Allied powers held war crimes trials at Nuremberg for Nazi war criminals. We indicted, tried, convicted, and sentenced to death Hermann Göring, the head of the German *Luftwaffe* (air force) for, among other things, the "indiscriminate destruction of cities" (Count I, Section III of the indictment). That is, we said that targeting civilian populations for ærial bombardment, even in a time of war, was a crime against humanity—indeed, a hanging offense.

How could it be, we pacifists ask, that the saturation bombing of cities is a crime against humanity when Germans do it, but is okay if we do it? Either an action is a shameful crime against humanity or it is not. It cannot be that the same action, killing the same number of innocent civilians, is a ghastly crime when *they* do it, but morally acceptable, even laudable, when *we* do it.

As the child of two Jewish refugees from Nazi Europe, I have always been acutely conscious of the lessons of Nuremberg and of the catastrophic consequences that can result when otherwise civilized people ignore their consciences because they are merely "following orders." That awareness often animated my thoughts and motivated my actions during the Vietnam War, and today can be seen reflected in my writing from that period.

Yet my commitment to nonviolence also has a very practical dimension. The great pacifist leaders of our time—Mohandas Gandhi, Martin Luther King Jr., A. J. Muste, David McReynolds—were not just moral leaders; they were extremely shrewd political tacticians as well. There are only two possible ways that activists can bring about social change: through violent agitation or through nonviolent action. And whichever way an activist hopes to change the world, he or she must concede that

more people are needed before we can create the kind of world we want.
That is, the very reason social change *advocates* have to be *activists* is
that the world of which we dream is not here yet; more people need to
be recruited to our cause.

Violent action turns people against the peace movement. Violence
engenders fear, and terrorism, which is an extreme form of political violence, engenders extreme fear. The social change movement needs more
widespread public acceptance of our views and aims. Movement violence isolates us and diminishes our public support.

This is true even in the case of carefully planned, narrowly focused
actions of political violence—so-called vanguard or exemplary actions.
In her autobiography, *Living My Life* (1931), Emma Goldman tells about
the assassination attempt that her political comrade and lover, Alexan-
der (Sasha) Berkman, made on Henry Clay Frick in Pittsburgh, Pennsylvania, on July 22, 1892, at the height of the Homestead steel strike.
This was a time of great political agitation; as Goldman writes elsewhere,
both the strike itself and the murderous anti-strike activities of Frick had
already "aroused the whole country to the slavery and exploitation in
the steel industry." Goldman and Berkman were certain that Berkman's
heroic action would be the spark that would ignite the toiling proletar-
ian masses to rise up in socialist revolution. In her autobiography, Goldman describes her own and Sasha's genuine bewilderment—indeed,
complete bafflement—that the assassination attempt did not have that
result at all.

Much the same tone of surprise emerges from the communiqués
of the Weather Underground, a violent faction of Students for a Democratic Society (SDS), in the early 1970s, when the organization was engaged in political bombings. As with the attempted Frick assassination,
the Weather Underground's bombings came at a time of great political
turmoil and upheaval. As with Berkman's carefully planned and narrowly focused attempt on one man's life, the Weather Underground's
bombings were of carefully selected targets such as the Pentagon and
the U.S. Capitol—unmistakable symbols, so they thought, of U.S. imperialism. Like Goldman and Berkman before them, the Weather Underground genuinely believed that their exemplary actions in bombing
these carefully selected targets would cause an uprising of the masses
in the United States, in the latter case in solidarity with Vietnamese

revolutionaries and oppressed people throughout the Third World. And like Goldman and Berkman before them, the members of the Weather Underground were amazed and astonished when their actions did not have the anticipated result.

None of these people should have been surprised. Radical social change is, and by definition must be, threatening to an entrenched status quo. Violence, even when it is carefully targeted, is particularly off-putting. The Weather Underground, by operating secretly, did nothing to put a more human, more palatable face onto their actions; they gave the public nothing with which it could identify.

Nonviolent direct action seeks to address these problems in a way that works. By acting openly and publicly, nonviolent activists seek to maximize the opportunities for explaining our motives and actions to the public. By eschewing violence—even carefully targeted violence—we seek to avoid alienating the very people we are trying to reach and influence. We see our deliberate use of tactical nonviolence as a way of broadening and strengthening our movement in a way that can never happen through the use of violence.

Yet, I was always concerned that my commitment to pacifism not be confused with passiveness. Through my actions—demonstrations, sit-ins, Selective Service nonregistration, raiding draft boards and destroying files—I hoped to show the real power and effectiveness of active nonviolence.

1
School

I WAS THE KIND OF STUDENT who caused even highly committed teachers to reconsider their career choice.

I know this to be literally, not just figuratively, true. In 1974, Congress passed, by overriding President Nixon's veto, the so-called Buckley Amendment that opened to students the records that schools kept on them. This was a huge and abrupt change in policy, for the files had always been secret. On the day Congress overrode the presidential veto, I went to Great Neck South Senior High School demanding access to my entire file, grades one through twelve. The Buckley Amendment was, at that point, only a few hours old, so it took a while for the school to dig my file out of the archive, but they did find it and I spent the afternoon reviewing its contents. One of my former teachers, a mid-career professional, had written that, after having had to deal with me in class all year, she was seriously thinking of leaving teaching.

I understand that there was something fundamentally unfair about the operation of the Buckley Amendment. All the comments I read had been written by teachers who had been promised that their comments would be kept confidential, and who had obviously relied on that promise when they had decided what to write. Nevertheless, understanding that the situation was unfair did not stop me from gleefully demanding my file the very day the law first permitted such access.

Throughout elementary, junior high, and senior high school, I was a classic underachiever. Some quarters, my grades were nearly all As; other quarters, my grades were all Cs and Ds. In ninth grade, I flunked Latin; in twelfth grade, I flunked third-year algebra. My algebra teacher that year, Mrs. Saunders, was a very good teacher. She knew her subject well, explained everything clearly, and was patient with the questions from students who didn't get it. It was not Mrs. Saunders's fault that I flunked her course. The reason I flunked algebra was that I did no work for the class.

"Jerry, you are such a bright student. You could do well in school if only you would apply yourself." "Jerry, you are so intelligent; there is no reason for you to be getting Ds." "If only you would buckle down and work, you would be able to get good grades." This was the litany I heard endlessly from teachers and from my parents. I felt that if I heard the word "underachiever" one more time I would throttle somebody.

But laziness—nay, an almost complete refusal to do any school-work—was not my only problem. I was also disruptive in class: inter-rupting, sassing back, and generally acting up. In sixth grade, I was sent to the principal's office endlessly. In seventh grade, I had to write some of the homeroom announcements 100 times because I did not listen when they were being read, and I frequently knocked the books out of classmate Steven Cohen's arms while we were in the halls between classes. Later, working in the peace movement, I spent much time as a guest speaker at high schools and colleges and, in retrospect, I can well understand how extremely frustrating and exasperating it must have been for my teachers to have had me as a student in class.

One brief exception to my almost uniformly bad experiences in ele-mentary and high school was fifth grade. My fifth-grade teacher, Miss Ely, was unequivocally the best teacher I ever had. Miss Ely was warm, humorous, and unorthodox in the extreme.

I am not sure how she did it, but Miss Ely really conveyed a sense of the joy of learning. At no other time in elementary school did I work as hard as I did in fifth grade; nor did I enjoy school so much; nor did I learn as much. The sense of excited curiosity I got in fifth grade was pretty well stifled in junior high and high school—so much so that after high school I had to have a fifteen-year hiatus before I was truly ready to go to college. But when I did go to college, I loved it and I did well, which showed that the seeds planted by Miss Ely had not been entirely killed off by the likes of later teachers like Miss Kozlarek; those seeds had merely been lying dormant for twenty-three years.

Among the most important of the ideas Miss Ely imparted was the concept of critical thinking. *Everything* was viewed skeptically and was open to question: *is that true or not? Is this a fact or opinion? Do you have facts to support that assertion? What is the source of your information? Is the source biased?* We carefully examined newspapers for hidden bias. Textbooks were scrutinized for opinion masquerading as fact. Jeff Grabelsky gave a report on Cuba and said that Batista had been a bad dictator; *did Jeff have facts to support that opinion?* I have always attributed my ability to think critically and skeptically to the influence of Miss Ely. It was probably her most valuable legacy to her students.

Miss Ely was very big on constructive criticism. When we commented on the oral presentations of our classmates—and we always did—our own comments had to be constructive. We were not allowed merely to observe what was wrong with a report but were supposed also to suggest how it could be improved. "This was an excellent report but . . . " became a commonplace.

Current events were important in Miss Ely's curriculum. (My parents were appalled. *How can mere children be expected to understand current events,* they wondered, *when they have no concept of history? Let them study the Peloponnesian Wars before they dip into the civil war in the Congo.*) In Miss Ely's class, students each chose a continent and had to collect newspaper clippings dealing with that continent. We pasted these into scrapbooks, side by side with the students' own commentaries about what the articles discussed, and periodically made oral reports on our continents.

For some reason, when it came my turn to choose a continent, they had all been taken. I got the United Nations and, unlike my classmates, who switched continents from time to time, I stuck with the UN all year. Kathleen Teltsch was the UN correspondent for the *New York Times* in the early 1960s; it was the time of the Congolese civil war; and the UN had its first big debt crisis because the Soviet Union refused to pay its special assessment for the UN peacekeeping force sent to the Congo. All this went into my current events scrapbook. On weekends I would take the Long Island Railroad into Manhattan and go to UN headquarters; I took the guided tour so often that I came to know much of the guides' commentary by heart. I started collecting UN stamps.

The idea of an international body dedicated to world peace became more and more important to me. I wrote to public figures asking their views on the UN, and received a wonderful reply from the U.S. Ambassador to the UN, Adlai Stevenson:

My own conviction, which I have expressed many times but am glad to repeat for you and your fellow students, is that the United Nations is the alternative to war. It provides a place for world opinion to be formed and felt, for the process of quiet diplomacy to explore solutions for difficult issues. It encourages words and discourages force.

Two years later, when my seventh-grade social studies teacher, Mrs. Gloth, asked her students to choose topics for current events, I again chose the United Nations and again kept my topic throughout the year while my classmates changed theirs from time to time.

Miss Ely's ideas were very often offbeat. For Christmas presents, she contributed a dollar in the name of each student in the class to the relief and development agency CARE, and then discussed with us poverty in the world, hunger during the holidays, and the spirit of sharing. When the Israelis kidnapped and tried Adolf Eichmann in 1962, Miss Ely's views were typically unorthodox. Hannah Arendt wrote, in her now-famous *Eichmann in Jerusalem* (1963), that Eichmann deserved death for the simple reason that he had sought to wipe an entire people off the face of the earth. I remember discussing the Eichmann trial with my grandfather. Although I knew that my family had had trouble with the Nazis (my entire family were refugees), I little realized at the time how directly Eichmann in particular had ruled the fate of my relatives. "Hanging is too good for Eichmann," my grandfather said. "They should kill him slowly, cutting off a limb per day." Miss Ely disagreed. It would be sufficient punishment, she argued, to make Eichmann—perhaps by means of psychiatric care—truly comprehend the magnitude of the evil he had perpetrated.

Miss Ely ran an "open classroom" long before the book about open classrooms was published and long before the idea came into vogue. The first thing we did each morning was to plan the day. This was done democratically, with each person in the class encouraged to make suggestions about how we would spend our time. Each suggestion was considered, debated, accepted or rejected. Like us, Miss Ely could make suggestions—"I have some math work I'd like to do with you today"—but, like ours, her ideas were evaluated critically and sometimes rejected.

Each day a student volunteer would write our agreed-upon schedule on the blackboard, along with a quotation or aphorism (often humorous) of his or her choosing. Some agenda items were standard each day: lunch, recess, and "smorgasbord" (the thirty minutes immediately after recess we all spent reading). What was fun for us each morning was crafting the rest of our day. The message that came through to the students through this unconventional process was that Miss Ely respected us. We knew this because she treated our ideas for how to spend the day respectfully.

My familiarity with Miss Ely's way of planning our school day got me into trouble with my new teacher, Miss Kozlarek, on the very first day of sixth grade. "The first thing we'll do each day in class," said Miss Kozlarek, her voice fairly dripping with condescension, "is we'll plan the day together." Miss Kozlarek then proceeded to write on the board her predetermined schedule for every minute of the day. A student raised a hand and made a suggestion for some activity or other and was promptly overruled by Miss Kozlarek. The student's suggestion was not on her prearranged plan. This certainly wasn't the process I had grown accustomed to in Miss Ely's class! I asked Miss Kozlarek why she had said we would plan the day *together* when what she obviously meant was that she would plan our time herself, announce her plans to us imperiously, and that we would have to follow her wishes whether we wanted to or not. This was the beginning of a very bad year.

I would love to be able to say that my general disruptiveness in school was a consequence of boredom—that I was an intelligent student who disrupted class merely out of boredom. Such an idea has some superficial appeal. After all, I did passably well in fifth grade because Miss Ely knew how to challenge me. But I do not think that boredom was the main problem. After all, many of the classes I took—physics, chemistry, algebra, trigonometry, Latin—were quite challenging and certainly kept brighter students than I productively occupied. I think the real problem was that at home I was locked in a constant battle with my parents and, as a result, when I came to school I was tense and angry, and I acted out a lot.

One thing that interested me in 1974 when I reviewed my school records was the high correlation between my emotional recollection of

certain teachers and what they had written about me. Many of my teachers wrote similar things: Jerry is a bright kid with poor social skills; he
could probably do reasonably well in life if he were able to get a grip on
his behavior issues; I hope he does and I wish him well in the future.
This struck me as rather insightful. But Miss Kozlarek had written that
I was a bad kid—bad in the sense of being truly evil. Her evaluation of
me jibed accurately with my recollection of her. I had thought she was a
witch (and, on one occasion, I had told her so to her face).

I was not a model student.

2
Students for Peace in Vietnam

MY PARENTS HAD COME OF AGE in this country and were liberals, but were not especially active politically. They supported Adlai Stevenson for president in 1952 and 1956, and although they had never been members of the Communist or Socialist parties, they had friends who had been. When I was growing up politics were not the most important discussion topic around our dinner table. Nevertheless, my parents and I read the *New York Times* every day, and we discussed the events of the day at the dinner table.

Because of their liberal views, my parents were mostly supportive of my anti-war work when I was a teenager. My father took me to my first Vietnam peace demonstration on Saturday, November 27, 1965, in Washington, DC. This was one of the first large demonstrations against the war. We went with one of my father's tennis partners, Bob Praver, taking a special train from New York chartered by the peace group SANE to bring demonstrators to Washington.

The large crowds of peace demonstrators made a big impression on me. I had been a bit tentative in my anti-war views and had felt myself part of an isolated minority. It felt exhilarating to be part of a crowd of 30,000 people who shared my views; I lost my squeamishness when I realized that, while I might be part of a minority, I was certainly not alone. For several years after that, when people asked about the efficacy of the large demonstrations, I thought about how they not only affected government policy but also provided encouragement and support to antiwar people by showing them that they were not alone in their heresy.

During the rally at the Washington Monument, I told my father that I was going to look for my social studies teacher, Mr. Foote, whom I

knew was there, and that I would be back in half an hour. When I look
back on that now, I cringe: a fourteen-year-old boy going off on his own
in a crowd of 30,000 demonstrators; the ever-present risk of violence;
the hopelessness of finding a particular person in that crowd; and the
virtual certainty of not connecting again with my father. But I walked
directly to where I figured Mr. Foote would be, found him, chatted
for a while, and then returned to my father without incident. After
that, I always made a habit of looking for people I knew at the big peace
demonstrations.

At that demonstration, I bought a large blue lapel button that read
"Peace in Vietnam." The following week, I wore the button to school.
One of my teachers, Mr. Ranhoeffer, who was pro-war, instructed
me to take it off. I refused, and Mr. Ranhoeffer sent me to the school
office to be disciplined. The principal supported Mr. Ranhoeffer and ordered me to remove the button, but I confronted him with a written
policy adopted by the Great Neck Board of Education that said students
were permitted to wear buttons to class. I returned to class wearing the
button.

After that initial demonstration in Washington, my involvement in
the peace movement grew rapidly and I became active in Great Neck
Students for Peace in Vietnam (SPV). The following spring I helped SPV
distribute publicity flyers for the March 26, 1966, peace demonstration
in New York. My father did not attend that demonstration, but I went
with Mr. Foote and Mrs. Kramer, a English teacher at my junior high
school. In Central Park, they introduced me to two social studies teachers from the high school whom I would soon come to know, Mr. Parker
and Mr. Horne.

In early October 1966, I heard that President Johnson was going to
make an appearance on Columbus Day, Wednesday, October 12, in
Salisbury Park, in East Meadow, Long Island. The event was to be a campaign rally for some local Democratic congressmen, including our own
Lester Wolff, a moderate Democrat, who represented New York's Third
Congressional District. I decided to organize a anti-war demonstration
in Salisbury Park to coincide with the president's visit.

In later years I would gain much experience in the mechanics and
logistics of organizing demonstrations, but in October 1966 I was a fif-

teen-year-old high school student who had never done anything like this before. First, I enlisted SPV. The group activated its telephone tree to get its members to participate in the demonstration. The head of the phone tree called twenty "callers" who each had a list of 10–12 students to whom to relay a given message.

This was a start, but more had to be done. For one thing, most of us did not drive and we needed transportation from Great Neck to East Meadow. So I called Alice Miller, the head of the local Women Strike For Peace. Would they join our demonstration (and, incidentally, provide car-pools for our student demonstrators)? Alice agreed.

Next, I called the press to let them know of the demonstration. I was amazed when, only a few hours after I made the first press call, I was called by a Secret Service agent in New York City who inquired in some detail about our plans. My surprise reflected my inexperience.

We made signs to carry at the demonstration, and I called a few other student peace groups on Long Island to see if they would join us. One from Friends World College in Westbury did. In the end, about 250 people participated in the demonstration, mostly from SPV and Women Strike for Peace.

Despite my complete lack of experience in organizing such events, the demonstration somehow took place without logistical problems. And we were big news in the local press. *Newsday*, Long Island's major daily newspaper, gave our small demonstration almost equal play with the president's speech. The headline in Thursday's newspaper was: "LBJ Slaps GOP and Backlash/LI Hecklers Give Him a Hard Time." The entire rest of the front page was taken up with two large photographs printed side by side. On the left was President Johnson addressing the crowd. On the right was a good shot of our demonstration, showing three signs: "Support Our Boys: Bring Them Home NOW," "War on Poverty, Not on People," and "Liar, Butcher, Jingoist" (a play on the president's initials).

On December 6, 1966, I attended a lecture in Great Neck on the draft, held in the auditorium of one of the public schools in town. The speaker was someone I had never heard of from an organization I had never heard of: David McReynolds, of WRL. McReynolds was an electrifying speaker—the best in the peace movement. He started out this way:

There are two words in the English language I am thinking of right now. The first is a very common four-letter Anglo-Saxon word that describes a form of lovemaking. When people do this, babies are sometimes produced. This word is considered obscene, and if I use that word here, you will read in the newspaper tomorrow how David McReynolds was arrested for obscenity. The second word I am thinking of is 'napalm.' Napalm burns babies. But 'napalm' is not considered obscene; I can say 'napalm' all I want and nothing will happen: napalm, napalm, napalm.

If you think that napalm is dirtier and more obscene than the four-letter words that got Lenny Bruce busted all up and down the United States, then you have a serious problem.

And he went on to talk about the draft, and especially about how young men should not *evade* the draft but rather *confront* and oppose it. I was so taken with the speech that, at the end of the evening, I went home and wrote it down, from beginning to end, from memory. I did not know it at the time, but this was a standard talk of Dave's—basically the same talk that was later made into a pamphlet, *Uptight With the Draft.* The pamphlet was a WRL best-seller during the late 1960s, and, like Dave himself, helped to influence a generation of conscientious objectors and resisters. Some years later, when I saw the pamphlet, I was amazed at how accurately and completely I had transcribed Dave's speech from memory back in December 1966.

I am sure that, like me, a significant percentage of the pacifist portion of the peace movement came into the movement through the influence of Dave's speaking or writing. I remember especially the flyer that WRL members distributed by the tens of thousands at the November 15, 1969, Moratorium demonstration in Washington, DC. The title was *Give Earth A Chance.* That piece, like all of Dave's writing, was in that classic, unique, and completely unmistakable McReynolds voice. By then I was on the WRL staff. We had a huge—in fact, unprecedented—response to the reply coupon at the bottom of that leaflet. I am sure that many WRL members today, a generation later, first discovered WRL through that flyer or through some other speech or article of Dave's.

At the same time, I do not want to overly idealize Dave. I also remember quite clearly that the text of *Give Earth A Chance* was due at the printer by a certain date so that we could get the copies back in time to distribute to our many volunteer leafleters. Dave, however, had trouble focusing his energies that autumn (more on this in chapter 4). At our weekly staff meetings at WRL that autumn, Ralph DiGia, who was as close to an office manager as the non-hierarchical WRL ever got, repeatedly pestered Dave for the text. But, week after week, Dave had nothing to give us. We finally got the text, just in the nick of time, the leaflet was printed and distributed, and it was a big success—but, due to Dave's tardiness, it very nearly did not happen at all.

As a result of hearing Dave's lecture that Tuesday evening in Great Neck, I started getting involved with WRL in addition to my work with SPV. WRL is a pacifist organization that had been founded in 1923 by opponents of U.S. involvement in World War I. The membership pledge of WRL was admirably simple:

> War is a crime against humanity. I therefore am determined not to support any war, international or civil, and to strive for the removal of all the causes of war.

(The text was slightly changed in the early 1970s.) Membership was open to those sixteen years of age and older. I thought a lot about whether I really was a pacifist, and on my sixteenth birthday I signed the pledge and mailed it in to WRL.

During the summer of 1967, I got the idea of having lapel buttons made featuring a famous quotation of pacifist leader A. J. Muste: "There is no way to peace; peace is the way." I planned to donate the proceeds to WRL. I found a button manufacturer in Manhattan and had 1,000 buttons made for $52, or 5.2 cents each. I sold the buttons for twenty-five cents each, the going rate for political lapel buttons at the time. That autumn, after I had made back my initial investment, I showed up at the WRL office with a wad of bills and a pile of coins, the proceeds of my little enterprise.

I became a regular visitor to the WRL office: first at 5 Beekman Street, near the Brooklyn Bridge exit of the Lexington Avenue subway, and later at 339 Lafayette Street. I came to know their staff: Jim Peck, who greeted visitors and put a short blurb about my button sales into the

WRL newsletter; Igal Roodenko, a part-time staff person who also ran a printing business on the Lower East Side; Dave McReynolds; and Ralph DiGia.

Jim, Igal, and Ralph had all been imprisoned during World War II as draft resisters. This was a real eye-opener for me; it cast the growing contemporary movement of draft resistance to the Vietnam War in a most interesting historical perspective. Draft resistance was not a recent development, newly invented in response to current events in Vietnam, but rather an older technique being adopted by a new generation of peace activists.

In the autumn of 1967, when I was starting eleventh grade, I started the first of two one-year terms as co-chairman of SPV. In October, we chartered a bus to bring our members to Washington for the October 21, 1967, "Confront the Warmakers" demonstration, which included the now-famous sit-in and civil disobedience at the Pentagon. Although I participated in the legal mass demonstration, I did not participate in the civil disobedience at the Pentagon the next day. I was sixteen years old, and dared not get arrested without my parents' approval (which I did not have).

The winter and spring of 1968 was the time of the Tet Offensive in Vietnam, launched by the liberation forces on January 29, 1968. This was a turning point in the war—perhaps not in the actual military situation on the ground in Vietnam, but certainly in the attitude of the American public toward U.S. intervention. Before the Tet Offensive, listening to U.S. officials talking about the war was like listening to Voltaire's Dr. Pangloss. Everything was going perfectly well for the United States in Vietnam and things were getting better all the time! Whenever our side suffered what appeared to be a setback, there was an American official on television telling us that we had turned the corner at last and could see the light at the end of the tunnel.

The Tet Offensive, during which American and South Vietnamese forces were for a time badly routed throughout South Vietnam, put an end to that view. It changed the outlook of the American people with regard to the war. In a nationwide Gallup poll released on December 7, 1967, just before the Tet Offensive, 52% of the people polled described themselves as "hawks" and only 35% described themselves as "doves." Less than a year later, in a Gallup poll released on August 7, 1968, when asked "Do you think the U.S. made a mistake sending troops to fight in Vietnam?" 53% answered yes and only 35% answered no. This was the first time that a respected national poll reflected an anti-war majority.

Americans' change of heart, however, was a shallow one. The problem for most Americans was mainly that it now appeared we could not win. As the *New York Times* put it in a lead editorial on March 24, 1968, "The futility of escalation has long been evident . . . the search for a military solution is futile . . ." A very similar tone emerges from the much-ballyhooed editorial against the war by CBS News anchorman Walter Cronkite, widely viewed at the time as "the most trusted man in America." On February 27, 1968, shortly after returning from a news-gathering trip to Vietnam, Cronkite startled hawks and doves alike by broadcasting an editorial critical of the war. But Cronkite's criticism, too, was rooted in the fact that the war did not seem to be working: "It seems now more certain than ever that the bloody experience of Vietnam is a stalemate."

To the *Times*, to Cronkite, and to many Americans, the problem with the war was not that the United States was perpetrating crimes against humanity, but rather that the crimes did not seem to be achieving their intended goal. In their view, it was the futility of the war, not its immorality, that was the central problem. Even the wording of the August 1968 Gallup poll was troubling because it failed to distinguish between the views of those who thought it a "mistake" to have sent troops to Vietnam because to do so was wrong and immoral, and those who thought it a "mistake" because it appeared we were not winning.

To be sure, there were a great many problems with the war, but the factor perceived by too many Americans at that time, that we were not winning, was emphatically not one of them. One actual problem was that we had gone in on the wrong side, fighting against the side struggling for freedom and independence for their country. We were supporting an unpopular and totalitarian puppet government whose own people were immolating themselves in the streets in protest against that government. We were committing atrocities beyond number and pursuing policies, including targeting civilians, which were internationally recognized as war crimes.

The Tet Offensive in the spring of 1968 turned many Americans against the war, but did little to deepen their perception or understanding of what exactly was wrong.

During the spring of 1968, I was organizing the local part of the national "academic strike" to be held on Friday, April 26, the day before that spring's big peace demonstrations in New York, San Francisco, and other cities. In Great Neck, instead of having students simply boycott regular classes as part of the academic strike, SPV set up a "peace school" at a local synagogue, featuring a full day of lectures and seminars conducted by local and national peace movement leaders. We spent months publicizing the project, contacting speakers and making the logistical arrangements.

On the day of the strike, 1,100 Great Neck high school students attended our Peace School, far more than the number that attended either of Great Neck's two high schools that day. The regular high schools looked like they had been hit by an epidemic: some classes that normally had twenty-five students in them had only two or three in attendance. During the lunch hour, a large contingent of teachers arrived at the Peace School, to a thunderous ovation from their students.

Discipline and decorum at the Peace School were spectacular. Although not all of the SPV members had agreed with me, I had exercised the prerogative of leadership and had insisted that boys wear ties and jackets and girls skirts or dresses. This was in the context of a student body that had just won a long and bitterly fought battle with the school authorities to eliminate the dress code (a battle in which I had not been involved, because I thought the issue trivial). Cut-off jeans, tee-shirts, slacks for girls—these were now all allowed at school. Although I had no enforcement powers whatsoever, not a single student came to the Peace School without proper dress. The insistence on proper dress was classic, idiosyncratic Jerry Elmer; nearly twenty years later, my colleagues in the American Friends Service Committee teased me by saying that they could always tell when I was going to get arrested by engaging in civil disobedience, because it was the only time I wore a suit.

The Peace School went without a hitch, and the publicity we received was extensive and very favorable. Multiple photographs (taken

Jerry Elmer (*in profile,* wearing armband) greeting high school faculty members at the Peace School, set up by Great Neck Students for Peace in Vietnam on Friday, April 26, 1968, during the nationwide academic strike to protest the Vietnam War. Mr. Parker is shown at far left, Mr. Horne at far right. Photograph by Philip R. Olenick.

by my good friend Phil Olenick) and an excellent article appeared on the front page of the *Great Neck Record,* the local weekly newspaper.

Parents did not attend the Peace School but my mother had wanted very much to come and I had told her she could. Afterwards she told me how proud she was of me. I had not had a bar mitzvah, but Mom said that she felt that, in a way, this had been similar to a bar mitzvah: it was a public event in which I had stood before the community and proved myself to be a man.

The spring 1968 period in the peace movement is widely misunderstood by historians. Charles DeBenedetti, considered by many to be the dean of historians of the peace movement, writes in *An American Ordeal* (1990) that, in the wake of President Johnson's announcement on March 31, 1968, he would negotiate with the Vietnamese in Paris and that he would not run for re-election, "anti-war activists tried to rouse people to the fact that . . . the war is not over" but that the effort was largely unsuccessful because "the country wanted to believe otherwise." The dovish historian Melvin Small, in *Johnson, Nixon, and the Doves* (1989), tells a very similar story: "With the withdrawal of Johnson from the primary campaign [and] the agreement in early April by Hanoi to open peace talks . . . the peace movement lost some of its energy." Even Dan Ellsberg, who ought to know better, writes in his Vietnam memoir, *Secrets* (2002), "For two years after Lyndon Johnson's decision not to run again for president, from his announcement on March 31, 1968, to Nixon's invasion of Cambodia on April 30, 1970, the Vietnam War more or less disappeared from the mainstream political debate as a major issue."

This view, widely held by historians, simply does not comport with the facts. Saturday, April 27, 1968, saw mass legal demonstrations in New York and San Francisco every bit as large as the mass legal demonstrations in New York on April 15, 1967, and in Washington, DC, on October 21, 1967. At another demonstration the same day in Chicago, perhaps 20,000 people took part and more than fifty people were arrested. The previous day, students at hundreds of colleges and high schools nationwide took part in the academic strike described earlier; in the New York metropolitan area alone, an estimated 200,000 students took part. The day after the Saturday demonstrations, a four-page advertisement appeared in the Sunday *New York Times* in which over 500 student leaders from small and large colleges in all parts of the country denounced the war as "immoral and unjust."

And there was much, much more.

April 1968 also saw the uprising at Columbia University. The war was one of two major issues for the protesters, who focused on the university's connection to the military through the Institute for Defense Analysis. (The other major issue was the university's plans to build a gymnasium in the adjacent Morningside Heights neigborhood, a plan opposed by local community groups.) The Columbia students' analysis of this military-university complex was remarkably sophisticated, and was all the more admirable because it came relatively early in the war. The Columbia students occupied several buildings for almost a week, and it took 1,000 of New York City's finest finally to evict them. Seven hundred and eleven students were arrested, making their protest the largest civil disobedience on an American college campus up to that point—or since.

On April 3, there were nationally coordinated draft resistance activities. (I discuss the April 3 draft card burnings and their significance in the next chapter.) On May 17, the Catonsville Nine draft-board Action occurred, signaling the beginning of what was to become a widespread tactic of peace activists invading draft boards and destroying files. (I discuss this development in chapters 4 to 6.) In August, thousands took part in the weeklong anti-war protests in Chicago at the Democratic National Convention. In fact, the sustained national press coverage of those demonstrations for nearly a week—and, especially, of the brutal police riot that the demonstrations sparked—was probably the longest continuous coverage of any peace activity during the entire war.

And, as I already mentioned, this period saw a majority of Americans for the first time turn against the war, as reflected in the Gallup poll.

In short, whether measured by quiet public sentiment, mass legal demonstrations, tumultuous student uprising, draft resistance, or other radical civil disobedience, the period following President Johnson's March 31, 1968, speech was *not*, as many historians seem to believe, a lull in the peace movement. In this sense, my own activities as a student anti-war organizer during this period tracked reasonably well what was going on in the wider movement.

In the summer of 1968, between our junior and senior years in high school, my friend Steve Dreisin and I took a bike trip together through New England. Steve and I had met in fourth grade, and throughout junior high and high school we frequently found ourselves in classes together.

When Steve and I were in elementary school, my mother frequently held Steve up as a paragon of good behavior. *Why can't you behave well, the way Steve Dreisin does?* my mother often asked me. Steve always found this amusing. He considered himself quite neurotic, and spent much time and psychic energy wrestling with his inner demons. Steve found it ironic and laughable that my mother would hold *him* up as an exemplar of good behavior.

In twelfth-grade English, Steve sat in the front row of the classroom; I sat directly behind him. I often twanged his ear with my thumb and forefinger, surely a most annoying habit. It was really most unfair: Steve would be paying attention to the teacher or concentrating on a test and suddenly feel an acute stinging of the ear. He would turn around in order to respond or to tell me to stop and then *he* would get into trouble for talking in class.

Before our trip, feeling full of hope, I bought a package of three condoms for Steve and me to take with us. Sadly, neither of us even came close to having an occasion to use them during our travels that summer. To begin our trip, Steve and I took the Penn Central train from New York to Providence, Rhode Island. From Providence we biked to Newport, where we had tickets to the Newport Folk Festival. We rode south from Providence along Route 114 through the towns of Barrington, Warren, and Bristol.

We had bought a tent for the trip, half paid for by Steve's parents and half by mine. After dark on the first day of our trip, we biked into a park, climbed over a low stone fence, set up our tent, and went to sleep. In the morning light, we saw gravestones all around us. We had slept in a cemetery.

From Newport, we biked along the Atlantic Coast out to Cape Cod. We met a young hippie, Chris Brown, who said we could set up our tent in his family's back yard in Wellfleet. We did so and stayed for a couple of weeks, helping ourselves to the Browns's indoor bathroom—and to their shower facilities, and to their kitchen. We must have been an incredible imposition on the family, but at age seventeen, Steve and I were cheerfully oblivious to this obvious fact.

From Wellfleet, Steve and I made our way to the Committee for Nonviolent Action (CNVA) Farm in Voluntown, Connecticut. We had heard about the Farm—I do not recall how—and decided to visit. This visit to CNVA, in mid-August 1968, was my first time there.

CNVA had started in 1957 as the direct-action component of the pacifist wing of the peace movement. CNVA had conducted vigils and civil disobedience at the Nevada sites where the government conducted atmospheric tests of nuclear weapons. When the first Polaris nuclear submarines were being built and launched, CNVA had organized civil disobedience projects in which activists in canoes and other small craft attempted to blockade the submarines to protest the deployment of nuclear weapons. In 1963–1964, CNVA had sponsored an integrated peace walk from Quebec, Canada, to Guantanamo, Cuba, via Washington, DC. Initially conceived primarily as a peace action, the project took on important meaning in the civil rights movement as well when the racially integrated peace walkers were arrested and jailed in the South, most notably by Police Chief Pritchitt in Albany, Georgia.

CNVA was a combination of a communal-living situation, a political action center and a peace office. The CNVA staff of 15–20 people lived in the various buildings at the Farm (as the headquarters was referred to by all) in Voluntown; the Farm also served as their offices and as a conference center. A few years later, when I was on the CNVA board, I came to realize what a problem it was that many aimless young people viewed the Farm as a convenient place to crash, live for free, hang out, and maybe meet some hippie chicks who were reputed to be easy. We board members viewed the Farm as a serious political action center and were always trying to devise ways (with distinctly mixed results) to keep these drifters away, or at least get them to work and pay while they stayed at the Farm. When Steve and I visited the Farm in mid-August 1968 during our bike trip, though, we were more or less precisely the type of people the CNVA staff were not happy to have as visitors.

During the first few days of our visit, we heard stories from the staff about incidents that had occurred there. Some of the incidents were relatively benign. It seems it was a popular pastime for the local teenage boys to get drunk on Saturday nights and go visit the "hippie encampment." Sometimes the guys from town would come to the Farm to make passes at the women there; sometimes they would set off firecrackers late at night to scare the pacifists.

Some of the incidents, however, were distinctly less benign. Two years before, in 1966, the Farm's barn had been destroyed late one night by an arsonist. Luckily, no one had been hurt. On the bulletin board in the dining room was a threatening letter from a right-wing paramilitary group that called itself the Minutemen. The letter had been sent to many peace groups; it showed the crosshairs of a rifle and bore the words: "Beware! Even now the crosshairs are at the back of your head!" Since the barn had been burned, fire was always a major concern. A dozen or more people slept in the old, eighteenth-century farmhouse; if nocturnal arsonists returned and went unnoticed, the results could be truly catastrophic. In order to avoid such an event, the CNVA staff had a night watch. One or two staff people would stay up all night on the first floor of the main Farmhouse to deal with whatever drunk (or worse) visitors might show up.

On Saturday morning, August 24, 1968, Steve and I were awakened at 2:45 A.M. by what we thought was the sound of firecrackers. "Well, well," I thought to myself. "Those stories we have been hearing about townies coming here late at night and setting off firecrackers to scare the pacifists are really true." I remembered what we had been told: in case of trouble, all Farm residents should gather and confront the unwanted visitors; be firm, but nonviolent. Sleepily, I walked downstairs to join the other Farm residents. I would do my part to be serious, firm, and nonviolent. Above all, I would be dignified. We'd soon deal with these trouble-making teenagers. I was so groggy, though, that I forgot I was wearing only underpants. Had I actually made it all the way downstairs to confront what I thought were rowdy local teenagers, I would surely have looked comical and ridiculous rather than serious and dignified.

But I never made it all the way downstairs. As I came partway down the stairs, I saw two big men with rifles rounding the corner at the bottom of the stairs, going into the main dining room. I was suddenly wide awake and realized that it was not firecrackers at all that had woken us up; it was gunfire. I turned around and went back upstairs.

About ten of us were now awake. We could hear the gunfire downstairs and outside, and we assumed that some right-wing crazies were rounding up all the pacifists and shooting them. We considered barricading ourselves into the room where we were sitting huddled on the floor. Then we remembered the danger of fire; barricading ourselves into the house was precisely the *wrong* thing to do.

There ensued a macabre debate. Some of us argued that we should barricade the doors because we were in imminent danger of being shot. Others warned of the danger of fire and said that barricading ourselves in was too dangerous. The debate went on until the shooting stopped. Eventually we figured out that the remaining men in plainclothes were police and we all made our way downstairs.

What happened that night was that five heavily armed members of the Minutemen, whose warning was posted in the CNVA dining room, had attacked the Farm. The Minutemen were masked and dressed in military garb, and carried bayonetted rifles, pistols, and knives. Some of the Minutemen had entered the Farmhouse with cans of gasoline to burn the building. Others had waited in the fields with high-powered rifles, ready to shoot the pacifists as they jumped out the second- and third-floor windows to escape the blaze.

The FBI had infiltrated the Minutemen, however, and had learned about the impending attack in advance. The FBI had tipped off the state police who, unbeknownst to us, had posted about a hundred troopers around the Farm. The authorities had deliberately not informed CNVA of the impending attack, believing, probably correctly, that the pacifists would have tried to put their nonviolent principles to work by contacting the Minutemen and trying to reason with them.

No one knows how the Minutemen slipped through the perimeter of police officers that night. There was some speculation at the time that the police had deliberately allowed the Minutemen to get through, but I saw no evidence of this and I seriously doubt if that is what occurred. When the Minutemen with the gasoline entered the Farmhouse, they found two members of the CNVA staff, Mary Suzuki Lyttle and Bobbie Trask, on watch in the dining room. The Minutemen blindfolded, bound, and gagged the two women at rifle-point. Meanwhile, the police realized that the Minutemen had gotten through their stakeout, so they chased into the Farmhouse after the Minutemen. (The two heavily armed men I had seen when I had tried to come downstairs to look serious and dignified were in fact state troopers, not Minutemen.)

A shootout ensued, during which seven people were wounded—three seriously, but none fatally. The two CNVA staffers—bound, gagged, and blindfolded on the dining-room sofa—were directly between the police and the Minutemen during the firing; the side of Bobbie Trask's leg was shot off when one of the officers' guns accidentally discharged (it had been knocked from the officer's hands by a Minuteman lunging with a bayonet). Four Minutemen were shot by the police before they surrendered, including one blinded in both eyes. Two of the police officers were hurt. Steve and I were unhurt.

All the police officers were in plainclothes, so there had been some confusion during the shooting about who was on which side. The confusion continued after all the Minutemen had been subdued and taken away by the police. The officers spent some time going to the various outbuildings of the Farm, rounding up the frightened residents. Understandably, the pacifists were a bit chary of the plainclothed officers, not knowing whether these obviously heavily armed men were the same ones who had just attacked the Farm. For their part, the police officers were also a bit skittish, for they too could not be completely sure that the people they were meeting were in fact pacifist Farm residents rather than additional Minutemen.

At dawn, we heard radio news reports about the shootout; these reports grew more lurid as the morning wore on. Steve and I realized that our parents would soon hear about the raid and worry about us. Both of us called home to say that we were safe, and that we would be home later that day; luckily, we reached our parents before the news did. It was probably a bit odd for my parents to get my phone call. I woke them up early on a Saturday morning when they had no idea that anything might be wrong in order to assure them that I was just fine and had not been shot during the night.

I have described how I was not an exemplary student. By high school I was still not doing assigned work but now I was channeling my energies into political activity—that is, the peace movement. One project I worked on was organizing opposition to air raid drills in school. When I was in high school, New York State education regulations (promulgated by then-New York State Commissioner of Education James Allen, later President Nixon's Commissioner of Education) required every public school in the state to hold three shelter drills per year.

The 1950s and 1960s were the era not only of air raid drills but of growing protests against them. The first organized protest against Operation Alert, the nationwide civil defense drill, occurred on June 15, 1955, when twenty-eight people from WRL, Fellowship of Reconciliation (FOR), Peacemakers, and the Catholic Worker were arrested at City Hall Park in New York City for refusing to take shelter. Among the twenty-eight protesters arrested were Ammon Hennacy, the anarchopacifist, and Dorothy Day of the Catholic Worker.

The civil defense protesters in New York continued their civil disobedience each year during the annual nationwide air raid practices: not cooperating with the drills, not taking shelter, and getting arrested. Between 1956 and 1959, between nine and nineteen people were arrested each year. In 1960, 1,000 people participated, with about 500 refusing to take shelter. The *New York Times* (which chronically underestimated the size of peace demonstrations) reported only 150 participants. Writers Dwight Macdonald and Norman Mailer, both of whom had joined the protest, published a letter to the editor in the *Times* criticizing the newspaper's coverage and saying, in part, "We are convinced that those 1,000 people gathered, fully aware of the possibility of arrest, in order to demonstrate their belief that there is no possible defense against an atomic attack other than peace." In 1961, about 2,000 people participated in the annual demonstration, with about 1,000 refusing to take shelter.

The insight that motivated these protests was that air raid drills and civil defense planning were part of wider, larger-scale preparations for nuclear war. At the purely practical level, it was idiotic to think that students hiding under their school desks or civilian urban populations going indoors would be safe from a nuclear holocaust. At the more important, political, level, civil defense preparation was an integral part of the Cold War, of the general demonization of the Soviet Union that helped fuel the Cold War, and of war preparations that made war more likely.

During the autumn of 1968, my senior year in high school, I organized a petition campaign in my school. The petition did not ask that shelter drills be discontinued. Instead, we merely asked that students who were morally opposed to participation in the drills be excused. In effect, we were seeking a special status for conscientious objectors to air raid drills just as there was a provision in the draft law for people who were conscientious objectors to military service. The petition I wrote and circulated said, in part:

> A society whose whole economic system and social structure are oriented toward war, and which is constantly preoccupied with preparation for war, is more likely to become involved in a major world conflict than one whose economic system and social structure is geared toward peaceful coexistence with her neighbors.

We presented our petition to the school authorities in the autumn of 1968. The school rejected our request. I also sent the petition to Commissioner Allen in Albany. The reply came from Herbert F. Mayne, Co-ordinator of Civil Defense for Schools:

> After studying the New York State Defense Emergency Act of 1951, as amended, and consultation with appropriate authorities, I can find no way in which the Commissioner of Education could grant your request without defaulting on his legal obligation to do all in his power in insure the safety of the students in the schools of New York State.

In response, I organized a noncooperation campaign in the school. If the school would not exempt conscientiously objecting students from participation in air raid drills, we objectors would exempt ourselves. We would refuse to take part. When the air raid drills occurred, we would refuse to leave our classrooms to go into the halls. We would, instead, remain quietly at our desks for the duration of the drill and put on armbands that said, "The Only Shelter Is Peace."

We did not know when the first air raid drill would occur—the date and time were kept secret from the students—but by early December we knew it had to be held soon because the state's regulations required that one of the three annual drills occur before Christmas. When Monday, December 16, arrived and there had been no drill, we knew it had to be that week. And when Thursday, December 19 passed without a drill, we knew it would be conducted the next day, Friday, December 20.

The air raid drill happened during third period. When the siren sounded, I stayed in my seat and put on my armband. I was terribly curious about what was happening elsewhere in the building: how many students were refusing to take shelter? Was the protest working? What would different individual teachers do with us? It was hard to imagine the liberal teachers like Mr. Parker and Mr. Horne punishing anyone, but would the school administration have issued a rule about how to handle the situation that even they would have to follow?

I soon found out what was happening throughout the rest of the school. I was sent to the office, where the other students who refused to take shelter had also been sent. About thirty-five students were there. All of us were wearing our armbands. We were put together in a room and the school principal, Mr. Gould, came in. He yelled at us for a while, and then told us to take off our armbands. No one knew what to do. Mr. Gould said that he would suspend any student who did not take off his or her armband immediately. (This threat, it turns out, was not without some irony. The U.S. Supreme Court case that established the right of students to wear protest armbands in public schools, *Tinker v. Des Moines*, had been argued the previous month, on November 12, 1968. The Supreme Court's favorable decision, however, was not handed down until early the following year, on February 28, 1969, too late to do us any good.) Everyone took off their armbands except me. Mr. Gould announced that I was suspended from school, and that he would call my parents to come to pick me up. My friend Dave ("Bug") Rosen stood up to tell Mr. Gould off. Mr. Gould told him to sit down. When Bug did not sit down but continued talking, Mr. Gould suspended him too.

But our protest was a success. Friday, December 20, 1968, was the last day an air raid drill was ever held in Great Neck South Senior High School. The New York state regulation requiring schools to hold drills stayed in effect for some years thereafter, but our high school never again sought to actually hold an air raid drill.

This was not the first time I had been thrown out of high school for political organizing. In March 1967, during my sophomore year, I was suspended for distributing flyers promoting a fast to raise money for medical aid for Vietnam. SPV had organized a three-day "fast" in which we asked students to eat nothing but rice and drink nothing but water, and to donate the money saved from the food they would otherwise have eaten. Mr. Gould warned me that the fast would be dangerous for students, and that I had to stop distributing the flyers at school. I tried to argue with him on a practical level, telling him that this was not a true fast and that it was perfectly safe for adolescents to subsist for three days on rice and water. Mr. Gould was not persuaded. I tried arguing on the political level—that I had a First Amendment right to distribute flyers. Mr. Gould was not persuaded. On the other hand, I was not dissuaded. I continued to distribute the flyers. I was suspended from school.

Let it be understood, however, that the fact that during high school I was becoming politically active did not in any way mean that I was becoming a better student, nor even a reasonably well-behaved one. In twelfth grade, Bug and I had the same late lunch hour, followed by social studies with Mr. Parker. We often spent lunch hour outdoors playing frisbee (and sometimes smoking marijuana) and would come into class noisily (and sometimes stoned), chatting or giggling loudly, halfway (or more) through the period. In physics, I slept soundly, head down on desk, nearly every day. (I sat in the middle of the front row, directly in front of the teacher, an amiable young man named Mr. Levitt.) I rarely did the assigned reading. If I turned in written assignments at all, they were invariably late.

One day while I was cutting class, I took a notion that I wanted to discuss something with Bug, who was in his advanced placement chemistry class. (Unlike me, Bug was an excellent student and graduated near the top of our class.) Bug's being in class was very inconvenient, so I walked in and told the teacher, Mr. Knapp, that the school's assistant principal wanted to see Bug.

"What did you do now, Rosen?" Mr. Knapp, an archconservative, asked Bug.

Bug himself was worried. "What did we do?" he asked me as soon as we were outside the classroom.

I explained that he had done nothing—that I had just wanted to get him out of class to chat. Later, Mr. Knapp had occasion to ask the assistant principal what he had wanted Bug for. (I had not foreseen this rather obvious outcome.)

On December 20, 1968, there was an SPV demonstration at Great Neck's draft board, Local Board #3. I do not remember now who organized it, but I do not think that I was directly involved. About forty students took part, and the demonstration became, shall we say, spirited, with students disrupting traffic on Great Neck's main street, Middle Neck Road, and shouting slogans at passers-by. Police were called , and were taunted by some of the demonstrators, but no one was arrested.

A lively debate appeared in our newsletter, the *SPV Bulletin*, about what had occurred. (The *SPV Bulletin* was largely a one-man show. I wrote many of the articles, solicited the rest, typed the originals, laid out each issue, and took it in to the printer.) In the January 1969 issue, Geoff Beckett published an article criticizing the tone of the draft-board demonstration the previous month. In the February issue, I ran two pieces, side by side, responding to Geoff's. On the left half of the page was a piece by my friend, Dave Helvarg, defending the strident tone of the December demonstration. Next to it was an article I had written. Part of my article said:

> As I have stated on other occasions, I believe that on demonstrations, we peaceniks ought to conduct ourselves in an orderly, polite, dignified manner. This is only good public relations. Many people are going to discount us for many things; some may call us hippies, others may call us Communists. *It must be our job to see that people have as little as possible to discount us for.* . . . We went to the draft board on December 20 to protest *against* the viciousness of the draft. Hurling things, even insults, at cops certainly does nothing to advance the cause of peace. . . .
>
> Please don't misunderstand me: I am not suggesting that anyone sacrifice basic principles on the altar of middle-class respectability. Rather, I am saying that we should make an effort to keep our future demonstrations orderly. . . . [As for] Dave [Helvarg]'s statement that he has seen "cops act like pigs," Dave has apparently never been on a farm where pigs are raised. . . . [Emphasis as in original.]

Every year on Memorial Day, Great Neck holds a parade. The route runs up Middle Neck Road, from Northern Boulevard through all of "downtown" Great Neck, north to the Village Green. The school bands and the one from the Merchant Marine Academy in Kings Point take part, as do Boy Scouts, Girl Scouts, and other community and civic organizations. The event is organized by the local American Legion post. Everyone in town comes out to watch.

In 1968, I suggested that SPV take part in the annual parade. We duly applied to the American Legion for permission to march and, not surprisingly, were immediately turned down. Not to be deterred, we showed up at the Village Green on Memorial Day with signs and placards. The front page of the *Great Neck Record* for Thursday, June 1, featured a picture of a group of SPV members, including Bug holding a sign that read: "For Their Memory: Peace in Vietnam."

Our peace demonstration infuriated the local American Legion, whose members castigated us in the *Record* for desecrating the memory of the war dead. Later, the *Record* published my response, explaining that we had sought permission from the American Legion to march in the parade, but had been turned down.

The following spring, SPV applied again to march in the parade. Still unhappy with how we had "spoiled" the previous year's event with our demonstration, the American Legion hit upon what they may have thought was a novel way to keep us quiet. They approved our request to march, but told us that we could carry no signs of any type. After some negotiation, we were allowed (like all of the organizations in the parade) to carry a single sign with the name of our organization. I bought a piece of cloth that stretched to nearly the width of Middle Neck Road. We painted "Great Neck Students for" in small letters, and in huge letters we printed "PEACE IN VIETNAM." In strict adherence to the policy, we all marched behind that one banner.

Great Neck is a liberal community, and we received huge cheers along the entire parade route. That could not have been what the American Legion had hoped for.

3
Nonregistration

I AM THE ONLY CHILD of two parents who were both Jewish refugees from Nazi Europe. Both of my parents were born in Vienna, Austria. Both of their families came to this country in 1939, the year after Hitler's takeover of Austria.

When I was growing up, my parents' circle of friends were all Jewish refugees whom they had known in Vienna. One of my mother's best friends, Annie Ross, had been a kindergarten classmate of hers. Mom's other best friend, Vera Van Gelder, was also from Vienna. The friends they had over for dinner and went with on ski trips—the Grünwalds, the Fürsts, the Eastons—were all friends from Vienna. My parents hardly knew their American neighbors and almost never socialized with them. When my parents spent an evening with friends, German was spoken as often as English. Frequently, my parents and their friends would switch back and forth between English and German, sometimes several times within the same sentence. Sometimes a single word was created by running together part of a German word and part of an English word. Inverted word order, syntactically correct in German, was common. ("Did you know that Steven was from high school *ausgedropped*?") I grew up with the Viennese dialect of German (*Zwetchken* instead of *Pflaumen*; *Marillen* for *Aprikosen*; *Erdäpfel* for *Kartoffel*); German spoken by someone from Germany sounds quite different to my ears than what I grew up hearing at home.

Dad's doctors, lawyers, and accountants were all Viennese refugees. I have no idea how he found them. In the mid-1970s, after my parents divorced and Dad moved to Piermont, New York, he had to find a new physician. Amazingly, he found one from Vienna.

Some of the bedtime stories Dad read to me were German books he had enjoyed as a child. I still remember him sitting on my bed, translating *Emil und die Detective* (*Emil and the Detectives*) and *Der 35. Mai* (*The Thirty-Fifth of May*), both by Erich Kästner—slowly, painstakingly, sentence by sentence. Kästner, a prominent left-wing intellectual in Germany between the World Wars, had gone into hiding after the Nazis seized power. My father was among the American soldiers who had liberated Kästner and his family at the end of the war.

When it came time to send me to summer camp, I attended Children's Colony in Lakeville, Connecticut. The owner, Trude Frankl, was another Viennese Jewish refugee. When she was a girl, Mom had attended Trude Frankl's camp in Austria.

My father's family name had been Epstein. All the family members (except one cousin) changed the name to Elmer when they arrived in the United States. When I was growing up, the explanation I was given by my parents was that, when the family fled from Vienna, many of its members had promised never to return. This was, in fact, a condition set by the Nazis for the departure of Jews, to aid Hitler's goal of making Europe *Judenrein* (cleansed of Jews). But some family members, my father included, later went into the United States Army and returned in uniform to Europe during the war. Had they been captured, the story went, they would have been in danger had it been discovered that they were Jewish emigrés who had broken their promise not to return. The name change was designed to make discovery less likely.

The story, however, was untrue. The first Epstein to arrive in New York as a refugee was Onkel (Uncle) Franzl, my paternal grandfather's younger brother. Onkel Franzl was something of a character. In Vienna, he had been an attorney. In this country, he became a professional photographer—until he suddenly developed a phobia about cameras. He then became a high-class smuggler. He had an elegant shop on Madison Avenue in Manhattan where he sold pre-Columbian Mexican artifacts that he smuggled into the United States himself. Twice a year Onkel Franzl went to Mexico on buying trips.

Onkel Franzl was an amazing raconteur and joke-teller. He not only knew every joke ever invented, but could discuss at some length the ætiology of families of jokes, as well as the similarities and differences of jokes between cultures. Many of Onkel Franzl's jokes had an edge to them—often a misogynist edge.

When Onkel Franzl arrived in New York, he was bitter and disaffected. He decided to change his name, and he did so with a vengeance. He kept the first letter of the family name, so the E in Epstein became the E in Elmer. For the rest of the name, however, he took a rough acronym from a common but vulgar German insult, *leck mich im Arsch* (literally 'lick my ass'). As the remaining members of the family arrived, each one in turn (save one) dutifully changed his or her surname to Elmer. I dare say it tickled Onkel Franzl's misanthropic sense of humor to think of future generations of Elmers growing up with that name, albeit not knowing the derivation.

Although, all in all, my parents assimilated themselves in the New World reasonably well, they never completely lost an aspect of seeing themselves as outsiders. Some of this was evident at an obvious and perhaps superficial level: because of their accents, my parents could not open their mouths and speak three words without being recognized as immigrants. Mom, especially, was sensitive about her accent. But their attitude toward American culture set them apart, too. Americans listened to rock and roll; my parents had grown up on Beethoven, Mozart, and Strauss. Americans watched television; when I was young, we did not even have a television, and when my parents later bought one, they almost never watched it. To them, America was the world capital of the lowbrow and kitsch; my parents had come from what was in their view the cultural capital of all civilization.

My parents also never lost the unsettled feeling of having been abruptly uprooted from what had seemed like a safe and stable environment. If we were eating in a restaurant (something that happened *very* rarely; restaurants were generally anathema to my frugal parents) and I said something out loud that would reveal that we were Jewish, my parents would shush me immediately.

"What's wrong?" I would ask. "Nobody will hurt us because we are Jewish."

"Why take chances?" they would answer rhetorically.

My mother inherited a roll of twenty one-ounce gold coins from Onkel Franzl. When Mom eventually passed the coins on to me, she acknowledged that I would be tempted to sell the gold and buy something with the proceeds. But she urged me to keep the coins as they were. "You never know when you might need gold," she said. "If anything happens, you can take your passports and the gold and try to get to safety with your kids."

I knew exactly what Mom meant, and I have always kept the gold in that form.

In the end, I think that I inherited from my parents the perspective of the outsider, of the skeptic, of the cynic. I do not think that this was something that my parents sought consciously to convey or to pass on to me, but I think it was a natural concomitant of who they were.

My family history is not one of high political consciousness or progressive political activism.

In Vienna, my Oma (Grandmother) Elmer's father was so patriotic that, although he was overage and obviously ineligible, he tried to enlist in the Austrian Army during the First World War. *Für Kaiser und Vaterland* (for emperor and fatherland) was a favorite saying of his. Despite the increasing anti-Semitism and Nazi activity after the *Anschluss* (the German annexation of Austria in March 1938), my paternal grandparents did not think of leaving Vienna until my grandfather Hans lost his job when the family textile business was "Aryanized."

Nothing will happen to us, they had thought; *we are patriotic Austrians. Hitler's ranting about Jews doesn't mean us; we are fully assimilated into Austrian society. We fought in the war for the Kaiser. Hitler means the Polish Jews who live in the Second District. They have recently come from Galicia and, in contrast to us, they are not assimilated. See their* peyis *(ritual earlocks) and* yarmulkes.

In part, of course, this attitude of my forebears reflected the all-too-common, condescending attitude held by many urban Jews in central Europe (themselves but a generation or two removed from the shtetl) toward more recent arrivals. (This phenomenon has been well described elsewhere.) But this attitude—this almost total insensitivity of the stark, deadly political realities all around them—also betrayed an abysmal lack of political consciousness.

On my mother's side, my Opa (Grandpa) was a successful businessman in Vienna, just exactly as he was later after emigrating to the United

States. Just months before the *Anschluss*, wholly oblivious to the disaster that lay just around the corner, he withdrew a large sum of money from the safety of a Swiss bank and brought it to Vienna to open a third branch of his upholstery fabric store. After the *Anschluss*, Opa was arrested by the Nazis and released from prison only after he promised to leave the country and not return. In effect, the arrest probably saved his life, for it is likely he would never have left of his own volition.

Opa had a cousin in the fur business who, even after escaping from Austria to the safety of England, returned repeatedly to the Nazi-occupied continent in order to conduct or conclude business transactions. He was finally caught and died in a concentration camp.

In retrospect, this inability of my family members to see the writing on the wall seems staggering. In contrast, on the very day of the *Anschluss*, Martin Ross (a family friend) collected his brother Karl and left the country on the first train to unoccupied Jugoslavia. The Gestapo was raiding Martin's home in Vienna just as he was crossing the border out of Austria. Martin and Karl had tried to persuade their father to come with them as they fled, but the father thought that Martin was exaggerating the danger. The father died in Buchenwald.

The difference in reaction between a Martin Ross and my relatives was that Martin was politically conscious, he was aware of events in the world around him and he knew what they meant; my relatives, while perhaps conscious of the events, were surely not aware of their import.

Although they were not activists, my parents were decidedly left of center politically. Nevertheless, when it came to civil disobedience and violating the law, my parents were clearly not supportive of my actions. I always understood this; their experience with the Nazis had taught them that to challenge the government openly can be very dangerous.

In early 1968, I organized a fundraising campaign for medical aid programs in Vietnam. The programs we were supporting were administered by the Canadian Friends Service Committee (CFSC). Because this Canadian organization had received no U.S. governmental licenses for their relief shipments, it was illegal for Americans to contribute to them—a violation of the 1923 Trading With the Enemy Act. SPV collected contributions for several weeks by standing outside Great Neck synagogues and churches before and after services.

My parents did not object to the fundraising, nor even to our send-ing the funds illegally to CFSC. But they put their foot down at publi-cizing the civil disobedience in the *Great Neck Record*. *Why provoke the U.S. government needlessly?* they wondered. I think they had visions of their son spending the next seventy-five years manacled in some dun-geon because he had sent a small check to CFSC.

As co-chairman of SPV, I felt I could not shirk my duty to publicize our action, but at the same time I was scared to disobey my parents. I waited until my parents took their annual vacation in early July and publicized our civil disobedience with a letter to the editor in the *Record* while they were out of town. The letter said, in part:

> We are now sending a money order of the money we raised to Can-ada. We are fully cognizant of the fact that such an action involves a direct violation of the 1923 Trading With The Enemy Act, and its ap-pended regulations. We violate this law because we do not recognize the Vietnamese as our enemies, but rather as our brothers. We com-mit this "crime" as a gesture of reconciliation, as an act of love, and of compassion. We are deeply distressed that our government still considers those who, in anguish cry, "They are our brothers whom we kill!" to be a fringe minority to whom it owes no exculpation.

I was naïve in the extreme. I carefully hid *our* copy of that week's *Record* so my parents would not see the article, but, of course, that didn't stop all their friends from commenting to them when they returned from vacation about my wonderful letter.

My father was furious. Not only had I violated the laws of the United States government but, maybe even worse, I had disobeyed him. He cast about for an appropriate punishment for my deed. He decided that I would not be allowed to attend the Pete Seeger concert at the Newport Folk Festival later that month for which I already had tickets. The con-cert was to be part of the bike trip through New England with Steve Dreisin that I discussed in the previous chapter.

I tried to persuade my father that this was not fair—that, in effect, he was punishing Steve by denying him a travel companion because of something I had done. Finally, we worked out a compromise: Steve and I would go together to Newport as planned, carrying two tickets to the concert, but because I was being punished I would simply not attend the concert on the appropriate night. To this day, I don't know whether my father really thought that I would not attend the concert under those circumstances or whether this was his face-saving way of rescinding the punishment.

Raising money for the Canadian Friends Service Committee in 1968 was my first act of civil disobedience. Several years later I learned that Carol Bragg, whom I was later to marry, had committed *her* first act of civil disobedience taking part in a public protest in which the demonstrators had carried money, perhaps including the money SPV had raised, across the border to present to CFSC. I was a high school student from Great Neck; she was a college student from Macalester, in St. Paul; and we wouldn't meet each other for another two years.

My second act of civil disobedience was publicly refusing to register for the draft. This was a decision I had come to gradually over a two-and-a-half-year period.

The central issue for me was what the appropriate response to the draft is for a person who is conscientiously opposed both to conscription in general and to the particular war that conscription was supporting at that time. Should one register as the law required, fill in the required forms, carry a draft card as required, accept a student deferment or conscientious objector status? Or was the way to manifest one's opposition to the draft to refuse to be any part of the draft at all: don't register, don't fill in the forms, don't carry a draft card, don't accept any classification? I believed that the latter course was the right one.

Of course, many people urged me to register for the draft and apply for conscientious objector status. If it was the draft and the war that I opposed, why not take the out offered by the law? After all, no one would be killed or wounded by my registering as a CO.

There were two reasons why I disagreed with this approach. The narrow reason was that the entire, elaborate Selective Service structure of exemptions and deferments was deeply discriminatory. It favored the wealthy and the middle-class—those who could get student deferments or a doctor's letter saying that the registrant had a minor psychiatric or physical problem—and it disfavored the poor. I was unwilling to take advantage of this special privilege.

At a deeper level, I thought it was fundamentally inconsistent to say that I was opposed to the draft if, at the same time, I cooperated with it by registering, filling out forms, and accepting a classification or deferment. The first task of somebody who opposes a particular system is to refuse to participate in it or to cooperate with it in any way. The analogy of involuntary servitude—slavery—seemed to me to be appropriate. The first responsibility of an abolitionist in the antebellum South was not to participate in the system of slavery by owning slaves. What would we say about the hyprocrisy of an abolitionist who crusaded against slavery but owned slaves himself? So it was with the draft: if one was truly opposed to conscription, then one could not in good conscience have anything whatsoever to do with the conscription system.

This period of deliberation about whether or not to register for the draft during the years leading up to my eighteenth birthday provided me with my first really sustained opportunity to examine deeply the issue of civil disobedience: Is it ever acceptable to violate the criminal laws of the country? Does not doing so invite lawlessness and dangerous disorder in society? If it is ever acceptable to violate the law, when is it acceptable and under what circumstances? I spent days considering these questions and discussing them with friends. I read and reread Thoreau's classic essay, *On the Duty of Civil Disobedience*. (Today, decades later, I still consider it the best single piece on the subject.) I also read Gandhi's writings on civil disobedience, A. J. Muste's essays, and the public statements of many contemporary draft resisters.

At some point during this period I heard an interview with the radical historian Staughton Lynd. I still remember his words, more or less verbatim:

> I endorse that form of civil disobedience in which an individual says, I believe that I *cannot* obey this particular law. However, I shall disobey it in such a way that any immediate adverse consequences fall on myself, rather than on others; and, if in the judgment of society, I am to be punished for my action, I shall accept that punishment in the hope that I will have accomplished something by violating the law that I could not have accomplished otherwise.

Each separate portion of that definition made sense to me.

First, civil disobedience should never be undertaken lightly or casually. Gandhi always emphasized that the first duty of the *satyagrahi* (one who engages in *satyagraha*, or civil disobedience) is to *obey* carefully all laws to which he is not conscientiously opposed. In civil disobedience, the participant says: for deeply held religious or moral reasons I just *cannot* obey a specific, particular law. This commitment to general lawfulness—violating only a specific law, and only for deeply held beliefs—is one of the things that prevents civil disobedience from degenerating into general lawlessness.

During this time, many of my friends used illegal drugs, especially marijuana. There were a number of reasons why I did relatively little experimenting with illegal drugs. (Although, as I have said, I experimented some with marijuana during high school, I stopped shortly after high school, and never used other drugs at all.) One was concern about the health consequences. But another, very important, reason was that I thought that drug use was incompatible with serious political action. I believed that Gandhi was correct: the first requirement of one involved in civil disobedience is to obey all laws to which there is no religious or moral objection. On a more practical level, I was very much aware of the damage it would do to the peace movement if a peace activist were arrested for illicit drug use.

The next requirement of civil disobedience is that it must be nonviolent. If I were to demonstrate my opposition to the draft by attacking the local draft-board clerks, that would not be civil disobedience, because it would not be nonviolent. Even burning down the draft boards would not be nonviolent because it would risk people being hurt in the ensuing blaze. Nonviolence is the essential, crucial part of what makes civil disobedience *civil*.

The final requirement of civil disobedience is that the participant must do his or her actions openly and be willing to accept the consequences for them. On an abstract level, this, too, distinguishes civil disobedience from general lawlessness. The bank robber (or embezzler or shoplifter) acts clandestinely and tries to get away with his or her actions. The person engaged in civil disobedience acts openly and does not try to get away with anything. Less abstractly, doing civil disobedience openly makes sense because, by acting openly, the participant can try to explain her action to the public, thereby helping to build and enlarge the movement of which she is a part.

Gandhi said that the *satyagrahi* had to accept prison or other punishment *cheerfully*. Gandhi, on coming to court for civil disobedience, sometimes told the judges either to give him the maximum sentence allowable by law or to resign. I thought a great deal about this; Gandhi was, after all, the world's foremost practitioner of nonviolent civil disobedience. But after much deliberation, I decided that Gandhi was wrong. Those who engage in civil disobedience, I decided, must, for both moral and practical reasons, do so openly and publicly, and must accept the consequences of their actions. But I'd be damned if I had to be *cheerful* about going to prison!

In thinking about civil disobedience in the years before I turned eighteen, I was very mindful of the Nuremberg precedent. At the Nuremberg war crimes tribunal, the victorious Allied powers, including the United States, tried and executed members of the Nazi high command for the crime of *not* disobeying the law of the land when those laws involved the perpetration of crimes against humanity. At Nuremberg, the defense was often, "I was just following orders." The prosecutors responded, "Following orders is no excuse." For me, the lesson of Nuremberg was that there are times when an individual must violate the laws of a particular country in order to uphold a higher law. Although I understood that the analogy was imperfect, I believed that there was a parallel between the deaths at Auschwitz and the deaths from American bombing in Vietnam: both situations involved the mass, indiscriminate slaughter of large numbers of innocent people. If we would have expected the "good" Germans to disobey orders and to violate the law of the land when those orders and laws involved the perpetration of unspeakable atrocities, then there was a moral obligation incumbent upon me to commit civil disobedience when crimes against humanity were being carried out by my country.

Igal Roodenko of WRL used to call himself and the rest of us who engaged in civil disobedience "misfits." I never liked the pejorative flavor of the word (which was, of course, part of the reason Igal used it: to shock or to jolt); but I did understand what he meant. If we peace and civil rights activists truly fit comfortably into contemporary society, we would not be getting ourselves arrested on freedom rides (as Igal had done) because we would just accept the Jim Crow status quo. If we really fit comfortably into society, we would not be getting ourselves arrested for draft resistance (as Igal had done during World War II, and I did during the Vietnam War) because we would accept conscription or, at least, accept conscientious objector status. The fact is, we who engage in civil disobedience are rather oddballs—although I prefer the less pejorative term "quixotic" to Igal's "misfits"—because of our difficulty or inability to accept certain unacceptable aspects of the status quo.

I thought a lot about prison during this period. I did not view going to prison as an end in itself, as something that would somehow strengthen or help the peace movement (as some resisters did). Instead, I viewed going to prison as the highly undesirable but nevertheless probable result of actions in which I felt morally obligated to engage. By the time I turned seventeen, I was sure I could not register. I had a copy of the *Handbook for Conscientious Objectors* on the desk next to my bed and I used to read and reread the section on what life was like in prison. Sometimes I cried while reading this—for the harshness of the world, for the hardness of life in prison, and for myself and what I was sure awaited me. I was a middle-class kid from the suburbs and I was frightened of going to prison.

I made the mistake of telling my parents about my decision not to register for the draft at the same time I told them that I was not going to go to college. As a high school senior from a middle-class, suburban, Jewish community, I had, of course, applied to colleges. In October 1968, the autumn of my senior year in high school, I had flown out to Yellow Springs, Ohio, with my classmates Bug Rosen and Ellen Gaine, to visit Antioch College. During the winter, I completed and sent in applications to Antioch; to Earlham College, a small Quaker school in Richmond, Indiana; to Beloit College, in Beloit, Wisconsin; to Washington University, in St. Louis; and to Bard College, in upstate New York. But as my senior year wore on, college seemed increasingly unrealistic. From my point of view, there was both an ethical and a practical dimension to the decision not to go to college.

As an ethical matter, I thought it would be wrong to attend college while there was a war on. People were being killed; babies were being burned alive with napalm. This was being done by my country, and in my name. College was safe and cushy, but there was a moral duty to oppose the war as completely and as fully as possible. In an ironic way, I agreed with some conservatives who complained about "college protesters." How could one devote oneself properly to one's studies if one is working hard against the war? I wondered. It seemed like a shameful waste of one's parents' tuition money to be enrolled in college but to spend all one's time at demonstrations. More importantly, how could one devote oneself fully to the peace movement if one was wasting one's time attending classes?

As a practical matter, it seemed foolish to start college when I would soon be headed to prison. To me, the connection between the decision not to register for the draft and the decision not to attend college was obvious. Although, in 1969, only about a third of all resisters were being prosecuted, public nonregistration was by far the riskiest method of resistance, with 96% of all public nonregistrants being prosecuted. The average sentence for resisters was thirty-six months in prison, but sentences in New York were generally longer. Even if, by some stroke of good fortune, I was not prosecuted for my own individual resistance, I was by that time also thinking about taking part in the public destruction of draft files. Why start college when I might only be there for a few weeks?

Unfortunately, the connection between my decision not to register and my decision not to attend college was equally obvious to my parents. How did I expect to get a good (that is, lucrative) job without going to college? they asked. And why do something as precipitous as not registering, something that would mark me for life and that I might later come to regret?

I thought a great deal that year about the you'll-regret-this-later argument. I decided that I could only act now according to my present beliefs and ideals, and hope that I would have the honesty and humility later to change my public position if my views changed. I could not refrain from acting now, in the way I believed right, on the chance that I might later change my mind. "Think of the options I am closing off by not studying Latin," I told my parents in the spring of 1969. "Maybe some day I will want to convert to Catholicism and become a priest. Then I'll wish I had studied Latin."

My decisions not to register, and later to destroy draft files, are ones I have never regretted. Seventeen years after refusing to register for the draft, I applied to law schools and knew that I might not be admitted because of my previous felony conviction. Even though I wanted very much to go to law school, I accepted the possibility of not being admitted with equanimity, knowing that it was the price I had to pay for taking actions that I believed, both at the time I took them and years later, were right. I would have regretted being turned down by law schools due to my previous acts of civil disobedience, but I would not for a moment have regretted having engaged in the civil disobedience.

Similarly, after I completed law school and applied for admission to the bar, I was acutely conscious of the risk that I would not be allowed to practice law because of my criminal record. This time, there was also an additional problem: I was deeply in debt from three years of law school. All the time and effort expended in attending law school, and all of the attendant expenses and debt, might have been for nothing if, in the end, I were not admitted to practice. Nevertheless, although I was certainly very aware of the risk, I did not for a moment regret my prior actions that resulted in my situation being what it was.

I spent the summer of 1969 in San Francisco. I had had a tacit understanding with my parents that I was under their control until I turned eighteen. I graduated from high school in June but would not turn eighteen until August 30. Thus there was a kind of two-month interregnum, after I was done with school but before I was technically free of my parents' control. Although my plan was to work for WRL at its New York office after high school, I wanted to spend the summer months, the period of the interregnum, as far away from my parents and their control as possible. I decided to go to San Francisco to work at the WRL office there for the summer. In the autumn, after my eighteenth birthday, I would move back east.

Classes and exams at Great Neck South High School that year ended on Friday, June 20, but the graduation ceremony was not until a week later, Friday, June 27. I considered staying for the ceremony; it would have been fun to play a practical joke on the superintendent of schools, the ancient John L. Miller, by placing a buzzer (or toothpaste or Camembert cheese) in the palm of my hand when it came time to receive my diploma and shake his hand. But it was not worth waiting an extra week just for a five-second joke. On June 20, I flew to San Francisco.

The disadvantage of my situation with WRL in San Francisco was that there was no specific work for me to do and no money to pay me a salary. This had been made clear to me when I had inquired about coming out. So I stayed as the guest of various WRL staff people and volunteers, from a few days up to a week or two at a time at different people's homes. Sometimes I slept on the floor of the WRL office. I bought my own food, using some savings I had from high school. I helped out around the office a bit—WRL West was rather more laid back than the office in New York—and I had lots of free time.

The advantage of the situation was that I was as far away from my parents as I could be without leaving the forty-eight contiguous United States.

The summer of 1969 was a wonderful time for me. It was my first experience of being on my own. When I slept in the WRL office I subsisted on peanut butter, Wonder Bread and milk. The milk started out at 27¢ a quart but I learned about inflation when, in midsummer, it went up to 29¢ a quart.

For a couple of weeks I was the guest of Paul Wesley, a tall, long-haired WRL staff member who was into brown rice, organic food, and the Incredible String Band. He was an Irish Protestant who had met Joan Baez on one of her concert tours of Europe, had briefly been her lover, and had moved to the Bay area to work for the peace movement. I was awakened every morning by the strains of the Incredible String Band on the record player.

The summer of 1969 was watching the sun set over the Pacific Ocean from a field of wildflowers atop Mt. Tamalpais, north of San Francisco. It was attending Randy Kehler's wedding on a windswept beach. Half of the wedding party consisted of the couple's friends, barefoot peace activists; the other half of the party was the couple's relatives in suits and leather shoes. The summer of 1969 was running naked on Wildcat Beach at Point Reyes National Seashore, wandering alone in Golden Gate Park, and hitchhiking back and forth across the Bay Bridge between San Francisco and Berkeley.

I was saved from loneliness by meeting John-i-thin Stephens at a pot-luck dinner sponsored by the Resistance, the organization of draft resisters. He and I became fast friends. John-i-thin was then on parole, having been released from prison for his own draft resistance. He had a straight job as a janitor at a local hospital, a job that, unlike movement jobs, allowed him lots of free time when he was not at work. Every weekend he took me on two- or three-day trips: hiking in the high Sierras, panning for gold in the Colorado River, the Muir Woods. John-i-thin had acquired his unusual nickname in 1964, during the CNVA Quebec-to-Guantanamo peace walk. There had been three men named John participating. In order to avoid confusion, each John took on a different nickname. John Stephens became John-i-thin because of his lean build.

That summer I wrote my public statement about why I was refusing to register for the draft. Nonregistration was far and away the most important thing I had ever done and I wanted the statement to be good and complete. If I was going to go to prison I wanted to express clearly to everyone I knew the precise reasons for my action. I prepared a draft of my statement and circulated it to some friends in July for comments. With 3,000 miles separating us, I even felt safe sending a copy to my parents. As expected, I received back from them lengthy letters attempting to dissuade me. Most of the other comments I received were supportive. One exception was a letter from my friend, Phil Olenick.

Phil and I had been linked during high school by our common interest in politics but even more by our lack of popularity with girls. Phil's parents had been radicals in the 1940s and 1950s and I had been adopted into their family as their "other son." We all used to have wonderful, long political arguments. Phil's parents were Marxists; I was a pacifist. Phil's letter about my draft said, in part: "I have heard everything in it many times before. What bothers me is that I've heard them in exactly the same words. Has it all become a ritual chant? Don't let yourself get wrapped up in catchphrases. . . . For starters try to rewrite the whole thing. . . ."

In part, Phil was correct; he *had* heard it all from me before, and in pretty much the same words. The point he missed, however, was that the reason he had heard it all before was that the positions in the statement had been honed through months and years of arguments in his living room with him and his parents.

That summer I also planned how I would conduct my nonregistration. Because of my views about the importance of civil disobedience being open and public, I could not keep my nonregistration secret. This was a key distinction. By 1969, there were tens of thousands of men turning eighteen and not registering, but they were doing it clandestinely. Not one was ever prosecuted criminally. At worst, if a quiet nonregistrant were found out, he would be obligated to register belatedly. But, as already noted, of the public nonregistrants—a much smaller number, to be sure—nearly all were prosecuted.

But it was not enough for me merely to refuse to register and do it publicly. I wanted to call attention to my protest, to publicize it as widely as possible. The Selective Service law at that time gave men five days after their eighteenth birthday to comply with the registration requirement. I decided to use the five-day period during which I was obligated to register to fast and conduct a vigil outside what would have been "my" draft board.

Given the sharp disparity in the treatment of public and clandestine nonregistrants, my parents were understandably unhappy about my plans. Perhaps having given up hope of persuading me to register, they tried to dissuade me from making my civil disobedience public. In a letter dated July 23, 1969, my mother wrote:

> It seems to me that one ought to consider, whenever one plans any kind of protest, what the likely consequences will be. I don't mean the consequences for oneself, but the results in influencing other people. That is, after all, the whole purpose and aim. . . . It seems not likely at all to me that you will influence a single youngster who is entering or leaving the draft board. . . . To stand in front of the draft board on the day you were supposed to register, but didn't, seems to me to call undue attention to yourself, which I could understand *if* it were likely to be of some value.

On August 1, my father wrote:

> By publicly demonstrating and/or announcing your act of civil disobedience you will not convince anyone to do likewise. I would like you to re-think and reverse your decision of staging this demonstration in front of your draft board. . . . I may remind you that in a similar case you felt the proper way to "go public" was with a letter to the editor of the *Great Neck Record* asking for contributions

which netted little compared to less flamboyant but more effective methods.

On August 18, twelve days before my eighteenth birthday, I left San Francisco in a Volkswagen minibus full of WRL staffers. WRL was the American affiliate of War Resisters International (WRI), a pacifist organization with chapters in fifty-three countries. WRI was holding its triennial conference at Haverford College, in Haverford, Pennsylvania, during the last week in August. This was the first time since WRL had been founded in 1923 that a WRI Triennial had been held in the United States. The conference would be attended by pacifist activists from WRI chapters all over the world.

We all took turns driving from San Francisco to Haverford. I had gotten my driver's license the previous January, but I had never driven a car with a standard transmission. Shortly before we left, I learned how to do so, so that I could share the driving on the trip east.

The week-long Triennial was an exciting time. Martin Niemöller, the famous German Lutheran pastor who had been imprisoned by the Nazis, was there, as were Gandhian activists from India such as Narayan Desai. There were also three American war resisters in three different stages of their resistance at the Triennial. The first was Bob Eaton, a Quaker from Philadelphia. Bob had already been convicted of draft resistance. One day, all the participants in the Triennial adjourned our conference and went to the federal courthouse in Philadelphia to hold a vigil at Bob's sentencing. He got three years. The second resister was Randy Kehler, my colleague and friend from the San Francisco WRL office. Randy had a trial date set for that autumn. At one point, Randy made a very moving speech about draft resistance to the conference participants. The third resister at the Triennial was me; I was set to publicly refuse to register for the draft the day after the conference ended.

At the Triennial, there was also a Pentagon analyst who had been working for some years on a secret study of the United States' involvement in Vietnam. He had become increasingly troubled about what he had learned about American policy, and he attended the Triennial because of his growing doubts about the war. This was his first experience with the peace movement. As a Defense Department employee, he was understandably a bit unsure what kind of reception he would receive from this group of peaceniks, but he was pleased with the openness with which he was greeted. He was deeply moved and impressed by Bob and Randy's actions, and he and Randy struck up something of a friendship. They shared some common background, including the fact that they both were alumni of Harvard, and they kept in touch after the conference was over.

I have always thought that the example of Dan Ellsberg attending the WRI Triennial in Haverford and being inspired by the draft resisters he met there is a prime example of how wholly unforeseen good results can spring, sometimes where least expected, from our actions. In August 1969, Ellsberg was an unknown Defense Department analyst. But in June 1971, the entire world learned his name when he released the study he had worked on to the *New York Times* and it was published as the Pentagon Papers.

There were additional remote consequences of those events in 1969 (the WRI Triennial) and 1971 (publication of the Pentagon Papers). Outraged by Ellsberg's action, President Nixon established a clandestine team of burglars known as the White House plumbers, so-called because they were supposed to stop leaks such as Ellsberg's leak of the Pentagon Papers to the *Times*. The plumbers' first operation was to burglarize the office of Ellsberg's psychiatrist in Los Angeles, trying to get negative information with which to discredit Ellsberg. Later the plumbers went on to burglarize the offices of the Democratic National Committee at the Watergate Hotel. In mid-1974, both burglaries formed the basis for articles of impeachment against President Nixon that were approved by the House Judiciary Committee.

When the Triennial ended, I returned to my parents' house in Great Neck to carry out my nonregistration plan. My birthday, August 30, fell on Saturday. Monday was Labor Day, and the draft board would be closed. On Tuesday, September 2, I appeared at "my" draft board. I was scared, but I was also exhilarated. I was finally doing what I had been planning for so many months and years. I went inside and explained to the clerk, Mrs. Abraham, that I would not register. We then had a most amusing dialogue.

Mrs. Abraham gave me the standard Selective Service forms to fill out: name, height, weight, hair color, eye color. In return, I gave Mrs. Abraham a copy of my nonregistration statement and a short lecture, explaining that, for deeply held moral reasons, I would not fill out the forms. So Mrs. Abraham decided to fill out the forms for me.

"What is your hair color, Mr. Elmer?" she asked.

Of course, I was noncooperating. "I am sorry, Mrs. Abraham. It would be against my principles to tell you that information." She glanced up at hair and filled in brown.

"What is your eye color, Mr. Elmer?"

"Mrs. Abraham, don't you get the message yet? I am not going to co-operate with you. I am not going to fill in those forms, and I am not go-ing to give you the required information so you can fill them in for me. I am morally opposed to telling you the color of my eyes." Mrs. Abraham looked at me for a moment and filled in brown.

And so it went. Mrs. Abraham asked my weight and I lectured her about how I would not tell her. She asked my height and I gave her an-other lecture. She filled in the form completely and then came to the signature line.

"Please sign here to show that you have properly registered," she said to me. It was almost comical.

"Mrs. Abraham, haven't you been paying attention? I am not going to register. I am not going to sign your forms. I oppose the draft and won't cooperate with it at all."

"Ah," said Mrs. Abraham. "I think I follow you now. You won't fill in the forms. You won't provide any information. You won't sign your name to anything because you are noncooperating. Is that correct?"

"That's right, Mrs. Abraham. I think you have it now."

"Well, in that case, would you please sign this *other* piece of paper here to show that you are not registering and not cooperating?"

After the discussion with Mrs. Abraham, I took up my vigil outside the draft board. Local Board #3, which had recently been relocated from Great Neck to Manhasset, was one of the busiest draft boards in the country, and there was a steady stream of men going in and out on draft-board business. I distributed leaflets to them explaining that I was in the same position they were in—that is, eighteen years old and legally obli-gated to register—but that I had decided to noncooperate. I urged them to do the same. As planned, I fasted that week. Each day I went down to the draft board and spent the day handing out leaflets to passers-by.

During the course of the week, Bug Rosen spent some time with me.

He had turned eighteen the previous spring. He had been contemplating draft resistance, but had registered anyway. My protest persuaded him to burn his draft card. Bug and I quickly organized a demonstration for Friday, September 5, the last day I was going to be at the draft board, at which he would burn his draft card. Considering the short notice, turn-out was remarkably good: nearly a hundred people attended. Bug tore his draft registration card into thirds; he and I each burned a piece, and our high school classmate Pam Fadem took care of the third.

Art and Cathy Melville were present. They had both been Maryknoll missionaries in Guatemala, and in 1967 had made headlines when they been expelled by the Guatemalan government because of their sympa-thies for the guerrilla movement. I had met them at the CNVA Farm the previous April, and we had become friends. Art spoke briefly at the demonstration.

The demonstration was not only well attended, but received good newspaper and television coverage. The civil disobedience, the visual

Instead of registering with Selective Service when he turned eighteen, as the law required, Jerry fasted for a week and vigiled outside what would otherwise have been "his" draft board, Local Board #3 in Manhasset, New York. He passed out leaflets to the men going into the draft board, urging them not to register or cooperate with the draft. On Friday, September 5, 1969, the last day of the vigil, this anti-draft demonstration was held at the draft board. Photo by Josh Zaret.

"We have chosen to say, with the gift of our liberty, if necessary our lives: the violence stops here, the death stops here, the suppression of the truth stops here, this war stops here."

--Rev. Daniel Berrigan, S. J.

THE DRAFT: WHAT TO DO ?

The Selective Service law requires all men to cooperate with the draft in certain ways: one must register at age 18, one must accept the classification or deferment one is given, one must submit to induction if one is called.

I AM 18 AND HAVE REFUSED REGISTRATION...

I REFUSE TO BE ANY PART

OF THE SELECTIVE SERVICE SYSTEM

It should be apparent by this time in history that war can no longer be used to solve international disputes. Organized violence cannot solve man's problems - it can only compound them further, especially at a time when the next global war threatens the annihilation of mankind. We must begin to explore newer, nonviolent approaches to the resolution of international conflicts.

At home, the Selective Service System oppresses poor people and Black people, on whom the burden of service falls disproportionately. Abroad, the United States military, fed by the Selective Service System, is used to bring untold suffering and anguish to the people of Vietnam in a senseless and criminal war. And our military involvement in Guatemala in 1954 and in the Dominican Republic in 1965 are just two more symptoms of the same disease that has led us into Vietnam. In addition, the Selective Service System represents a form of involuntary servitude, which is specifically prohibited by the thirteenth amendment of the United States Constitution.

If you feel that the draft is wrong, is it right for you to cooperate with it by registering and accepting a classification? I feel that the draft is so murderously wrong that I in conscience cannot be any part of it. Thousands of young men have taken this same step. We are not draft evaders; we are draft resisters. If we wanted to evade the draft we could easily: by accepting a student deferment, or conscientious objector status, or by skipping off to Canada. But rather, we choose to stay here, in order to make our challenge to the Selective Service system open, honest and direct. We act publicly, rather than clandestinely, and are fully willing to accept the consequences of our actions.

There is implicit in my loud and forceful "no" a quiet but hopeful "yes." For in saying "no" to war, and to the misery, death, and exploitation associated with it, I am saying "yes" to the forces of peace and life and joy.

I APPEAL TO YOUR HEARTS AND MINDS. JOIN ME.

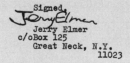

Signed,

Jerry Elmer
c/o Box 125
Great Neck, N.Y.
11023

The leaflet Jerry handed out to men going into the draft board during his week-long vigil in September 1969.

impact of the draft-card burning, and Art and Cathy's celebrity status combined for a newsworthy event.

By publicly refusing to register for the draft, I was "joining"—if that is the right word—the Resistance. The Resistance was something less than an organization; today it would probably be called a network. The Resistance was a loose national confederation of young men who had taken an absolutist position with regard to the draft; these were the complete noncooperators.

Members of the Resistance were draft *resisters*, not draft *dodgers*. This was an important distinction. Draft dodgers were primarily motivated by self-interest. They sought to evade military service because there was a war on and they might get killed. Draft evaders tried to game the system legally by cooperating with Selective Service and applying for deferments or exemptions. If they could not get a draft deferment legally, they might try to fake a disqualifying medical condition or they might flee to Canada. In contrast, draft resisters were more likely to be motivated by an altruistic political or moral opposition to the war. Most resisters were (like me) eligible for easy, safe outs from the military draft themselves (such as a student deferment or CO status) but deliberately chose not to avail themselves of those outs. Instead of evading the draft, members of the Resistance sought to throw the whole weight of their being against the draft through their total noncooperation.

The Resistance had no national board of directors—indeed, no central decision-making body of any sort. It had no formal structure, no dues, no membership cards, and no membership requirements. To be sure, there were offices of the Resistance in many major cities, carrying out anti-draft projects and providing support to resisters and their families. If one was a draft resister, one had "joined" the Resistance.

A few members of the Resistance (that is to say, draft resisters) were pacifists like me, opposed to participation in any war under any circumstances or pretext. A large majority, however, were not pacifists. These were men willing to fight if our country were attacked, but who believed that the Vietnam War was wrong and immoral.

Some members of the Resistance were heavily into the 1960s counterculture of drugs, sex, and rock and roll. Others had strictly conventional lifestyles as college students or professionals and wore ties

Earlier in the week, David "Bug" Rosen had decided to sever his ties with
Selective Service by publicly burning his draft card at the demonstration on
September 5. Bug tore the card into thirds, and three people each burned a
portion of it *(left to right:* Bug Rosen, Pam Fadem, Jerry Elmer). At the time,
even burning part of *someone else's* draft card was a felony, punishable by five
years' imprisonment. Photo by Josh Zaret.

to demonstrations. To call the Resistance "diverse" would have been a
quaint understatement. In fact, the Resistance rather bordered on the
anarchic, with the tone and activities of each chapter or office as varied
as the politics and cultural predilections of the local members.

A few members of the Resistance came to their absolutist position
with regard to Selective Service, as I had done, before their eighteenth
birthdays. These men refused to register. A large majority, however,
came to their position after their eighteenth birthdays. These men then
stopped cooperating with Selective Service. Since the law required men
of draft age to be in possession of their draft cards at all times, some men
burned their draft cards publicly as a symbolic way of showing that they
were severing their ties with Selective Service. Other men mailed their
cards back to the government. Others wrote to their draft boards saying
that they would no longer cooperate.

The act of draft-card burning has an interesting history that goes back at least as far as 1947. That year, there was a proposal introduced into Congress for post-World War II conscription. The proposal was controversial. The United States had never had peacetime conscription (I am not counting here the Selective Training and Service Act of 1940, which immediately preceded U.S. entry into World War II), and many Americans had ancestors who had fled to this country in order to escape conscription in Europe or Russia. In 1947, the proposal for a peacetime draft was especially alarming to pacifists, who saw it as part of a trend toward militarism in American society. Many American pacifists were just then being released from federal prisons, having served sentences for draft resistance during World War II. These men were especially sensitive to the unprecedented proposal for peacetime conscription.

On February 12, 1947, in response to the proposal, WRL and FOR organized Break With Conscription demonstrations in thirty-six states across the country. Among the organizers were A. J. Muste, Dave Dellinger, Bayard Rustin, and Jim Peck.

Dellinger, Rustin, and Peck had all been draft resisters during the war and had all been recently released from prison. Dellinger later became famous as one of the Chicago Seven defendants in the conspiracy trial stemming from the Vietnam peace demonstrations at the Democratic National Convention in Chicago in 1968. He had graduated from Yale and had been a seminarian when he had refused to register for the draft at the beginning of the war; his book about his draft resistance (among other things) was called *From Yale to Jail* (1993). Rustin later was the principal organizer of the 1963 March on Washington at which Martin Luther King Jr. made his "I Have a Dream" speech. In 1947, Jim was already on the staff of WRL; he was still there when I joined the staff in 1969. Both Rustin and Jim Peck had participated in the first Freedom Ride in the South in April 1947; organized by FOR, that early project was called "Journey of Reconciliation."

The largest demonstration on February 12, 1947, occurred in New York, where forty-two draft-age men tore up their draft cards. There was an amusing twist to this event. After an outdoor demonstration, the anti-draft group went indoors to the Labor Temple, on East Fourteenth Street. The forty-two men intended to burn their draft cards there, and had announced their intention in advance to the press. The New York City fire marshal, however, informed the men that they could not burn the cards indoors, so the well-behaved demonstrators tore up the cards instead. The torn up cards were later burned outdoors. One of the speakers in New York was Dwight Macdonald, then a member of the WRL Executive Committee. Twenty-one years later, he was one of our speakers at the Peace School in Great Neck during the academic strike in April 1968.

In Washington, DC, twelve men burned draft cards in front of the White House. In a secret memorandum dated that same morning, FBI Director J. Edgar Hoover advised the Attorney General not to arrest them: "To try and stop this action would make martyrs out of those responsible, which is just what they want." Unmentioned by Hoover was the fact that burning draft cards was not then illegal. (The memo was released in 2004 in response to a Freedom of Information Act request filed by FOR. It was part of a 76-volume FBI file on the organization dating back to 1923.)

One of the draft-card burners in February 1947 wrote to President Truman about his decision to break with Selective Service. The letter (also part of the FBI surveillance file) sounds much like the personal statements of Vietnam-era draft resisters a generation later:

> This is to inform you of my intention to break with conscription by publicly burning my draft card. This is not only a protest against the present Selective Service Act but against any proposal for compulsory military training. . . . My draft card is a symbol of acquiesence to the conscriptive system when in my possession; I will not even passively submit to the act. . . .

During the spring and early summer of 1965, as the Vietnam War heated up, there were a few sporadic cases of individual resisters burning their draft cards at demonstrations. For example, five men burned their draft cards on July 29, 1965, at an anti-war demonstration at the army induction center at Whitehall Street in Manhattan. The act of burning a draft card was still not itself illegal, although it did clearly put a man in jeopardy of prosecution for not having his draft card in his possession. And, naturally, a man's subsequent noncooperation with Selective Service *always* put him at risk of criminal prosecution. Most often this came about by the man being reclassified 1-A (immediately eligible to be drafted) by his draft board because he refused to fill out the forms that might lead to an deferment or exemption. Then the resister, newly reclassified 1-A, would receive a draft notice. Of course, he would refuse to be inducted. Then he would be indicted, almost always for refusing induction, and sometimes also for other Selective Service violations as well.

Nevertheless, in early 1965, draft-card burning was really just a catchy, photogenic way for a draft resister to announce to the world that from then on he would no longer cooperate with Selective Service. But catchy it was, and the tactic soon drew the attention and ire of those who supported the war. During the summer of 1965, Congressman Mendel Rivers, chairman of the House Armed Services Committee, introduced a bill to make burning a draft card a felony punishable by five years' imprisonment. Rivers was not only an outspoken hawk but an ardent racist and segregationist as well. In 1948, he had supported Strom Thurmond's Dixiecrat presidential race; Thurmond had decided to run because the Democratic Party had included a mild civil rights plank in its platform. As late as 1966, Rivers was the only member of either house of Congress to admit openly that he was a member of the white supremacist White Citizens Council. He had staunchly opposed every civil rights bill ever introduced, regardless of how moderate.

On August 11, 1965, the House passed Congressman Rivers's bill on draft-card burning by a vote of 393–1. "This bill places these birds where they belong," Rivers said, referring to draft-card burners, "behind bars." There was not much floor debate on the bill, but some of what was said was truly purple. Referring to peace demonstrators, one congressman said, "These mobs of so-called students and Communist stooges attempt to create fear and destroy self-confidence in our country ... they publicly mutilate or burn their draft cards ... they [are] generally a filthy, sleazy beatnik gang. ... ." The Rivers bill moved on to the Senate, where its chief sponsor was Strom Thurmond. On August 20, *Life* magazine, a popular weekly at the time, carried a picture of Chris Kearns burning his draft card. This was just the push the bill needed in the Senate. It quickly passed the following week, and it was signed into law by President Johnson on my birthday, August 30.

The first person to burn a draft card publicly after the new law was enacted was David Miller. Miller was described in one contemporaneous account as "a recent graduate of LeMoyne College, a tall, Nordic athlete who could grace any [military] recruiting poster." On October 15, 1965, there were peace demonstrations all across the country. What may have been the largest started at UC Berkeley with demonstrators marching to the Oakland Army Base. More than three dozen demonstrators were arrested at the draft boards in Ann Arbor, Michigan. Miller had been asked to speak at the demonstration in Manhattan at the Whitehall Street induction center. He appeared at the demonstration in a suit and tie, next to a large American flag. Rather than delivering himself of a long harangue, Miller just burned his draft card. Two days later, Miller was arrested—again in suit and tie—in New Hampshire, where he was traveling, doing speaking engagements on college campuses about draft resistance.

The government had hoped, no doubt, that making it a felony to burn a draft card would stem the tide of these protests. If so, that hope was cheated. The same day Miller was arrested in New Hampshire, a demonstration was held at the federal courthouse at Foley Square in New York, at which ten men, most but not all of draft age, announced that they, too, were draft resisters. Their leaflet said, in part: "We ourselves have destroyed or returned our draft cards. By these acts we have hoped to reach the conscience of our fellow Americans—to open their eyes to the crimes their government is now committing in Vietnam."

One of the Foley Square demonstrators was Jim Peck. To be sure, Jim *had* burned his draft card, and *was* a draft resister (and, in fact, had served three years in prison for his draft resistance); but what the Foley Square leaflet did not say was that Jim had been a resister during World War II, and had burned his draft card as part of the Break With Conscription events in 1947.

After Dave Miller burned his draft card, the tactic spread like, well, wildfire. In their individualistic, unorganized ways, draft resisters all over the country started burning draft cards alone or in small groups. One such event took place on November 6, 1965, when Dave McReynolds, Tom Cornell, and three others (all in white shirts, dark suits, and ties) burned their draft cards at a demonstration in Union Square, New York, while A. J. Muste looked on. What had until recently only been a public symbol of an underlying decision not to cooperate with Selective Service now became—because of the new law—a powerful act of

On November 6, 1965, five men burned their draft cards at a demonstration at Union Square in New York City. *Left to right:* Tom Cornell, Marc Edelman, Roy Lisker, David McReynolds, and Jim Wilson. A. J. Muste (in hat and top coat) looks on. Photo by Neil Haworth, from Records of the *WIN Magazine* Collection, Swarthmore Peace Collection.

defiance in and of itself. By burning their draft cards, first dozens, then scores, then hundreds of men said openly to the government that, in order to continue to prosecute the war, the government would have to lock them and a lot of their friends up in prison for long periods of time. Especially threatening to the government was the fact that many of the resisters were middle-class kids who, like Dave Miller, were from respectable families and had attended good colleges.

At the large, legal anti-war demonstration in New York City on April 15, 1967, the first mass draft-card burning of the Vietnam era was held. Almost five hundred men participated. There was some squeamishness on the part of the Fifth Avenue Vietnam Peace Parade Committee, the organizer of the legal mass demonstration, over the proposed civil

The first large-scale burning of individual draft cards by resisters took place on Saturday, April 15, 1967, in Sheep's Meadow in New York's Central Park, on the same day as a mass, legal anti-war demonstration. The cards were collected and burned in a coffee can. Photo by Diana Davies, from Records of the *WIN Magazine* Collection, Swarthmore Peace Collection.

disobedience. An accommodation was reached whereby the draft-card burning was separated slightly in time and geography from the main event. The slight separation fooled no one, and the draft-card burning figured prominently in the news coverage of the day's events. This first mass draft-card burning was a success, and a new organization was born, the Resistance, to promote draft resistance and support the resisters.

The first nationally coordinated event of the new organization was held on October 16, 1967, when 1,400 draft cards were burned by men in simultaneous demonstrations, small and large, in thirty cities across the country. This was also the first stand-alone mass draft-card burning—one not associated with or a part of a larger, legal demonstration. Whether or not the organizers were aware of the fact, the October 16 event was highly reminiscent of the Break With Conscription demonstrations that had taken place nationwide in 1947.

The next nationally coordinated draft-card burning—the third one to occur, and the second one organized by the Resistance—took place on April 3, 1968. Charles DeBenedetti writes in *An American Ordeal* that this event "generated fewer resisters than previous ones and little public interest." Even at the strictly factual level, DeBenedetti is wrong: fully 1,000 men turned in draft cards at coordinated events nationwide. In Boston alone, 235 men turned in draft cards at a support demonstration attended by 15,000 people. By any reasonable, objective measure, the April 3 events were successful *both* in increasing actual draft resistance *and* generating public interest.

But DeBenedetti misses a wider point, too. After the April 3 draft-card turn-in, there *was* something of a change in how new resisters made their stands public, but it was a change that reflected the growing success and public support for draft resistance—not the opposite (as DeBenedetti incorrectly suggests). In early 1967, draft-card burning had been a relatively new tactic. Because of both its perceived newness and the long prison terms which resisters were inviting, it was a scary step for many men to contemplate. If there were not true safety in numbers, at least there was some comfort, and it was natural that those contemplating total resistance would seek a single large event where their morale could be boosted by the presence of many like-minded men undertaking similar risk. But after October 16, 1967, draft resistance grew by leaps and bounds. Resistance offices, disorganized and anarchic though they were, sprang up all across the country. Draft-card burning was no longer seen as new. Over time there was a metamorphosis. In the place of rare, mass draft-card burnings, where resisters sought to take heart from whatever strength there might be in numbers, there were now many smaller events in which one, two, or a few men burned draft cards. The point which historians like DeBenedetti miss is that it was precisely the *growth* of the draft resistance movement that made mass, coordinated draft-card burnings less necessary in 1968 than they had been in 1967, and even less necessary in 1969 than they had been in 1968.

The threat to the government that undergirded everything the Resistance did—that in order to prosecute the war the government would have to imprison thousands of middle-class kids—was becoming a reality. By December 1968, there were 729 members of the Resistance in federal prison. More than a thousand others had already refused induction and were thus subject to indictment at any time.

Based on the forms that Mrs. Abraham had filled in for me, Selective Service considered me to be registered "in absentia" (even though I had not signed anything), and I was sent a draft registration card in the mail a few weeks after my vigil and fast at the draft board. The card arrived with a form letter that said, "This is to certify that, in accordance with the law, you have registered with Selective Service." In November, I organized another demonstration at the draft board, at which I publicly burned the registration card. A while after the registration card, I received my classification card. Because I had not filled in any of the Selective Service forms that would have been necessary to apply for a deferment or exemption from the draft, I was classified 1-A.

Before I could be drafted, however, the government put into place the draft lottery. The Selective Service System had been severely criticized for being unfair—for allowing middle-class white kids to buy their way out of the draft with college deferments, while poor black kids were drafted and sent to Vietnam. The lottery system had been designed to counter those charges of unfairness. Each registrant received a random number based on his date of birth. The lottery was a sham, though: the entire, elaborate system of deferments and exemptions that favored the rich and the middle-class over the poor remained completely intact. All that changed was that there was now a randomized procedure for deciding the order in which the minority of men classified 1-A would get their induction notices.

My draft lottery number, 187, was neither high nor low. (My friend Michael Shapiro lucked out and got a very high number, 333, guaranteeing that even if he were ever classified 1-A, he would never receive a draft notice.) My number was low enough that, since I was classified 1-A, I eventually did receive a notice to appear for a pre-induction physical examination. Of course, I refused to go. But my number was also high enough that, in the end, I never actually received an induction order.

Still, I had violated the draft law repeatedly. Refusing to register was a felony, punishable by up to five years' imprisonment. Each time I burned a draft card—Bug's on September 5, my own in November—that was an additional felony punishable by another five years' imprisonment. Refusing the pre-induction physical, even though I later never received an induction order, was a felony.

Nevertheless, I was never prosecuted for my individual draft resistance. This was a bit unusual, since public nonregistrants always had the highest rate of prosecutions of any form of resistance. Although I was never sure why I was not prosecuted, I think part of the reason probably was that, by the time the government would have gotten around to prosecuting me, I was already under indictment for draft-related offenses in Providence. The government could send me to prison for as long as it wished in Providence; why waste time and money with a duplicative prosecution in New York?

After their initial horror, my parents came to understand, and even respect, my nonregistration. My act was, in a sense, my parents' chickens coming home to roost. It was, after all, my father who had brought me to my first peace demonstration four years earlier. It was political discussions with my parents at home that had stirred my early conscience. More significantly, it was my family's history with the Nazis that helped to motivate my nonregistration.

All my years growing up there had been an unspoken *leitmotif* in the background of my life, of my family's life: trouble with the Nazis. Some of my family members had escaped Hitler; others had perished. Something had puzzled me my whole life. I had no trouble understanding Hitler and the Nazis; human cruelty was not nice, but it was not incomprehensible either. Human history was largely the history of humankind's inhumanity to humankind. But what *was* incomprehensible was the silence of an entire people in the face of unspeakable atrocities. I knew that my act of nonregistration might not end the war, but while my country was perpetrating crimes against humanity it would at least break the silence.

4
Draft-File Destruction
Six Draft Boards in Boston

YOUNG CHILDREN TEND TO MAKE unwarranted extrapolations of broad principles based on their own peculiar, personal experiences. For instance, when I was six years old, I knew that women drink coffee in the morning but men drink tea, because that was what my parents did. In the same way, I knew that only women smoke cigarettes but men smoke pipes.

I was embarrassingly old—perhaps already in junior high school—before I came to understand the religious composition of the United States. Until then, I had assumed that the United States was religiously the same as the friends and neighbors I knew in Great Neck: 97% Jewish, 3% Christian—that is, Catholic. The fact that "Christian" is not synonymous with "Catholic" never entered my consciousness since the only Christians I really knew—the Conés across the street and the Bachors next door—were Catholic. I had probably never even heard the word "Presbyterian."

When, after high school, I became deeply involved with "Catholic Left"—the Berrigans and others who were involved in draft-file destruction and other acts of war resistance—my parents tried to tell me that these people were not representative of the Catholic Church as a whole. But I would not listen.

In certain respects, I was correct: my new friends in the Catholic Left *were* in many ways representative products of typical Catholic upbringings. Many of the women were either nuns or lay parochial-school teachers. The men were priests: Jesuits, Josephites, Servites. Almost all were themselves products of Catholic parochial schools. Words like Eucharist and Holy Father and eschatological and Blessed Virgin, words that I had never heard before, rolled off their tongues with great regularity.

Nevertheless, my parents were, of course, correct: the Catholic Left was not representative of the Catholic Church as a whole. The members of the Catholic Left were heavily involved in radical politics. Many of the priests had married; occasionally one of the nuns became pregnant.

In a way, those in the Catholic Left were as insular and isolated in their overall *Weltanschauung* as I was. Theirs was a world of catechism and confession and mass. They may have known intellectually that the United States was not 97% Catholic, but they were like me in the sense that all of their friends and associates were of the same religion as they were. In fact, in their case, their friends were not merely nominally Catholic, but Catholics for whom Church policy, theology, and institutions stood at the very center of their lives.

I was interested in draft-file destruction from the very first Action. On October 27, 1967—the week after the "Confront the Warmakers" march on Washington—Phil Berrigan, Tom Louis, Dave Eberhardt, and Jim Mengel walked into a Baltimore draft board, poured blood over the files, handed out Bibles to the startled Selective Service clerks, and prayed while waiting for the police to arrive to arrest them.

Their Action had an immediate and strong fascination for me. I had been disturbed at the Pentagon demonstration, as I often was at such events, that some of the participants would sing songs, shout rude slogans, and dress like hippies. To me, issues of war and peace were serious business; ending the war should be a solemn undertaking. The tone of our demonstrations, I believed, should reflect the seriousness of the issue we were confronting. Children were being burned alive with napalm—this was not an occasion for levity.

The Baltimore blood-pouring appealed to me because I felt that the protesters, by risking twenty-three years in prison each for their action, were demonstrating that they *were* taking the war seriously. And the symbolic shedding of blood over draft files, to protest the real shedding of blood in Vietnam, stirred me deeply.

I had already thought long and deeply about the war and about civil disobedience in connection with my then-developing decision to refuse to register with Selective Service. The similarities between nonregistration and draft-file destruction were obvious: refusing to register and destroying draft files both involved civil disobedience. Many of the questions posed by the two different types of actions were the same: is it ever permissible to break the law? If so, when and in what ways? What about going to prison?

But there were important differences, too. One difference was that, by publicly refusing to register, one was "merely" declining to take part in the war oneself. I understood the old anti-war adage that "wars will end when men refuse to fight." I certainly understood the central importance of young men like me who *said* they opposed the war refusing to participate in it. Still, it seemed to me that "just" refusing to take part myself was not enough—that, in addition to that, I should go out and actively do the most powerful, most active, most effective thing I could think of to stop the war. Destroying draft files seemed to be that thing.

Another difference had to do with how a person could come to either decision. Individual draft resistance was very much a decision thrust upon a man whether he wanted to face the issue of the draft or not. The legal requirement to register for the draft at age eighteen meant that every man of draft age *had* to decide what to do, whether he wanted to or not. Not deciding not to register was to decide.

But draft-file destruction was different. With draft-file destruction, not to decide was merely not to decide.

In May 1968, I was moved again by an act of draft-file destruction, this time in Catonsville, Maryland. After being convicted of the previous blood-pouring, two of the Baltimore defendants, Phil Berrigan and Tom Louis, joined with seven others to destroy Selective Service records at a draft board in the Baltimore suburb. They entered the draft board, cleaned the 1-A files into trash baskets, carried the files outside, and burned them in a parking lot with napalm they had made themselves from a recipe found in a Green Beret manual. The symbolism of destroying draft files with napalm went straight to my heart. In October, when the Catonsville Nine were tried in federal court, I clipped the daily reports of the trial from the *New York Times* to read and reread. I still have those yellowing clippings today.

The Catonsville Nine was typical, in both composition and outlook, of the various groups of Catholic Left draft-board raiders that followed. The group consisted of two priests (Phil Berrigan and Dan Berrigan),

The third draft-board Action (raid on a draft board to destroy files) occurred on May 17, 1968. Nine Catholics entered Local Board #33 in Catonsville, Maryland, cleaned the 1-A files (of men immediately eligible to be drafted) into a trash can, and took them outside to a parking lot where they burned the files with napalm they had made themselves from a recipe found in a Green Beret manual. *Left to right:* Father Tom Melville, Father Phil Berrigan and Father Dan Berrigan. Courtesy of the *Baltimore Sun.*

an ex-priest (Tom Melville), an ex-nun (Marjorie Melville, Tom's wife), a Christian Brother (David Darst), and four others (Tom Louis, George Mische, John Hogan, and Mary Moylan). The group's public statement said, in part, "We are Catholic Christians who take the Gospel of our

Faith seriously." Fully one third of their statement, five out of fifteen paragraphs, consisted of lengthy excerpts of a papal encyclical, *The Development of Peoples*.

During the autumn of 1968, I organized an evening seminar on the draft for SPV. One of the speakers was to have been Jim Forest, but he was unable to be in Great Neck on the night of the program because he was on trial in Milwaukee. He had taken part in the Milwaukee Fourteen draft-board Action in which files at several draft boards, all in one complex, had been burned on September 14, 1968. The Catonsville Nine/Milwaukee Fourteen Defense Committee sent as a substitute speaker Paul Mayer, with whom I subsequently became friendly. Paul, who was then in his early forties, had been born in pre-war Germany into a Jewish family and had had a bar mitzvah at age thirteen, but had later become not only a Catholic priest but a Benedictine monk. He had still later left the order to marry (a former nun, Naomi), and had become involved with the Catholic Left.

When Paul came to Great Neck to speak at our SPV seminar, I told him privately of my interest in draft-board Actions and in possibly participating in one myself. We met a second time, at his home in Edgewater, New Jersey, to discuss the matter further. He arranged a third meeting for more discussion, this time in Central Park on a weekday. I cut school for the day to attend this meeting and forged an excuse note to the school with my father's signature. It was 1969, the winter of my senior year in high school.

By spring, I had also had many long, intense discussions about draft-file destruction with my classmate Bug Rosen. On Monday, May 26, 1969, Bug and I met, as we often did, before school at my locker outside Mr. Postiglione's classroom in the science wing of the school. I showed Bug an article in that day's New York Times—about the Action of the Chicago Fifteen the previous day, during which files had been destroyed at a Selective Service complex on the South Side of Chicago that housed thirty-four draft boards. Bug and I whooped for joy. At that moment, I knew that he and I would end up in a draft-board Action together some day.

Bug and I discussed taking part in an Action with another classmate, Ellen Gaine. I continued to be in touch with Paul Mayer, and he said that if we really wanted to pursue the matter further, we needed to go to Baltimore to talk with Phil Berrigan. Phil was using his time before prison to organize additional Actions involving new people.

Bug, Ellen and I decided to go by Greyhound bus to Baltimore over Memorial Day weekend to meet Phil. Paul Mayer made all the necessary arrangements to let Phil know to expect us. I told my parents that we were going to visit Art Levine, a friend from Great Neck who had graduated from my high school the previous year and was now a freshman at Johns Hopkins.

After school, on Friday, May 23, Bug, Ellen, and I took the Long Island Railroad from Great Neck into Manhattan and took the Eighth Avenue subway one stop uptown to the Port Authority bus terminal. When we got to the Port Authority, the place looked like Coney Island on the fourth of July. The station was so jammed with holiday travelers that one could scarcely move. All the buses to Baltimore were full and even with extra buses it would be late at night before we would be able to board one. Bug and Ellen decided to go home. I was too determined, however, to be deterred by the wait, so I stuck it out. (Ellen never did participate in a draft-board action. Bug did, eventually, but not that year.)

It was after 2:00 A.M. when I got to Baltimore. City buses did not run that late so I walked to Art Levine's frat house (where I was, in fact, spending the night). At dawn, before anyone else in the house was awake, I walked to the Josephite Fathers house at 1130 North Calvert Street, where Phil Berrigan lived.

Phil Berrigan was undoubtedly the most charismatic person I have ever met. His size—he was tall and broad-shouldered—probably played a role in that, but he also had a commanding presence that could not be fully explained either by his physical stature or his keen intellect. I did not always agree with him politically, but his power in a room was one that could never be ignored, one that a person had to experience personally in order to understand fully.

It must have been a strange meeting that day: the Jewish high-school student from Great Neck coming, in effect, to apply for a job, to seek a position, in a draft-board Action from the Catholic priest who served as the clearinghouse for much of that recruiting. We sat in the front parlor of the Josephite Fathers house during our meeting. The sun streamed in through the windows facing North Calvert Street. We talked for several hours. Phil offered me no refreshment during that time. He questioned me closely about the history of and reasons for my interest in draft-board Actions, about my own Selective Service status, and about my background in the peace movement. He seemed not at all perturbed by the fact that I was not Catholic, but was concerned about my age. "We've had mixed success with young people," he said.

Phil thought it would be good for me to meet two other people. One was Ann Speltz, who lived in Washington, DC; I could see her that weekend before returning to New York. Ann lived in a communal house at 1620 S Street NW, which served as both an office and living quarters for the defense committee of the DC Nine, the group that the previous March had poured blood on files at the Washington offices of Dow Chemical Corporation, manufacturer of the napalm used by the United States in Vietnam. Art and Cathy Melville, who had attended the demonstration in Manhasset when I had refused to register, had been participants in the DC Nine Action. When I arrived at S Street, Ann was out. I explained to the person who answered the door that I had come at the suggestion of Phil Berrigan. Soon a small group of people from the house had gathered around me to meet the emissary from the Great Man, as Phil was universally regarded at that time by nearly all in the Catholic Left.

The second person Phil suggested I see was Liz McAlister, a nun in Manhattan. Phil had a certain tone in his voice when he spoke of her, which I did not understand at the time. Years later it was revealed that Phil and Liz had been secret lovers. They eventually married.

Despite the fact that Phil had been noncommittal during our meeting about my actual participation in a draft-board Action, we kept in touch during the summer by letter. While I was in San Francisco that summer, I sought out contacts there with people associated with the Catholic Left. I met Tom Durkin, who ran the Society of Priests for a Free Ministry, a group of married (ex-)priests. Tom encouraged me to meet a nun from St. Louis, Missouri, who was passing through town: Joann Malone, another a member of the DC Nine.

Joann was staying with an old friend of hers, Phil Trainor, a priest who lived in the Servite Fathers house on Stanyan Street, adjacent to Golden Gate Park. I walked there from the WRL office on Haight Street and met Joann on Wednesday afternoon, August 13. Although Joann and I were different in many respects (to take but a single example, she was a nun who taught Latin in a parochial school; I was a Jewish kid from Great Neck who had flunked Latin in high school), we shared a certain irreverence for authority. Joann was hitchhiking across the country with her friend, Laura Zygnowicz, a topless dancer from Detroit. Joann gleefully showed me an article that had just been published in the liberal *National Catholic Reporter*, describing her (with an appropriate photograph) as the "nun who wears mini-skirts and hitchhikes."

I had planned a trip for that weekend to Pt. Reyes National Seashore with John-i-thin Stephens. I asked Joann whether she and Laura would like to join us. They agreed. John-i-thin, always interested in meeting women, was delighted. That weekend, John-i-thin glommed onto Laura, while Joann and I talked for hours about her participation in the DC Nine Action, about my interest in taking part in a future Action, and my upcoming nonregistration, which was then only two weeks away. These were intense discussions on exciting, heady topics.

We went to Wildcat Beach, which was inaccessible by car. To reach the beach, we had to hike in from the trailhead for several hours. Both the trail and the beach itself were totally deserted. At one point, I took off my bathing suit and suggested to Joann that she do the same. She did, and we spent much of the weekend romping naked on the sand and in the surf. Joann got badly sunburned on those portions of her body that were not normally exposed to direct sunlight. I started necking with Joann on the beach, and when she did not turn me down, I slowly got bolder and bolder. I couldn't believe what was happening.

When we returned to the city at the end of the weekend, Joann and I slept together. In the next room of the apartment where we were staying, there was a very conventional Christian Brother, Gerald ("Chris") Montesano. Chris also couldn't believe what was happening. I lost my virginity to a Catholic nun on a mattress on a living-room floor in Oakland, California, on Sunday evening, August 17, 1969, directly under a draft-resistance poster that showed Joan Baez and her two sisters sitting primly on a sofa under the words, "Girls Say Yes to Boys Who Say No."

My parents were right: the Catholics I was meeting were *not* typically representative of the Roman Catholic Church.

I left the next week for the drive east to the WRI triennial conference. Then, after my week at the draft board, I went to work for WRL at its national office at 339 Lafayette Street, in New York City. At first, I did not have a place of my own, so I stayed as a guest at Dave McReynolds's apartment, a small walk-up on East Fourth Street, near the WRL office. The apartment was a so-called "railroad flat," so named because there were no hallways between rooms; the rooms were laid out like a railroad train, in a line, with each room opening directly into the next. Dave made his bedroom in the living room, which opened onto the kitchen at one end of the apartment. The only bathroom was at the opposite end. Dave had to walk through my sleeping room to use his bathroom. Whenever I used the kitchen I was, in effect, in Dave's bedroom.

That autumn, Dave was working on—actually, agonizing over would be more accurate—the article in which he would come out publicly for the first time as being gay. This was the cause of his tardiness with the *Give Earth A Chance* leaflet. The article was published in the November 15, 1969, issue of *WIN Magazine*, a special gay rights issue, as "Notes For A More Coherent Article." Watching Dave struggle nightly with the article, I had no idea what he was working on, but it was clear to me that for Dave the process was excruciating. (I was correct. In the article, Dave wrote, "It is hard to write this. It has become a three-Miltown-a-day article.") He worked late into every night, writing until two or three A.M., long after I had gone to sleep; he was also drinking heavily, arriving at the office each day around noon, terribly hung over.

I was not a good guest. For reasons that baffled me at the time, Dave was not happy that I made liberal use of his kitchen and left piles of dirty dishes in the sink. He finally blew up at me and insisted that I wash the dishes I used. I resolved to clean up my act (and Dave's kitchen). The next day, Dave arrived home and was aghast to find me scrubbing his cast iron pan—a pan he had carefully seasoned for over a decade, never allowing it near water (much less hot, soapy water). I had not done it out of malice; I just did not know any better.

After a couple of weeks of this, when I showed no signs of finding a place of my own, Dave finally gave me an ultimatum. I would have to move out in a week, whether or not I had my own place.

With the help of a friend, Brad Lyttle, I found a small apartment in a tenement on Tenth Street, between First and Second Avenues. The place was unfurnished and I had no money for furnishings. It was infested with roaches and bedbugs. I had the place sprayed with malathion to kill the vermin. This worked for a while, but within a few weeks the roaches and bedbugs were back. I had the apartment sprayed again, but once again the benefits were short-lived. My bathtub was in the kitchen; the bathroom was in the hall. The realtor had admonished me to put a padlock on the bathroom door. When I moved in, I had not yet done so; when I went to the bathroom for the first time, I found two heroin addicts shooting up in it.

I viewed the job at WRL as a temporary expedient: I assumed that I was going to prison fairly soon, either as a result of my individual draft resistance or because of participation in a future draft-board Action, and I viewed the job at WRL as little more than something to keep me busy in the meantime.

I was an abysmally poor employee. This was the first office job I had ever had and I was not ready for a situation without clearly defined work hours—in which flexibility was permitted but self-discipline and a sense of responsibility were expected. My major responsibility in the office was maintaining the mailing list, a task that I found boring and for which I lacked the necessary stick-to-itiveness.

I took two-hour lunch breaks. I left for the weekend at 11:00 A.M. on Fridays and didn't get back until noon on Mondays. At first these week-ends were recreational; once, I accompanied Joann, who had moved to New York that autumn as well, on a hitchhiking trip to Detroit to visit Laura. Soon, however, my weekends were devoted to retreats in and around Boston in preparation for an Action there. I am ashamed to say that I used the position at WRL to provide a paycheck ($65 per week) in return for a job that I performed poorly while my heart and soul were really concerned with participating in a draft-board Action as soon as possible.

The way to become part of a group planning a draft-board Action was to attend a series of preparatory weekend retreats. The retreats were primarily organized and run by Phil Berrigan. Several other priests and nuns from previous Actions played a variety of supporting roles, from cooking for the group to helping run the discussion sessions.

These retreats served two separate and distinct functions. First, they were similar to the encounter groups that were becoming popular at that time. The theory was that if you were going to become involved in a high-risk public action together with other people you should first know them very intimately. In the context of possible twenty-three-year prison sentences, it was perfectly reasonable to want to know your partners well and to understand their motivations, their strengths and their weaknesses—in short, to feel comfortable with them. Nevertheless, the encounter-group aspect of the retreats sometimes got out of hand, with a whole room full of high-powered, articulate people focusing relentlessly on some perceived shortcoming or inadequacy of a particular individual until that person was reduced to tears or felt constrained to withdraw from the group and its process.

One of the questions we analyzed in excruciating detail at these retreats was the feelings of each group member about going to prison. There were lots of discussions about prison among peace movement activists in the late 1960s. It was the height of the draft-resistance movement, and there were many white, middle-class guys who, had they been born a few years earlier or later, would have been at Princeton or Yale, but found themselves in federal prison instead. Yet the discussions about prison at these retreats were certainly the best I was ever a part of. There was little superficiality ("You'll be more effective on the outside"), probably because of the nature of our shared enterprise.

Like most of the group, I was scared—very scared—of prison. But I also had a sense that, unlike some of the others, I was not confronting the issue for the first time. I had already thought deeply about prison pretty consistently for two years or so in connection with my own draft nonregistration. Thus, many of the issues raised by the possibility of going to prison were by then familiar emotional territory for me.

In other respects, however, there was a gulf separating me from some of the other people at these retreats on the issue of prison. I remember some of the priests who had already been to prison saying that their prison time had been relatively easier and had involved relatively less personal sacrifice than their time as novices in their respective religious orders. Although it was never really discussed at the retreats, it was always apparent to me that draft-board Actions had a disproportionately large share of principled, religious celibates taking part, and it is clear why. Not only were these celibates not held back by entangling family commitments, but prison did not mean for them a newly enforced sexual abstinence. But I had taken no vow of celibacy. I was just beginning to learn about myself as a sexual person and the possibility of cutting off that exploration abruptly weighed heavily in the scales of my decision-making.

The second function of the preparatory retreats was logistical. This involved detailed planning of the burglary being considered. In Boston, we planned to destroy files simultaneously at six draft boards at four locations in the city (two locations had one draft board at each; two locations had two draft boards at each). Each of the four sites was cased and analyzed in minute detail. We studied the neighborhoods, the bus lines, the buildings in which the draft boards were located, and all the neighboring buildings. We drew maps of each building to be burglarized, paying special attention to doors, windows, locks, security. We asked, and answered, what seemed like a thousand questions of detail: *Were the doors wood or metal? Were the hinges on the outside or inside? Where were the electrical outlets? What was the electrical current in the building? Who worked in the building and what were their hours? Was there a guard on duty at night? What about a janitor?* We drew maps of the inside of each Selective Service office, locating 1-A files and each portion of the cross-reference system. Every small piece of information was scrutinized; we spent weeks casing and planning. The retreats leading up to the Boston Action were mostly held in and around Boston; soon after starting my office job at WRL in Manhattan, I was splitting each week between New York and Boston.

Encounter groups in general were a relatively new phenomenon of the late 1960s and these retreats were not necessarily run by people experienced or knowledgeable about group dynamics or collective process. Yet the retreats worked. They worked to build a cohesive group. They worked to build mutual trust, respect, and even love among members of the group. Finally, they worked as a way to get a very large job done in a relatively short period of time. There were problems, but the shared political commitment and dedication of the participants acted as a powerful countervailing force to overcome whatever deficiencies there may have been in the process itself or the people leading it.

The group that was coming together at the retreats I attended was more or less typical of groups coalescing around that time for draft-board Actions. The group was predominantly (but not exclusively) Catholic and predominantly (but also not exclusively) under the philosophical sway of Phil Berrigan.

Tony Scoblick, 29, was, like Phil, a Josephite priest from Baltimore. When discussing his motivation for taking part in draft-file destruction, he referred often to a black Josephite friend of his, Phil Linden. Tony's friend had experienced discrimination throughout his life; Tony's participation, he seemed to be telling us, was a means of proving himself to Linden. It seemed to me to be an odd motivation.

One of the themes running through the draft-board Actions was the idea of being driven to extreme action when other, milder routes had failed. *We are Americans who have exhausted legitimate means of dissent,* stressed Phil at the Catonsville trial. *We have marched, picketed, and demonstrated legally. Our civil disobedience comes, at least in part, because these other methods didn't work.* The same message emerges from our press statement after the Boston Action: "We have marched, written letters, conferred with officialdom, spoken against the war . . . If you feel as we do that marching and demonstrating are unproductive, we encourage you to take responsible action . . ." This idea of having tried other, less drastic, methods before resorting to the more extreme method of destroying draft files was certainly true for me. I had been active in the peace movement since 1965. In 1966, I had campaigned for Stanley Millet, a peace candidate for Congress. As a member of SPV, I had taken part in weekly peace vigils in Great Neck. I had written letters to members of Congress, taken part in legal peace demonstrations, fasted, signed petitions, publicly refused to register for the draft. But Tony Scoblick told us that he had never taken part in any peace activity until this one. For Tony, draft-file destruction was not the logical culmination of years of gradually increasing involvement in the peace movement. It was his first contact with the peace movement.

Mary Cain, 30, was a nun who lived in New York and had taught in parochial schools. She struck me as cold and aloof. Once, between retreats, I called her mid-week from my office at WRL. Since we were going to be involved in a draft-board Action together, I thought it might be good to get to know her a little better. I suggested we get together for lunch. Her curt, negative reply left me feeling like my suggestion had involved some obscure, Catholic sin. Shortly after the Boston Action, Tony and Mary were married.

Claudette Piper, 27, lived in Washington, DC, where she worked full-time for the then-newly-formed National Council to Repeal the Draft. (For Claudette, unlike Tony, the Boston Action was a culmination of gradually escalating involvement in the peace movement.) Claudette had been recently divorced from Harold Piper, a reporter for the Baltimore Sun, and seemed different from most of the group. For one thing, I don't think she was Catholic; religious beliefs were certainly not at the top of her list of motivations for participation in the Action as they were for Tony and Mary. And Claudette was a sexual person. At one of the retreats, Claudette and I slept in adjacent sleeping bags on the floor and she came on to me. "I am a very earthy person," she said. "I have earthy, physical needs." I kissed her but she kept moving my hand to her crotch. But I was young, bumbling, and inexperienced and had no idea what to do, so nothing happened.

John Galvani, at age 32, was the senior member of our group. John was a priest, a Jesuit, and an Arabic scholar. He had lived for several years in the Middle East.

Paul Couming, 21, was a draft resister from Boston. Paul was a paradox. In certain respects he fit into the group perfectly: he was from a good Catholic family in the Dorchester neighborhood of Boston. In other respects he seemed out of place: he came from a working-class family and sometimes he seemed a bit at sea amidst the cerebral, Jesuitical discussions to which some of the others were prone.

Bill Au, 20, was a seminarian from Baltimore and obviously under the influence of Phil, whom he called "Uncle Ho." Bill was not alone in this. The reference was to Ho Chi Minh, the venerated head of the Communist Party of Vietnam, who had led the resistance struggle against the French. As used by Bill to refer to Phil, it was a term of fawning obsequiousness.

Darrell Dewease, 22, was a peace activist from Philadelphia. Like Claudette, he was not noticeably religious.

Barb Shapiro, 20, joined the group rather late and I did not get to know her well. Despite the name, she was apparently not Jewish. She had taught at a Catholic parochial school in California and, shortly after the Action, married Jesuit Mike Dougherty, one of the DC Nine; it was he who had recruited her for the Boston Action.

This group could only have come together in October and November 1969. A few months earlier, or a few months later, each of us would have been unavailable, with other commitments. The group was geographically diverse; we came from places from Boston to California. It would be tempting to say that a common thread was commitment to the ideology of the Catholic Left, but this would not have been true for all of us. The common denominator in the group was our outrage at the war, our shared vision of how we would act to stop it, and, crucially, the coincidence of our availability at that particular moment.

In the autumn of 1969, I had just turned eighteen. It was an autumn filled with firsts for me. I lost my virginity. I had my first paying job. I lived on my own in my first apartment. And I participated in my first large-scale clandestine operation.

The sustained level of excitement and focused energy and attention I felt about the Action were incredible. I was fascinated with the idea of "credentials." My friends from high school were all in college during the autumn of 1969. After four years of college, perhaps they'd go to law school for three years. After that they might work in a law firm for seven years. Then maybe—maybe—they'd be asked to become a partner in that firm. (Or they might go to medical school, internship, residency . . .) I was eighteen years old, had never been to college and yet, by participating in a draft-board Action, I would have "credentials." I would be a celebrity. I would be making history in a few weeks.

My mind focused on the upcoming Action day and night. I thought about it in bed before falling asleep in my squalid apartment in Manhattan on weekday evenings between retreats. I woke up energetic and alert, thinking about the Action. I have experienced peaks of excitement at other times in my life, but I have never sustained a level of excitement approaching what I experienced contemplating the Boston draft-board Action during the autumn of 1969.

There would be nine of us: the Boston Nine, just like the Catonsville Nine. The Action was set for early November. On November 3, President Nixon addressed the nation, announcing a modest U.S. troop withdrawal as part of his program of "Vietnamization." We barely noticed. What was clear was that Nixon was not ending the war.

A major anti-war demonstration was planned for Washington, DC, on Saturday, November 15—it turned out to be the largest such demonstration of the war, with 500,000 people participating. We decided to conduct our Action clandestinely the weekend before the demonstration, and have our group "surface" in Washington during the weekend of the big demonstration.

Then, during the last week before the Action, a political disagreement emerged in our group concerning the way in which we would surface after the Action. I was on one side of the issue; the other eight prospective actors were on the other side. A brief historical digression is necessary to explain the nature of the conflict.

The earliest draft-board Actions had all been so-called "stand-by" Actions. They were conducted in broad daylight, on weekdays, during normal business hours. Draft-board clerks were in their offices when the blood was poured in Baltimore and when the files were burned in Catonsville. The participants literally stood by after these Actions, waiting for the police to arrive, waiting to be arrested. The Actions were, by their open and daytime nature, more symbolic than effective in actually stopping the draft. In each of these early cases only handfuls of files were actually mutilated, by blood in Baltimore, by burning in Catonsville.

Then, earlier in 1969, a change began to take place. It happened in three stages, each of them a distinct move away from the concept of "stand-by" Actions.

In May, the Action of the Chicago Fifteen was a stand-by Action in the sense that the participants had waited at the scene of the burglary for the police to arrive and arrest them. But the Action was conducted on a weekend when the draft boards were closed. This gave the participants hours to remove, burn, and otherwise destroy files before they were apprehended.

On July 2, five women in New York City, calling themselves Women Against Daddy Warbucks, destroyed files at a single complex housing thirteen draft boards while the boards were closed. Unlike earlier groups, they did not "stand by" at the scene of the crime to be arrested. Instead, they "surfaced" two days later, on July 4, tossing around shredded draft files at a news conference in Rockefeller Center.

Finally, the New York Eight hit upon a new and novel idea. On

Kathy Czarnik, one of the Women Against Daddy Warbucks, at
Rockefeller Center in New York City. The draft-board Action of the
Women Against Daddy Warbucks began the evolution away from
so-called "stand-by" Actions. The group raided a New York complex
housing thirteen draft boards on July 2, 1969, when the offices were
closed. In contrast to earlier Actions, the women did not stand by to be
arrested. On July 4, the group surfaced at Rockefeller Center, tossing
around confetti made of shredded Selective Service records. Photo by
Bradford Lyttle.

August 1, they raided a draft-board complex located at 881 Gerard Avenue in the Bronx. Two weeks later, on August 15, they raided a separate complex at 165–08 Jamaica Avenue in Queens. Together, the two draft-board complexes housed eleven local boards. They raided both complexes at night and were not caught in the act.

At the time, the police were quoted in the press as referring to the burglaries as "professional and methodical." The group surfaced later, *but without any incriminating evidence* (unlike the Women Against Daddy Warbucks and their shredded files the previous month). Furthermore, at their surfacing, the participants said to the authorities, in effect, *Some of us burglarized the draft boards in Queens. Others of us hit the boards in the Bronx. See if you can guess who did which.* They had taken pains not to leave evidence such as fingerprints at the scenes of the crimes.

For the first time ever, participants in a draft-board Action were not arrested or indicted. We all presumed that this was because the authorities felt that they did not have sufficient evidence to indict the people who had appeared at the press conference. After all, how could the police even know whether these were the people who had actually done these burglaries? What would happen if these people were arrested but could produce alibis at trial? How embarrassing for the authorities! We also speculated, probably incorrectly, that the indictments would have had to specify the location or building each defendant was alleged to have burglarized and that, because the authorities had no way of knowing which of the eight people had burglarized which location, they (the authorities) were unable to secure any indictments at all.

As the stand-by nature of the draft-board Actions evolved into a format of surfacing later, the focus of the Actions changed from being only symbolic to an increased emphasis on actually putting draft boards completely out of commission. As people spent more and more time in draft boards destroying files, it became clear that by destroying certain specific records one could effectively stop draft boards from functioning. People were careful to destroy 1-A files—the files of men eligible to be drafted. The raiders became sophisticated in understanding and destroying all three critical portions of each local board's cross-reference system.

In Boston, I argued that we should follow the model of the New York Eight: burglarize the four separate offices clandestinely and then surface later *without* evidence. Surfacing publicly was a crucial part of our Action since truth and openness are an essential ingredient of nonviolence, I argued. But don't give the government evidence to use against us in court.

I was the only one who held that view. My eight colleagues all felt that their Action and the statement it sought to make would be more powerful if they surfaced with evidence. The specific scenario they agreed on was to distribute purloined draft files at a press conference in Washington during the big demonstration there the week after the Action.

I argued that the Action derived its power from the combination of its public nature and high risk. Adding risk by surfacing with evidence seemed unnecessary and foolish. I was willing to risk suffering (that is, arrest and imprisonment) as an unfortunate but perhaps inevitable consequence of actions I felt morally constrained to undertake; I did not feel any need to help the government prosecute me by giving them evidence to use to lock me up.

At the root of the disagreement was a profound difference in how we, as individuals, viewed suffering. In my view, suffering was not something to be wished for in itself; it was, rather, a possible result of actions done for other reasons that made sense. In contrast, most of the others in the group, especially the religious Catholics, viewed suffering as redemptive—a good in and of itself. The world was saved through the suffering of Christ; now they would help cleanse the world of the scourge of war by suffering themselves.

Since I was out of the consensus about surfacing, the Boston Nine became—just days before the Action took place—the Boston Eight. But the change was only partial. I had come too far with the group to drop out entirely. As a result, I participated fully in the draft-file destruction in Boston; since my disagreement had only been over the method of surfacing, I did not participate in the surfacing in Washington a week later.

The eleventh-hour decision that I would not surface, arrived at jointly by the rest of the group and me, left me with some strong feelings in the weeks following the Action. On the one hand, I had nagging, lingering doubts about whether I had decided not to surface with the rest of the group as a result of genuine political differences or whether these were merely a convenient excuse for simple fear, fear of prison. I also felt, however, a certain satisfaction at having had the strength to stand my ground on a matter of principle, even in the face of the united opposition of my friends and colleagues. Looking back now on my judgment call then, I still think my position was correct.

During 1969, there was a lively debate within the peace movement as a whole, and especially within WRL, about the propriety of draft-file destruction. Within the League, this issue was discussed among the staff and debated in the pages of *WRL News* (the League's house organ) and *WIN Magazine* (published jointly by WRL and the New York Workshop in Nonviolence). Some WRLers, like Jim Forest, approved of the tactic and had participated in draft-board Actions themselves. But many, perhaps most, in WRL, including staff members Dave McReynolds, Jim Peck, and Igal Roodenko, disapproved of the tactic.

There were two major reasons for their disapproval. One was that they felt that burglary and destruction of property were simply not nonviolent actions. As Jim Peck wrote in the September 1, 1969, issue of *WIN Magazine*, "raiding, looting and destruction are still not actions than can command respect." The second reason was the belief that the secrecy necessarily involved in planning the Actions was incompatible with truth and openness which, in turn, were central to the concept of nonviolence.

This was a debate that I felt especially keenly and poignantly since Igal Roodenko and Dave McReynolds were my political mentors. These were older men—Dave was forty at the time, Igal about fifty—who served as role models for me; these were men I sought to emulate. I was eighteen, and too full of myself to appreciate fully how strange it was to be the new person on the WRL staff arguing complex political points with these experienced movement leaders. It is a measure of the openness of the League, and of Dave and Igal in particular, that they took my arguments seriously.

The core of this argument was whether raiding draft boards and destroying the files did or did not qualify as nonviolent actions. In my view, the Actions clearly did qualify as being nonviolent; indeed, as a pacifist, had I not believed them to be nonviolent, I would not have taken part.

To me, the heart of nonviolent philosophy is the sanctity of human life. The Quakers have a simple but elegant way of saying this: *there is that of God in every man and woman*. I am not a Quaker but, like them, I believe that human life is sacred. Actions that kill or harm people are by definition violent. Actions that do not kill or hurt or harm people are not violent.

In draft-board Actions, we participants destroyed *property*, but we took great care not to hurt or injure any *people*. There is a fundamental difference between actions against property and actions against people. Damaging or destroying property might properly be called "destructive," but I do not think it can properly be called "violent." Property is not sacred; human life is. In order for an act to qualify as violent, there must be harm to a person.

Throughout history certain property has been highly destructive to human life. If a saboteur could have damaged or destroyed the rail lines leading to Auschwitz—and by doing so saved human lives—that would not have been a violent action. I think our draft-board Actions were on a similar moral plane with destroying rail lines that led to concentration camps. Both actions involved the destruction of inanimate property in the direct defense of human lives.

Thus, I believed that destroying draft files was not merely a nonviolent action, but was a moral imperative.

At the same time, I also believed that we had to be very careful about *how* we destroyed draft files. It would have been a relatively easy matter simply to bomb the building that housed the draft boards or to burn the building down. In doing so we would have saved ourselves a great deal of time, trouble and inconvenience during the months spent casing draft boards. But bombs are dangerous. The Weather Underground and others were at that time bombing buildings. In August 1970, a researcher was killed when political activists bombed the University of Wisconsin mathematics building, which housed the ROTC offices. Similarly, burning down buildings also would have been dangerous: people could have been working late in another part of a building that housed a draft board; a fire could have spread to other buildings; firefighters could have been injured or killed putting out a blaze that we had set. Because of the serious risk to human life and safety, destroying draft files by bombing or torching the buildings that housed draft boards simply was not non-violent.

By ripping up the files by hand, however, nobody could have been hurt or killed except us. The most immediate physical risk—something that was always in my mind and consciousness—was that we might be surprised during the actual burglary by a young and inexperienced police officer who would panic and shoot us. The most likely overall risk, of course, was that we would be arrested, prosecuted, and imprisoned.

The second part of the argument about draft-file destruction, within WRL as well as within the wider pacifist movement, concerned whether the secrecy and clandestine nature of the Actions should preclude pacifists from taking part. Truth and openness have always been an important part of the pacifist ideology. The question here was how did clandestine casing comport with this tradition. This question of openness tied in very closely with the equally important tradition with nonviolent civil disobedience of being willing to go to prison for one's actions. Raiding draft boards and destroying files secretly and remaining secretive by never surfacing is something I would have had deep moral qualms about, but announcing ourselves to the public after a secret raid seemed to me amply to satisfy the requirement of openness. After all, one would hardly succeed in destroying draft files if one announced one's intentions in advance. At the same time, after one holds a press conference announcing that one has burglarized a certain set of draft boards, and explaining why one has done so, it hardly seems right to call that action secret and clandestine any more.

Nevertheless, there was one respect in which I wholeheartedly believed that the arguments of my WRL friends against the philosophy of the Catholic Left and the specific tactic of draft-file destruction were most emphatically correct—that is, the elitist attitude of many of the participants. By this the WRL critics meant not that draft-file destruction was a tactic that only a few could undertake, but rather that the attitude of so many in the Catholic Left was that this was the one right action necessary to end the war and that all other anti-war efforts that activists engaged in were worthless.

I remember clearly a debate in August 1969, at the WRI triennial conference in Haverford. On one side of the debate, supporting draft-file destruction, was Joe O'Rourke, a Jesuit co-defendant of Joann Malone and Mike Dougherty in the DC Nine. On the other side of the debate was WRL staffer Jim Peck.

When I worked at WRL in 1969, Jim had already been arrested thirty times for nonviolent civil disobedience. For just one of those thirty separate arrests, he had served three years in prison for draft resistance during World War II. While in prison, Jim had helped organize a prisoners' strike to desegregate the mess hall of Danbury Federal Prison. In fact, the prison strike Jim helped to lead, at tremendous personal risk to himself, was instrumental in ending official racial segregation in U.S. prisons. As I already mentioned, Jim took part in the first Freedom Ride in 1947. In another Freedom Ride, in 1961, Jim was beaten to within an inch of his life by an angry white mob.

Jim was independently wealthy; his family had owned the Peck and Peck clothing stores in New York. After his release from prison after World War II, Jim worked half-time for the Congress of Racial Equality (CORE) and half-time for WRL, editing the newsletters of both organizations. Jim believed that the two biggest problems in the world were racism and war; by his division of time, Jim felt he was addressing both issues. Jim's work was all volunteer; although he worked full time and more for peace and civil rights, Jim had never drawn a single paycheck from either group.

After CORE expelled whites from the organization at the beginning of the Black Power movement, Jim came to work full-time at WRL. When I worked at WRL, Jim was always the first person in the office in the morning and often the last one out at night. He did the tasks no one else would do, including cleaning the lavatories. On weekends, he took mailing-list work home with him. He was a mainstay of the Times Square peace vigil against the Vietnam war, participating every Saturday, rain or shine, for over ten years.

In a way, Jim was a sad and pathetic person. He had no personal life and lived a joyless existence. The only time I remember seeing Jim smile was in March 1970, in a paddy wagon after we had both been arrested for a nonviolent sit-in at the draft boards at Varick Street in Manhattan. On the way to the police station, Jim came alive. He lit a big cigar and regaled his fellow prisoners with tales of past arrests. This was my first arrest and I felt it was quite a treat to share a paddy wagon with an old-timer like Jim.

Jim was the most tireless, dedicated, self-effacing, self-sacrificing, and humble peace activist I have ever met. He also disapproved of draft-file destruction.

At the WRI Triennial in Haverford, a large discussion group carried on a lively debate about the propriety of draft-file destruction. In the end, it developed into a debate between Jim Peck and Joe O'Rourke. Joe ended up making a scurrilous attack on Jim. The gist of Joe's attack was, "You have not done what I have done; therefore you have made no contribution whatsoever to the peace movement. I have found the one right tactic to end the war, raiding draft boards; nothing else has any value."

This was elitism at its most outrageous, but it was highly typical of the attitude of many in the Catholic Left. To Phil Berrigan, the entire world was divided into two parts: actors (those who had taken part in draft-board Actions), and everybody else. If you were not an actor, Phil had little use for you, unless he thought he could recruit you to be an actor. A word that Phil used frequently was "serious." People were only "serious" about anti-war work if they took part in a draft-board Action.

There is a story that was told about Phil. He had been invited to a small meeting shortly after Catonsville to speak about war resistance. In his talk, he denigrated individual acts of draft resistance as being passè and essentially useless; only draft-file destruction was worthwhile. At the time of this talk, both Dave Miller and Tom Cornell were in prison serving their sentences for draft-card burning. In Phil's audience were both men's wives. It is easy to imagine what their feelings must have been when they heard Phil's glib dismissal of their husbands' courageous stands for peace. I was not at that meeting, and I do not know if the story is apocryphal, but as one who worked closely with Phil over a period of time I can say that it certainly rings completely true. If it did not happen, it certainly could have.

There are explanations for this unfortunate attitude. Some of the Catholic Left activists like Tony Scoblick had never participated in any other peace activities. Destroying draft files was literally their first introduction to peace work. How easy it must have been to believe that the one and only tactic they knew about was the one tactic that mattered! In addition, it was easy for people who had been raised to believe that theirs was the one correct religion (I can still remember Phil Berrigan giving me a cross on one occasion, a New Testament on another, and trying to convert me to Catholicism) simply to transfer that belief to their new "religion," the Catholic Left, and believe that theirs was the one right tactic. It was an astonishingly, incredibly narrow perspective.

One other unexpected twist occurred a week before our scheduled Action in Boston. During the previous weekend (November 1 and 2) the Copley Square draft boards, one of the four sites we were planning to hit, were raided by another group, not connected to us or the Catholic Left. The job they did was shoddy. The group merely threw files around the office. They seemed to have no knowledge of the three-part cross-reference system maintained by Selective Service and, consequently, no idea how to effectively put a draft board out of commission.

Our group was very angry at this turn of events. We feared that, because of the other group's Action, security at Copley Square and our other three locations would be tightened, thereby making our more effective Action impossible. We had visions of our weeks of careful casing and planning having been all for nought. But when we checked, we found no additional security at any of our four locations. We were set to go Friday evening, November 7.

Meanwhile, at the Copley Square draft boards, the clerks spent the entire week of November 3–7 cleaning up the mess that had been left by the previous group. We knew this because, through our casing, we were closely monitoring their progress. On Friday, they put the finishing touches on the clean-up and went home for the weekend. It had not been an easy job but they had gotten it done. The following Monday, those clerks arrived at their office to find their boards hit again, but this time much more thoroughly, carefully, and completely. I have often wondered what those clerks must have felt going home Friday afternoon the weekend following our Action. Did they wonder whether their boards would be hit a third weekend in a row?

All of the records kept by draft boards were on paper. The main record was a manila file folder kept on each registrant. These folders contained the man's original classification questionnaire, the paperwork for any exemption or deferment he had ever applied for, and a record of any administrative decision made with regard to such application. The folders were grouped or filed within the draft board according to each man's draft status. In other words, draft boards kept conveniently together all the 1-A files—those of men immediately eligible to be drafted and thus the first files to be destroyed by raiders.

Each draft board also maintained a three-part cross-reference system. First, there were huge ledger books containing Selective Service Form 102s, with the records of the registrants kept in chronological order by date of birth. Second, there were four-by-six-inch file cards, Selective Service Form 1s. These were arranged alphabetically without regard to birth date. The card of a man currently classified 1-A might be directly next to the card of a man who had died in World War I (because of the coincidence of a similar last name). A copy of the alphabetical file card was kept in the state headquarters—the only type of duplicate record kept outside the local draft board. Finally, the minutes of local draft-board meetings, because they contained the names of registrants along with classification decisions, could be used to partially reconstruct destroyed files.

Part of my role in the Boston Action was to serve as door-opener at the two Copley Square draft boards. The draft boards were in Room 510 of a medium-sized office building at 25 Huntington Avenue. I would go into the building Friday afternoon before closing time. There was a back stairway and I would hide there between the sixth and top floor and the door to the roof. During the course of the late evening, I was to check every office on all six floors to make sure that no one else was in the building. At the appropriate time, I was to go down to street level and open the back door, which was next to a late-night bar, and let the others in. Copley Square was the largest office we were doing; the arrangement was that the eight other people in the group would divide up the other three locations, hit them first, and then rendevous to finish off Copley Square last.

The night of Friday, November 7, 1969, was drizzly in Boston. I entered the building around 4:00 P.M., carrying a bag with three scrambled-egg-and-green-pepper hero sandwiches and two cans of ginger ale; I was going to have a long vigil. I stationed myself on the platform above the sixth floor. Around 10:00 P.M., a janitor opened the sixth-floor doorway leading to the back staircase where I was hiding. I was sitting on the landing directly in front of him, but slightly above his normal field of vision. Had he but looked up for a moment, I would have been in plain view. Luckily, he did not look up; he was after cleaning supplies. Later in the evening, when my bladder filled up, I opened the door to the roof just a crack and urinated out onto the roof. Around midnight I started, ever so slowly and carefully, checking the building to make sure it was empty. It was.

At 2:00 A.M. I looked out a back window facing out from the sixth floor of my stairwell and across two streets for the signal that my friends were on their way. The streets were deserted. I saw Darrell Dewease walk briskly in front of the Radio Shack store that we had determined in advance was in plain view of my window. He bent down to tie a shoelace and then lit a cigarette. It was an unmistakable signal at that hour on those deserted streets. I went downstairs to let my friends in by opening a door to the street that, for reasons of fire code, had to open freely from inside the building. We knew from our casing that there was no alarm on the door.

I had had a silent, solitary ten hours alone at night in a huge, but totally empty, building. But each of the others had just come from destroying files at one of our other three locations; their adrenalin was really flowing. In a moment we were back up on the fifth floor; in another moment we were all inside the draft boards. The hours between 2:00 A.M. and dawn that we spent in the draft boards went quickly.

We tore up the files manually. On 1-A files, for example, we tore the folder so that each registrant's first name was separated from his last name, the identifying number was torn in half, and the number was separated from either portion of the name. We made sure that the torn contents of each file was separated from the outer folder. At one point, Mary Cain handed me a stack of files and suggested I might have a special interest in destroying those. She was right: these were the files of the eighteen-year-old new registrants. I myself had just turned eighteen a few weeks before.

All at once it was morning and time to go. We went down the stairs and out the same back door where I had let the others in, then walked several blocks to where we were to be picked up. Dawn was just breaking over Boston on Saturday morning, November 8, 1969. As we walked to our pick-up point, I stopped at a pay phone and called Bug, whom I had earlier told in a vague way about what was being planned. He was then a student at Harpur College, in Binghamton, New York. I woke him up in his dorm room. I said, "This is an anonymous caller." I described the draft-board Action in some detail but was careful to use the passive voice and the third person, but my voice would have been unmistakable to my old friend.

"Do you understand?" I asked at the end of the call.

"Yes," Bug replied, "and congratulations."

After we returned to our base of operations, it was time to deliver statements to the press. This, too, was my job. I was driven to the offices of the *Globe*, the *Herald-Traveler*, and several other media outlets. At each place I walked briskly in, dropped a typed statement at the city desk, and left immediately without waiting to answer questions.

The statement we gave out to the press had almost not been written. In the excitement leading up to the Action, we had all forgotten that we needed to produce a statement explaining ourselves. Phil, working alone, drafted a statement for us in about thirty minutes the evening before the Action. This accounts for the rather tiring similarity between the tone of our statement and statements issued after draft-board raids in New York and elsewhere.

After the statements had been delivered, the rest of the group traveled to Washington, DC, to prepare for the surfacing the following weekend. I rode with them as far as New York. I was dropped off at the George Washington Bridge, took the subway to Penn Station, and then took the Long Island Railroad to my parents' home in Great Neck. I got there at mid-day on Saturday. I was exhausted, because I had not slept since the morning of the previous day, and I told my parents that I wanted to go straight to bed because I had been up at an all-night party in Boston.

The next day my parents were reading the Sunday *New York Times* and came across the article about the draft-board raid in Boston. They put two and two together and asked me if that was the party I had been referring to. I told them it was. I also showed the article in the *Times* to Bunny and Arnold Olenick, parents of my high school friend Phil, and proudly pointed out the reference to me: "An editor at the *Boston Herald Traveler* said [our statement] had been delivered there by a 'short youth, with unkempt bushy hair, who was wearing a short-sleeved shirt and gloves.'" For years afterwards, the Olenicks referred to me as that 'short youth with unkempt bushy hair.'

The surfacing of the Boston Eight in Washington, DC, the following week went off without a hitch. Despite the fact that they distributed (to FBI agents, among others) stolen draft files at the surfacing, the group was never arrested, indicted, or tried. This was ironic. I had argued with the group against courting arrest by surfacing with evidence, but they had insisted on doing so—not *despite* the fact that this would drastically increase the likelihood of their arrest and prosecution, but *because* of that fact, and I did not surface with the rest of the group because of that disagreement. The irony was compounded in the Providence draft-board Action the following June, where we followed my preferred course by surfacing without evidence and were nevertheless prosecuted.

5

More Draft-File Destruction: The Rhode Island Political Offensive for Freedom

AFTER THE BOSTON DRAFT-BOARD ACTION, I returned to my job at WRL and stayed there until the end of December. Then I moved to Washington, DC, to organize support events surrounding the upcoming trial of the DC Nine—Joann Malone, Art and Cathy Melville, Mike Dougherty, Joe O'Rourke, and four others. During the trial, which started on Tuesday, February 3, 1970, we picketed each morning outside the federal courthouse. While court was in session, we sat in the courtroom to show support for the defendants. Each night, we held a rally at St. Stephen's Episcopal Church at 16th and U Streets NW. Pete Seeger sang one evening; Ernest Gruening of Alaska, one of only two senators to have voted against the Tonkin Gulf Resolution in August 1964, spoke another evening.

I lived at the communal house at 1620 S Street NW, which I had visited the previous May. All of the DC Nine defendants stayed there too. Joann, who was still a member of her religious order, slept with her old friend Mitch Ratner, and I felt jilted and hurt. Each commune member was expected to contribute $15 per week toward rent and food. I had no money and no source of income. I wrote to Phil Berrigan about this and he promptly sent me a check for $75—enough for my four-week stay at S Street, plus some left over for pocket money. He sent a very friendly note with the check: "Voilà," he wrote. "See that none of it comes back."

After Washington, I went to Bard College for the semester that began in early March. I had originally decided not to go to college, in large part because I had thought I would soon be going to prison, either for my own public nonregistration or for a draft-board Action, and I had wanted to work full-time in the peace movement until that happened.

But now it was almost spring: I had not participated in the surfacing of the Boston Eight and I had not yet been indicted for my own non-registration. My decision to attend college then was made partly out of curiosity about what college would be like, and partly out of boredom, not knowing what else to do.

Bard College is in Annandale-on-Hudson, New York, a tiny hamlet about 100 miles due north of New York City that essentially consists only of the college. The size of the student body had grown recently, but the school's housing facilities had not, and my dorm room was really the anteroom of a two-bedroom suite. Each of my two suitemates had to traipse through my room in order to reach their own. One of the two was rarely visible behind a dense cloud of opium smoke. I met Kirk Bjornsgaard, my neighbor across the hall, who was a Quaker conscientious objector from Doylestown, Pennsylvania, when he alternately urinated and vomited (from too much beer) into our communal sink.

I took four courses at Bard: Old Testament, Introduction to Philosophy, German Literature, and Constitutional Law. Despite the times, there was virtually no political activity on the Bard campus. In fact, I found little to do except schoolwork. For the first time in my life, I had papers finished before their deadlines. I felt restless and bored. Within a few weeks of the beginning of the semester, I was planning another draft-board Action.

Because I had participated in the casing and planning for four separate locations in Boston, I figured I knew enough to pull off my own burglary somewhere else. This time I would not join a group organized by Phil Berrigan and the Catholic Left. I clearly did not fit in with that subculture. Instead, I would pull together my own group from people I knew. Bug had dropped out of Harpur College and had been in Cuba that winter cutting sugar cane with the Venceremos Brigade. He wrote to me when he got back saying he would be interested. Two other classmates from Great Neck were also interested: Michael "Supo" Shapiro and Debbie Elkin. Suzi Williams and DeCourcy Squire would complete the group.

Michael Shapiro had been the first person I met when my family moved to Great Neck two months before my sixth birthday. Michael and I were the same age and he lived across the street. It seems like I spent twelve years—after school, on weekends and during vacations—playing kickball in Michael's back yard; there were three apple trees positioned just right for bases. When Michael and I were in third grade, our mothers coincidentally bought us identical jackets. That year we were often mistaken for twins.

In high school, Michael had served as treasurer of SPV when I was co-chairman. Michael and I opened a joint checking account for SPV at the local branch of Chase Manhattan Bank. Michael was extremely bright and, like me, did little homework or studying. But, unlike me, Michael had had the courtesy and good sense to listen in class; thus, unlike me, Michael had gotten consistently good grades in school.

When we were in fourth grade there was a girl on our school bus named Christine Kelly who fancied herself a bus monitor. Once Michael and I were doing something she didn't like so she told us that she was going to report us. "How do you spell Shapiro?" she asked Michael. "S-U-P-P-O?"

"No," Michael answered. "There is only one P." After that, Michael's nickname was "Supo." Forty years later, we still call Michael "Supo."

David "Bug" Rosen had also been an excellent student and had graduated near the top of our class. Bug and I often did things together. Some of these were political, like our work with SPV, or starting the Peace Club at school, or publishing an underground newspaper using an old mimeograph machine in my basement. But some of the things were manifestly nonpolitical: cutting classes, playing frisbee, and smoking dope. His nickname, which appeared years later without explanation in his FBI dossier, had a simple origin: he had been studying Russian in school. In Russian his name was pronounced "Da-bug." From there it was a simple step to "The Bug" or just "Bug." High school friends from Great Neck still refer to him as "Bug."

In high school, by contrast, Debbie Elkin had been a quiet, studious goody-two-shoes. She and I were friendly but not close. She also had been in Mr. Parker's class (as was Supo) and she looked down on Bug's and my antics. Occasionally I had used her excellent notes to cram before a test. In eleventh grade, Debbie had dated Supo. I was attracted to Debbie myself and had been jealous of Supo.

Suzi Williams was from Amherst, Massahusetts, and was a few years older than we were. Suzi was a peace-movement celebrity, having gained tremendous media attention from two earlier civil-disobedience actions. One was at CNVA's protest in July 1966 against Polaris submarines. Quite a few people had been arrested, but only Suzi had refused to stand in court for the judge at the arraignment. As a result, she had been sentenced to thirty days in prison for contempt—without having been arraigned. At the end of the thirty days, Suzi had been brought back into court for another attempted arraignment (before a different judge this time). Suzi again had refused to stand for the judge. This time she had been sentenced to sixty days for contempt. She still had not been arraigned.

Suzi was seventeen years old at the time, and had been an honor student. (In fact, she had scored a perfect 800 on all of her college boards except Latin, on which she had scored 798.) Her father was an ordained minister and, as a teenager, Suzi had won a Citizenship Award from the local chapter of the right-wing Daughters of the American Revolution. The story of the high school honor student in jail for not standing for the judge had received widespread news coverage. In the end, the judge had relented, arraigned Suzi in her cell (without her having to stand), and released her.

The second act of civil disobedience for which Suzi was known was an act of draft-file destruction in Boston in 1968, in which she and one other person had poured black paint on draft files at the draft board located in the Boston Custom House.

I had met Suzi at S Street in January 1970, during the month I lived there; like me, Suzi was then in Washington for the trial of the DC Nine. She had recently been released from the federal prison in Alderson, West Virginia, after serving a one-year sentence for the Boston paint-pouring. Suzi and I had become fast friends in Washington. We had bunked in the same communal bedroom (but were not romantically or physically involved at that time), and were both big fans of *The Lord of the Rings,* playing Tolkien trivia together on long walks through Washington. It was Suzi who provided our group in Providence with some of the money necessary for living expenses while we lived in Providence and planned the Action.

DeCourcy Squire was a friend of Suzi's originally from Morgantown, West Virginia. Like Suzi, she was quite young but had been a longtime pacifist activist. There was a certain purity about DeCourcy: she was not at all a sexual person. Like Suzi and me, DeCourcy was a vegetarian, but unlike us she was also a vegan; that is, she ate no eggs, milk, or dairy products.

Because I had been involved in the Boston Action, I was the resident "expert" who "knew" how to plan such an Action. (Suzi's 1968 Action in Boston had involved little planning or casing; she and her partner simply went into the draft boards and poured black paint on the files.) I conducted the planning sessions the only way I knew how: copying more or less exactly what we had done in Boston, without regard to whether or not it was appropriate to the new situation. For example, our first retreats were held in Boston, at the same house that had been used for several of the Boston retreats, even though New York would have been more convenient for most of us.

Our little group decided that, in addition to destroying files at local draft boards, we also wanted to do a Selective Service State Headquarters, because we wanted to destroy the duplicate records kept there. We also knew that we wanted to stay in the northeast part of the country. Before deciding where our Action would be, we cased the State Headquarters in Boston, Hartford, Albany, Trenton, and Providence.

My job was to do preliminary casing in Boston and Albany. When I got to Boston, I found that the Massachusetts State Selective Service Headquarters was located on the ninth floor of the then-new JFK Federal Building, with the FBI directly underneath on the eighth floor, twenty-four hours a day. Any attempted burglary of the draft offices during off-hours would almost certainly have alerted the FBI. When I went to Albany, I found the New York State Headquarters most intriguing. On the one hand, based upon my burglary experience in Boston, I believed that the Albany draft headquarters was eminently doable; that is, quite susceptible to being burglarized successfully by peace activists. On the other hand, New York was the most populous state in the Union and the State Selective Service Headquarters was huge, with far too many records for a relatively small group like ours to destroy comprehensively. Bug reported that the Hartford State Headquarters was located in a National Guard Armory.

We settled on the Providence office, which was in an easy building to burglarize in a relatively isolated location with no night guards. The Providence site held four local draft boards, 35% of the state Selective Service, plus the Rhode Island State Headquarters, all under one roof.

As our planning progressed, it emerged that Bug and I would be the only two members of the group to surface publicly. Supo dropped out of the group early on, but not before he made one important change in our proposed public statement. A critical sentence in our public statement read, in an early draft, "Despite government claims to the contrary, this [our Action] renders these boards inoperable." Supo changed the word "despite" to "regardless of." "We don't know in advance what claims the government will make," Supo said, correctly.

Debbie, Suzi and DeCourcy would help both with advance planning and on the night of the Action but would not surface with us. Suzi and DeCourcy were already planning an Action for Rochester, New York, where DeCourcy lived, and they viewed their participation with us as a way of gaining experience in casing and general burglary techniques for use in Rochester.

One other person also helped with our planning: Art Melville, the former Maryknoll priest who had spoken at the draft-board demonstration in Manhasset the week I had refused to register. His wife, Cathy, was serving a three-month term in Alderson Federal Prison for the DC Nine Action; Art was out on appeal and felt that he had time available to help us. Art was twenty years older than we were, and had lots of real-world experience and skills that we did not have. We welcomed his assistance.

At this early stage of our planning, Bug and I also decided on a name for our group. Calling ourselves the Providence Two would never do; that name was not nearly creative enough. After some discussion, we decided that we would be the Rhode Island Political Offensive For Freedom. We chose the name for the fine acronym it created.

Debbie Elkin rented an apartment for us in Providence at 178 Ives Street that we used as our base of operations. Bug and I worked out a simple code whereby he would give me over the phone the address of our new apartment by reversing the order of the digits but using the correct street name. The code was probably unnecessary but we viewed it as a precaution against possible FBI telephone taps. One of us got the code confused and I went at first to 187 Ives Street and couldn't find Bug and Debbie.

The draft-board complex was located at 1 Washington Avenue, in the Washington Park section of Providence. It was near the docks and the Shipyard drive-in movie. Late at night the neighborhood was deserted. Most of our casing at night was done in teams of two. A man and a woman would sit in a car together; if a police patrol passed, the couple casing could embrace and pretend to be necking. With the drive-in nearby, we reasoned that this was a scene that would blend in naturally with the surroundings. We drew maps of the area, noted the schedule and movements of the night janitor (and, especially, his nights off) and kept a record of police patrols in the neighborhood. We studied the building itself to figure out where and how we would break in. We drew maps of the interior of the building, and even figured out what electrical current was available in the wall sockets because we bought a paper shredder (which we ultimately decided not to use) to help with shredding the draft files. The Action did not take place until June, but we started our casing in March.

On March 21, Cambodia's head of state, Prince Norodom Sihanouk, was deposed in a CIA-supported coup that installed Lon Nol into power. Sihanouk had been a neutralist and so had managed to keep Cambodia out of the war that was consuming Vietnam. Sihanouk had been critical of both the North Vietnamese, for violating Cambodian sovereignty, and of the Americans, for wantonly bombing Cambodia in an effort to attack or interdict North Vietnamese forces. The Nixon administration needed a more pliable leader in Phnom Penh—a government that would not oppose American bombing of Cambodian territory—and so backed the Lon Nol coup. Ironically, at the time he was deposed, Sihanouk was in Moscow, attempting to persuade the Soviet government to bring pressure on the North Vietnamese to stop violating Cambodian sovereignty.

On April 30, the United States invaded Cambodia. Anti-war demonstrations, some of them violent, occurred throughout the United States.

On May 4, four protesting students were shot dead by National Guard troops at Kent State University in Ohio. Further demonstrations followed.

Campuses across America were shut down by striking students.

Interestingly, although I was fully aware of these events at the time, they were not uppermost in my mind as we planned the Providence draft-board raid that spring. To me, there was a crucial difference between the big picture and its various, relatively less important, constituent parts. The big picture was that the United States was conducting a criminal war in Southeast Asia that must be opposed. That was why I was planning the draft-board Action. Events like the invasion of Cambodia were merely details. We had started planning the Action well before the invasion, and would have conducted the Action even in its absence.

Wednesday, June 10, 1970, was a sweltering hot day in Providence. Around 11:00 A.M., Art appeared at our apartment after an absence of several days. He helped himself to a drink and then sat around chatting casually with us about the progress we had been making. After a while he asked us whether we were still looking for additional hands to come into the draft boards with us during the Action. We replied that we were. He suggested that he knew someone who might be interested. We pointed out that we'd have to meet this person rather soon since the Action was only a few days away. Art said that this could be arranged since the person was waiting downstairs in his car. We were a bit taken aback and told him to bring the person up so we could meet him or her. Art disappeared and reappeared a moment later with Carol Bragg, who was living at the CNVA farm in Voluntown. We "interviewed" her for the job, were favorably impressed, and invited her to join us.

On Thursday, June 11, Carol went into the draft-board complex as Mary Mulligan, from a non-existent group called Catholics for Peace. Her ostensible purpose was to copy the names of men newly classified 1-A by the four draft boards, information that is public. Her real purpose was to draw maps of the inside of the draft-board complex. That day, I went to Great Neck to borrow a van from David Greenberg, another high school friend of ours. Art borrowed a second van from Ted Webster, a friend of his in Boston.

Much of our post-Action publicity said that the Action had occurred "over the weekend of June 12 to 14." To be precise, we entered the draft boards just after dusk on Saturday evening, June 13, and came out just before dawn on Sunday morning, June 14. Four of us worked inside the draft boards: Bug, Carol, DeCourcy, and I. Debbie and Suzi provided assistance by driving us to and from the draft boards (so we would not leave telltale cars outside the supposedly deserted building) and covering the phone at Ives Street.

The plan was that Bug and Carol would be driven to the back of the Selective Service complex and break in through a window leading to a conference room. The window had no burglar alarm on the glass. Bug spent some time before the Action practicing with glass cutters that Art had taught us how to use. While Bug and Carol were breaking into the draft boards, DeCourcy and I would drive to the nearby Howard Johnson's restaurant on Narragansett Boulevard. At a pre-arranged time DeCourcy and I would receive a call from Bug and Carol at the phone booth in the restaurant parking lot. They would be calling from inside the draft board to say that they were in and that we should join them.

I pulled into the Howard Johnson's parking lot. The lot had a fairly steep incline; I was, consequently, forced to park the car on something of a hill. I was quite nervous and I forgot to pull the handbreak. After DeCourcy and I had both gotten out of the car and were walking in to the restaurant, the car started to roll backwards—directly toward a police car parked behind us. Although panicked, I nevertheless was able to jump into the driver's seat and stop our car just in time. Having a collision with a police car is often considered very bad form when one is in the midst of committing a major burglary.

At Howard Johnson's, I ordered apple pie à la mode. I was very keyed up but also very conscious of danger. Is apple pie served in prison? I wondered. Would this be the last apple pie I would have for a while?

DeCourcy and I received our call at the telephone booth in the restaurant parking lot right on schedule, and we went directly to join Carol and Bug inside the draft-board complex. Each of us had a job to do. I shredded 1-A files from the local draft boards using a utility knife. Each file folder needed at least three cuts—one to separate the registrant's first name from his last name, another to separate his name from his registration number, and a third to cut the number itself in half. Similar shredding was required for papers in the files. The files themselves varied greatly as to their thicknesses. Many contained nothing but the man's original classification questionnaire. Others were thicker, with documents reflecting a history of different classifications applied for or granted.

Bug used a crowbar to open locked storage cabinets to get at the chronological ledgers (Selective Service Form 102). Carol's job was to work on the alphabetical four-by-six-inch cards (Selective Service Form 1). We had realized that there would be far too many of these file cards for us to be able to destroy them in the draft offices, so we brought in with us dozens of collapsed cardboard cartons. Carol set up the boxes, filled each one with file cards, and neatly sealed each box with duct tape. The plan was to load these boxes into the two vans, carry them away, and burn the file cards later.

After Carol had neatly filled and sealed all of the cartons, we faced an unexpected problem. The filled boxes turned out to be so heavy that no one could move them. In fact, Bug and I together could barely budge a box! For all our careful planning, we had not anticipated the weight of the filled boxes. Carol had spent most of six hours meticulously filling boxes that now could not be moved. She had to open each box and rearrange the contents into additional boxes so that we could lift the boxes and carry them into the vans.

We filled the first van with three-quarters of the file cards. I drove the van back to Ives Street and switched vehicles, driving back toward the draft boards in the empty second van in order to retrieve both the remaining cartons of files and give Bug and Carol a ride away from the scene of the crime. But, a block away from the draft boards, I was stopped by a Providence police officer. Although I had been careful not to arouse suspicion by driving in any way improperly, the officer was suspicious of a young man driving an empty van in a deserted neighborhood in the middle of the night. He checked the license and registration and did a stolen-car check by calling the license-plate number in to headquarters. While the officer waited for a response, I struck up a conversation with him. I gave him a story that would jibe with my having a New York driver's license in one name (my own) but driving a Massachusetts van registered in another name (the van was Ted Webster's). I was a student, you see, visiting friends at Brown. I couldn't sleep; I was out looking for a drive-in. Oh, the drive-in here is not open at 4:00 A.M.? Gosh, officer, back in New York the drive-ins are open all night. Stealing lumber at these lumber yards? Gosh, no, officer, what would I do with the lumber anyway? I'm from New York.

The van checked out as not having been stolen and the officer let me go, but I had to drive straight back to Ives Street without picking up the remaining cartons of file cards—and without picking up Bug and Carol, who had to leave the draft boards on foot to be picked up by another driver in another vehicle.

Once we were all back at Ives Street, we left almost at once for Suzi Williams's family's home in Amherst. When we arrived there it was still early morning and we tried to get some sleep. But we were all much too excited to be able to sleep and we spent much of the rest of the day out in the fields behind the house, burning the thousands of pounds of file cards from the draft boards. We were amazed how long it took, even with a huge outdoor fire.

Unlike other groups of draft-board raiders, we had decided not to leave a statement behind in the draft boards. On Monday, June 15, however, Bug called the *Providence Journal* and the local television stations to say that the group responsible for the Action "would reveal themselves to the public at a time and place of their own choosing."

Also on Monday, Bug and I drove to Great Neck to return one of the vans to Dave Greenberg and to tell our parents what we had done. Carol accompanied us. Bug and I took turns driving.

Neither Bug nor I relished the task of telling our parents about the Action. My parents' reaction was, "Not again," referring to the Boston Action the previous November. Bug's mother's reaction was that Jerry Elmer had (once again) led her son astray.

On Friday, June 19, Bug and I held a press conference, surfacing in Burnside Park in downtown Providence—without evidence. We read our public statement, which was carefully worded to say that we "claim responsibility" for the Action, not that we had done it. Unlike the statements of most other groups of draft-board raiders, which were longer and more filled with flowing rhetoric than ours, our public statement was terse and factual. There was an important reason for this. Bug and I disagreed politically on a great many issues; most importantly, I was a pacifist and he was not. The only way Bug and I could agree on what to write in a joint statement was to keep it very short and limit it to just a dry factual recitation:

We, the Rhode Island Political Offensive For Freedom, claim responsibility for the destruction of records at Local Boards 7, 8, 9, and 10 in Providence, and at the Rhode Island State Selective Service Headquarters on June 13, 1970. We took this action because of our opposition to United States military involvement in Southeast

Asia, U.S. imperialism elsewhere in the Third World, as well as conscription and racism at home.

At each of these four Local Boards, all 1-A and 1-Y files, as well as files of new registrants, were destroyed. In addition, all portions of the cross reference system, including minutes of draft board meetings, chronological ledgers, and alphabetical files cards, were eliminated. In the State Headquarters, duplicate records and files on appeal were destroyed. Regardless of government claims to the contrary, this renders each of these draft boards totally inoperable in their ability to draft.

By revealing ourselves to the public, we hope to encourage others to conscientious actions against the U.S. institutions of war, racism, and conscription.

After Bug read our prepared statement for the TV cameras, Bug and I took questions from the audience, which consisted of reporters, United States Attorney Lincoln Almond, a large number of FBI agents, Providence Police detectives, and some peace activists from CNVA. There were many questions and answers, and some considerable sparring, on the question of whether we had actually *done* the Action or were merely "claiming responsibility" for it. One questioner asked repeatedly, "But were you really *there*?"

Bug and I held firm in our response that we were "claiming responsibility" for the Action.

"But how can you claim responsibility if you weren't there?" our persistent questioner asked.

Bug's and my responses to these questions were in keeping with our decision, based on my earlier experience with the Boston Eight, not to give the government evidence to use against us.

The FBI transcript of our surfacing, which I obtained years later through a Freedom of Information Act request for my entire FBI file, also quotes me as directing some comments to Federal Judge Edwin Robson. Earlier in June, the Chicago Fifteen, which had destroyed files at thirty-four draft boards in Chicago, had been tried and sentenced by Judge Robson. The sentences had been unusually harsh: five years for some members of the group, ten years for others. These were the longest sentences ever given to draft-board raiders. In giving such stiff sentences, Judge Robson had said from the bench that he hoped that these sentences would serve to deter future draft-board raids. The FBI transcript of our surfacing quotes my response to Judge Robson:

> We'd like to make one point very clear. Recently we've been witness-ing large amounts of repression coming down from the Govern-ment. . . . We see that in the recent trials of draft board liberators in Chicago. . . . Just about a week and a half ago, 15 people who de-stroyed records at 34 Chicago draft boards were tried and convicted. Judge Robson handed out sentences of five and ten years for this. In handing out those unprecedented sentences he said he hoped that these severe sentences would deter people from committing similar acts in the future. We surface today publicly to say that we will not allow Government threats or Government repression to deter us from our peace making efforts. The movement will not be stopped by . . . Government threats.

There was also one amusing thing in the same FBI transcript. Be-cause there were several peace activists at the surfacing, Bug's and my comments were occasionally punctuated by shouts of support from the crowd. These were transcribed by the FBI as people shouting, "Ride on, ride on!"

One other item related to our surfacing appears in my FBI file. After the press conference, Almond recommended prosecuting us for con-spiracy: "USA [United States Attorney], District of Rhode Island, on scene and advised that based on subjects' statements, he feels that con-spiracy charges to violate pertinent statutes are the best vehicles to be utilized in prosecution in this matter."

At our press conference on June 19, we took pains to refute at length government claims, made in the local press during the week since our Action, that the draft boards could still operate, and we issued a plea to young men not to re-register at those draft boards.

Despite our expectations, we were not arrested at our surfacing in Burnside Park. When we concluded the press conference, we waited around for a while, finding it difficult to believe that we would *not* be arrested. In the end, I drove to the CNVA Farm in Voluntown, where Carol lived and I was staying as a visitor.

That evening I watched the coverage of our surfacing on all three Providence television stations. Each of them ran long portions of our press conference unedited, including our highly detailed discussion of how these draft boards were now inoperable and our lengthy and several-times-repeated exhortations to young men not to re-register. I was amazed and delighted.

6

Still More Draft-File Destruction (And a Plot to Kidnap Henry Kissinger?)

BUG AND I HAD FULLY EXPECTED to be arrested on Friday, June 19, 1970, when we surfaced for the RIPOFF Action in Burnside Park. When we were not arrested, I found myself free to carry out some previously-made plans that summer.

Four More Draft Boards in Rochester

One of the things I did that late spring and summer was to spend considerable time in Rochester helping Suzi and DeCourcy plan the burglary of four draft boards there. I stayed at the Friends Meeting House, where DeCourcy lived with her friends, Bruce and Miriam Palmer, the resident caretakers of the Meeting House. Miriam was an excellent cook. Several times at dinner I was rather liberal about helping myself to seconds and thirds of whatever wonderful dish Miriam had prepared for us that evening. It was not until many years later that DeCourcy informed me that, on those earlier occasions, Miriam had been cooking for two nights and that I had several times unwittingly finished off meals that had been intended to last through the following nights.

Early in our planning we considered doing a simultaneous Action at draft boards in several cities in upstate New York. I spent a day with Miriam, traveling to and casing the two draft boards in Rome, New York. I spent a day on my own casing the medium-sized draft-board complex in Troy, New York. We all discussed the mechanical and logistical issues that would be presented by our conducting a simultaneous Action in Rochester, Syracuse, Rome, and Troy.

I personally found that idea exciting and appealing, and urged that we attempt a simultaneous Action in all four cities, cutting a broad swath across upstate New York. The Rome draft boards were housed in a small building on a quiet street in a sleepy city. After casing them with Miriam, I was convinced that this would be a relatively easy building to hit successfully, and I offered to take out that location personally. I was also excited by the prospect of our group doing the Troy draft-board complex. I had cased the Albany draft-board complex as a possible site for Bug's and my Action earlier in the year, but we had decided not to attempt Albany because of the huge volume of duplicate records at the New York State headquarters. But Troy was a medium-sized complex: much larger than the small two-board complex in Rome but small enough for a group our size.

Arguing in favor of a simultaneous raid in four different cities, I imagined what the publicity would be like after the raid. In Providence, after Bug and I had surfaced, a local Selective Service official had told the press that Bug and I could not have been responsible for such a professional burglary as the RIPOFF Action because we were "just kids." Now I wanted to outdo our previous success with simultaneous draft-board raids in four different cities. If they didn't think that mere "kids" could successfully handle a sophisticated burglary of *one* location, I thought happily to myself, what will they say when we hit *four different cities* all on the same night?

But it was not to be. For a variety of reasons, we decided to limit the Action to Rochester. The four Rochester draft boards were all located in a single complex in the downtown Federal Building. Also in the Federal Building was the local FBI office. This was a hard target to resist, and we didn't; we decided to liberate the FBI office at the same time we took out the draft boards. However, instead of destroying the FBI files, people would carry the FBI files out and publish them.

Over the Labor Day weekend I was in Rochester to assist with the draft-board/FBI-Action there. Eight people would go into the offices over the weekend; five of the eight planned to surface publicly later. I would help from the outside by driving people to and from the Federal Building from the apartment we were using as our base of operations and by calling the press after the Action.

On the night of the Action, two cars left our small apartment. I drove one, with four of the eight people who went go into the draft boards.

I dropped them off at the Federal Building, and then returned to the apartment to await their call the next morning when they were ready to be picked up. By having drivers who were not going into the Federal Building, there were no suspicious cars parked overnight at the scene of the crime while the burglary was in process.

Everything went smoothly as the group entered the Federal Building after dusk. They worked hard all night destroying draft files and gathering into bags the FBI files to carry out with them. But when I went to pick them up just before dawn I was greeted by an unexpected sight at the Federal Building: a large number of police cars with flashing lights. I drove on past without stopping and returned to our base of operations. I, and the several remaining friends who were working on the raid but had not gone into the Federal Building, quickly emptied out the apartment, trying to be careful to take with us any objects that might have our fingerprints on them. When the apartment was clean, I took my few personal effects and left.

Miriam drove me by New York Route 20 (rather than Interstate 90) from Rochester to the Syracuse Airport where, under an assumed name, I took the first flight to LaGuardia airport in New York. From LaGuardia I went to Penn Station in Manhattan, where I used pay phones to call the local newspapers and radio and TV stations in Rochester as well as the wire services in New York. Because of the unexpected arrest at the scene of the crime, all eight people inside the Federal Building "surfaced," not just the five who had initially intended to do so.

This was a sobering example of the extent to which, despite our elaborate planning and careful execution, events were not solely under our control. In both Providence and Rochester some members of the group destroying draft files had made careful decisions not to surface. But while in Providence things worked out as we had planned (Carol, DeCourcy, Suzi and Debbie did not surface), in Rochester they had not; three of the eight people who were arrested in Rochester had actually decided not to surface.

Hitchhiking to California

My other previously planned project that summer was a hitchhiking trip to California with Steve Dreisin. Throughout the spring, even while planning the draft-board Action with Bug, I was also planning this trip with Steve. I was not naïve; I fully realized that the Action in June might well preclude the trip in July. But I continued planning both nonetheless. When Bug and I were not arrested by the beginning of July, it seemed that my trip with Steve would take place after all.

Steve and I used the tent that we jointly owned from our 1968 biking trip on our cross-country hitchhiking adventure. Along the way, we stayed with friends or relatives whenever possible, but we slept out in the tent when necessary. Steve and I were both fans of J. R. R. Tolkien's *The Lord of the Rings*, and Steve, who was very artistically inclined, had sketched and painted on the door flap of our tent the design and runes that appeared in Tolkien on the door to Moria.

We left Great Neck on Sunday evening, July 12, 1970. My parents were away for their annual July vacation at Crystal Lake Lodge; Oma (Grandma) Elmer was staying in Great Neck with me. Her sister, my Tante (Aunt) Steffi, was visiting too. That evening, Steve and I took the bus and subway and bus into Manhattan, to and over the George Washington Bridge, to Edgewater, New Jersey, just across the Hudson River from Manhattan. That night, we stayed with Paul and Naomi Mayer, in order to get an early start the next morning. We almost did not make it out of Great Neck, though. Steve and I got to the bus stop and, a few minutes before the bus was due to arrive, we realized that we had left the tent at home. We dashed back for it, and returned just in time to board the bus.

Bright and early on Monday morning, July 13, Steve and I set out. We hitchhiked north on the Palisades Parkway to Spring Valley and from there we took the New York State Thruway to Rochester, where we spent the first night of our trip with DeCourcy Squire and Miriam and Bruce Palmer. The first ride we got in Fort Lee was in a Mercedes. Steve and I both took this as an omen that we would have a good trip and not have trouble getting rides. The omen turned out to be largely correct.

After the first night in Rochester, we spent the second night in Cleveland, with Bob Begin, one of the priests in the DC Nine. Our third night we stayed in a Chicago suburb, in the home of Steve's Uncle Oskar and Aunt Luba. The fourth night we camped on the banks of a lovely lake in rural Wisconsin; in the evening we took a refreshing swim and watched the full moon rise red over the lake. We cut across North Dakota on

Interstate 94, camping the next night in a roadside rest area about forty miles west of Jamestown.

On the eastern end of Montana, we got stuck, and it took us some hours to get a ride. Our plan was to go three quarters of the way across Montana on Interstate 94 to Livingston. There, we planned to leave the Interstate and travel south through Yellowstone National Park. We eventually got picked up by a young man named Les who worked for the railroad at the far western end of Montana; he was planning to drive through Livingston all the way to Missoula, Montana, near the border of Montana and Idaho. This was perfect for Steve and me; we would ride for some hundreds of miles, and get out of the car in Livingston.

After a bit, Les offered us a cautionary word about safety. We should be wary near Livingston, he told us, because there had recently been an incident with a hitchhiker; the locals might be reluctant to pick us up. Steve and I decided to change our route and continued on with Les through Livingston to Missoula, where we spent the night as his guest.

We spent the next morning in Missoula, and then went on through Idaho, where we camped in the mountains near the banks of a clean, clear river. Then we hitched west across Oregon to the Pacific Coast. We then went down the Pacific Highway to the San Francisco Bay area. During the course of the cross-country trip, every other day either Steve or I would call our respective parents to let them know where we were and that we were okay. Whichever boy's parents were called would call the other set of parents with the news.

Along the way, Steve and I took turns by the roadside, one standing with his thumb out while the other one sat on a backpack and rested. If we had trouble getting a ride, we would have a little competition with each other, betting on who would be the one who would succeed in getting a car to stop. The usual bet was a soft ice cream cone upon arrival in Berkeley. By the time we arrived in California, each of us owed the other more than a dozen ice cream cones. This was fine with me. In California, we stayed with John-i-thin, who took his vacation from work to coincide with our visit. Luckily, there was a soft ice cream stand quite close to John-i-thin's apartment, and Steve and I had jolly fun paying each other back the many ice cream cones that each of us owed the other.

John-i-thin took us around California hiking and camping. The three of us visited Point Reyes, and went panning for gold on the Colorado River. After a few weeks in California, we hitched home, directly across country, through Nebraska and Kansas. It had been an altogether wonderful, memorable trip.

A Plot to Kidnap Kissinger?

One more aspect of our 1970 cross-country trip must be related. On Monday evening, July 13, the first day of our cross-country hitchhiking trip to California, Steve and I had stayed in Rochester with DeCourcy. By coincidence, Phil Berrigan's then-girlfriend (later wife), Liz McAlister, was in town that night, at a meeting arranged by a local dentist, George McVey. Liz and George knew nothing about the Action that De-Courcy and Suzi had been working on. Oblivious to what was being planned, Liz was trying to recruit participants for possible future Actions which the Catholic Left might organize. I was invited to go to the meeting, and, after dinner at the Meeting House with DeCourcy and the Palmers, I excused myself to do so.

Before I left, however, DeCourcy admonished me in the strongest way not to tell Liz or George about the Action being planned. DeCourcy (with considerable justification) was very wary of the Catholic Left—not just of their elitism, but especially of their lack of security. Folks in the Catholic Left would show off, engage in games of one-upsmanship by bragging in oblique terms about secret, planned Actions that *they* knew about but that *you* didn't. DeCourcy found this anathema.

I attended the meeting with George McVey and Liz McAlister and, of course, honored my promise to DeCourcy not to mention anything about the Action we were planning. The next morning, Steve and I were off to Cleveland, and I thought no more about the meeting with George and Liz. Unbeknownst to me at the time, however, that meeting would have some considerable significance in the coming years.

The Rochester Action had taken place over the Labor Day weekend of 1970. The trial of the eight people arrested began on November 17, 1970. On November 27, during the trial, FBI Director J. Edgar Hoover testified before Congress, seeking $14.1 million in supplemental appropriations for the FBI in order to hire 1,000 additional agents and 702 additional clerks. It was the work of anti-war radicals, Hoover said, that made this additional funding for the FBI necessary. In particular, Hoover testified that there was a plot, organized by the imprisoned priests, Phil and Dan Berrigan, to kidnap National Security Advisor Henry Kissinger and blow up underground heating tunnels in Washington, DC. The group planning these actions, according to Hoover, was the East Coast Conspiracy to Save Lives.

Hoover's sensational charges made the front pages of newspapers across the country, and were immediately denounced by the anti-war movement in general and by the Catholic Left in particular. The charges were untrue, it was said; this was a transparent attempt by Hoover to get additional funds for the FBI by means of cheap scare tactics and, moreover, a reprehensible effort to prejudice the Rochester jury that was hearing the trial. This latter was true because there were multiple connections between Hoover's testimony and the trial then under way in Rochester.

The most general connection was that the Rochester trial involved people accused of destroying draft files. In his Senate testimony, Hoover stated that Phil and Dan Berrigan, who were known publicly for destroying draft files, were the masterminds of the supposed plot. Hoover seemed to be saying: see what people accused of destroying draft files are capable of; raiding draft boards is closely linked to plots to kidnap and bomb.

There was a more specific connection as well. In February 1970, a group largely made up of priests and nuns had destroyed files at several draft boards in Philadelphia; they called themselves the East Coast Conspiracy to Save Lives, the same name as that cited by Hoover for the supposed kidnap/bombing plot. One of the Rochester defendants was Ted Glick, a Catholic Left activist, who had been a part of the Philadelphia Action, the East Coast Conspiracy to Save Lives.

Actually, Ted had not been part of the Rochester group planning the Action over the course of the summer; in fact, the first time I ever met Ted was when I arrived in Rochester on the weekend of the Action there. Suzi and DeCourcy had carefully not involved anyone from the Catholic Left in their advance planning, but they were pleased to make use of Ted's labors on the night of the Action.

The potentially prejudicial effect of Hoover's Senate testimony was huge. Here was an ongoing trial of eight people in Rochester accused of burglarizing the local draft boards (and FBI office). During the course of the trial, the Director of the FBI offered testimony before Congress that suggested that these defendants were somehow connected to a group that was planning a political kidnapping and bombings! Moreover, at least one of the defendants on trial in Rochester was an *admitted* member of the group that was supposedly planning these other heinous crimes. Several of the people alleged by Hoover to have been part of the kidnap/bombing conspiracy held a press conference denying Hoover's allegations and, in effect, challenging Hoover to put up or shut up: *if we are guilty of a criminal conspiracy,* they said, *indict us; if we are not, then retract your inflammatory allegations.*

On January 12, 1971, a grand jury in Harrisburg, Pennsylvania handed up an indictment charging Phil Berrigan and six others with the precise charges Hoover had alleged in his congressional testimony: seeking to harm national security by conspiring to kidnap Kissinger and blow up underground tunnels in Washington. In addition to Phil, the other defendants were Phil's then-still-secret lover, Liz McAlister; Eqbal Ahmed, a Pakistani-born scholar; Father Neil McLaughlin, a priest who had been part of the New York Eight during the summer of 1969; Tony Scoblick and Mary Cain Scoblick, whom I knew from the Boston Eight Action; and Father Joe Wenderoth, a priest who had taken part in an earlier Action. In addition to those actually charged, the indictment listed additional unindicted co-conspirators, including Dan Berrigan and Paul Mayer. Attached to the indictment was a so-called "bill of particulars," a detailed listing of specific overt acts that the government alleged had been carried out in furtherance of the supposed conspiracy. The Justice Department hired a Special Prosecutor, William Lynch, to prosecute the alleged conspirators.

What can I say about the indictment? It was a mixed bag, a mélange of fact and fantasy. Also attached to the indictment was a series of letters between Phil Berrigan (writing from Lewisburg prison) and Liz McAlister. As soon as I saw the letters, I knew that they were genuine. I had had a long correspondence with Phil; his handwriting is highly distinctive. And there he was, in his own handwriting, discussing with Liz a plan to kidnap Kissinger (a "citizen's arrest," as they quaintly called it) and blow up the underground heating tunnels in Washington. There, too, were Liz's letters back to Phil keeping him apprised of her progress on this project.

At the same time, it was also clear that Hoover and the FBI had gotten much of the story wrong, and had blown things way out of proportion. For example, one of the overt acts listed in the bill of particulars was that Liz (whom I barely knew) and I had traveled together to Rochester on July 13, 1970, in order to recruit people for the kidnap plot. The bill of particulars listed the meeting that I had attended that night in Rochester, with Liz and George McVey, as being part of the plot. This was absurd. I had, of course, been at the meeting at the date, time, and place set forth in the indictment. But, far from recruiting people to kidnap Henry Kissinger (a plot I never knew about, and would never have participated in had I known), I had been under DeCourcy's strict instructions not even let slip that an ordinary draft-board Action was being planned.

Much of the indictment followed that pattern: a germ of truth, surrounded by layers of mischaracterization or outright falsehood. There was, for example, an East Coast Conspiracy to Save Lives. Hoover had not made the name up. However, the East Coast Conspiracy was not really an ongoing organization; it was the name given to those who had earlier destroyed draft files in Philadelphia. The name East Coast Conspiracy to Save Lives was rather like Bug and me calling our Action the Rhode Island Political Offensive For Freedom. The people indicted in Harrisburg were not part of the East Coast Conspiracy to Save Lives at all, and that group had had nothing whatever to do with kidnapping Kissinger or bombing heating tunnels.

But, still, how could there be even a germ of truth in the indictment? What on earth had happened that peace activists could even contemplate a political kidnapping—and seriously argue that it would be a nonviolent act because, in the end, the victim would be released unharmed? (Phil did argue just that in one of the letters.) And, if they were going to consider such an immoral and reckless scheme, how could they be so stupid as to get caught?

The getting caught part was relatively easy to explain. Phil and Liz had for some months been smuggling letters to each other while Phil was in the maximum-security federal prison in Lewisburg, Pennsylvania, using as a conduit a fellow prisoner of Phil's who was a trusty and who turned out to be a government informant. En route to delivery, each letter had been photocopied by the FBI. The magnitude of Phil and Liz's stupidity is amazing: discussing such a scheme *in writing* and using a virtual stranger to smuggle the incriminating letters into and out of a maximum-security federal prison!

How the plan could have been hatched in the first place is a bit harder to explain. Obviously, shortly after Phil had gone to prison, he and Liz actually *had* considered their ridiculous kidnap/bombing plan, and had discussed it in their intercepted communications. Realizing both the mechanical difficulties of the scheme and the moral problems with it, they had abandoned the idea relatively quickly. Months later, a distorted form of it was resurrected by Hoover. Some of the particulars were obviously correct—certainly enough to be an embarrassment to the peace movement and to make Phil and the Catholic Left look bad—but Hoover and the FBI had most of the details dead wrong and had failed to mention the minor detail that, while the plan had, in fact, been briefly discussed seriously, it had been voluntarily and completely abandoned some time before.

One of the most troubling parts of the whole Harrisburg business was the light it shone on Phil Berrigan's elitism, particularly his scathing observations about some of his closest colleagues. Recall that the FBI had attached to the indictment many pages of handwritten correspondence between Phil and Liz. Granted, the writers had assumed that their remarks were going to remain private. Granted, people speak differently in private, intimate conversations than they do for public consumption. Nevertheless, the correspondence, excerpts of which were widely reported in the mainstream press, cast Phil in a highly unfavorable (though entirely accurate) light. After Liz had written to Phil explaining that Eqbal had raised the possibility of a political kidnapping, Phil had written back to her about Eqbal:

> Just between you and me, I have never been overmuch impressed w/ Eq. He's a dear friend, very helpful in the last months, lovely guy, good ideologue, but still to produce. I think the role of the man from Missouri is the safest one with him. (I have this terrible suspicion regarding academics.) With few exceptions, the bastards will let others go to the gallows without a *serious* murmur. They did it in

Germany and they're doing it here. And E is from that strain. [Emphasis as in the original.]

Here is the quintessential, elitist Phil Berrigan. The "still to produce" reference meant that Eqbal had not participated in a public draft-board Action which, to Phil, was the only "serious" way to oppose the war. Nothing else the man might have done for the peace movement was worth mentioning. Lovely guy, but yet to produce.

In another letter, Phil even trashed his brother Dan, who *had* participated in the Catonsville Action: "But getting back to the bruv thing–that's an essentially different scene, you know . . . I remember how we operated with him—always happy to have him in a rap, but undisturbed when he couldn't make it. His talents grab on a different level than ours. . . ." And, of course, there was no use gainsaying the letters, as they were all in his handwriting.

On April 30, 1971, the Harrisburg grand jury handed up a superceding indictment, replacing the January indictment. The new indictment was radically different from the old one. It charged the same seven defendants—plus Ted Glick—with conspiring to harm national security *not* by kidnapping or bombing, but rather by destroying draft files! The government had apparently concluded, probably correctly, that there was simply not enough evidence to obtain a conviction on the kidnap and bombing charges.

The charge of conspiracy to harm national security by destroying draft files was terribly unfair because it made it much, much easier for the government to obtain convictions. Most of the Harrisburg defendants were either already in prison for destroying draft files (Phil Berrigan and Ted Glick), or had surfaced publicly, claiming responsibility for one or another draft-board Action (Tony Scoblick, Mary Cain Scoblick, Neil McLaughlin, and Joe Wenderoth). Accusing them of allegedly conspiring to destroy draft files was like "guessing" the winner of the Kentucky Derby on the day after the race is run: it rather takes the challenge out of the entire enterprise.

The original Harrisburg indictment in January had made the front page of the *New York Times*. The top of the *Times* the next day, in fact, had run no fewer than three photographs with the article: Phil and Liz, the alleged plot's masterminds, and Henry Kissinger, their supposed intended victim. The superceding indictment in April, however, was not even mentioned in the *Times*. The change in the government's theory— that the supposed plot was not at all to kidnap and bomb, but rather to destroy draft files—was entirely lost on the general public. Thus, if a conviction *were*, in the end, obtained, most people would think that the defendants were convicted of the original kidnap/bombing plot. Such a conclusion, although wrong, would have been entirely reasonable under the circumstances.

In early autumn 1971, I had a discussion with the U.S. Attorney in Providence, Linc Almond, and a local FBI agent, Tom Lardner. They talked about the Harrisburg case and about my supposed part in it. They told me that the special prosecutor, Bill Lynch, wanted to come to Providence to meet with me to get evidence for the forthcoming trial, and they told me that I could expect a lighter sentence in my own forthcoming trial if I were to cooperate with Lynch. I politely declined the invitation.

In the winter of 1972, the Harrisburg defendants went on trial. Former U.S. Attorney General Ramsey Clark was the lead defense attorney. The original defense plan was to go through all of the minutiæ of the indictment and show how wrong the government had been. For example, I was subpoenaed by the defense to testify that, yes, I had been at the meeting in Rochester on July 13, 1970, as alleged, but no, there had been no plan to kidnap Kissinger and, no, I had not been recruiting for it, as alleged. I was at the Providence airport for the flight to Harrisburg when I was paged to an airline phone. The defense plan had changed, and my testimony was not needed, after all. I could go home.

In the end, Ramsey Clark put on not a single witness for the defense. At the end of the prosecution's case, he made a closing speech in which he said that the government's case was so weak that, back when *he* had been Attorney General, such a case would never even have gone to a grand jury. (Since becoming an attorney myself, I have learned that it is a violation of the ethical rules of the court for an attorney to make reference to such firsthand views or opinions when addressing a jury.) Despite the almost complete absence of any defense, the jury deadlocked 10–2 for acquittal. The judge declared a mistrial, and the defendants were never retried.

On Monday evening, July 13, 1970, when I met with George McVey and Liz McAlister, I was completely unaware of all of the eventual fallout that would result from that meeting.

I Return to Providence

Steve and I were back on the East Coast by late August. Returning to college that autumn was not an option I considered seriously. Although I had technically finished the semester and received my grades, I had made my emotional break with Bard the previous spring and felt that I was done with school. Before I had left for California with Steve, Carol Bragg and I had become increasingly interested in each other, and when I returned from the West Coast I moved in with her at the CNVA Farm where she was on the staff.

On Saturday, September 12, one week after my narrow escape in Rochester, I called my mother on the phone from Voluntown. She reported that FBI agents had been to my parents' with a warrant for my arrest. "Damn," I thought to myself, "it's all I need to be indicted in Rochester while awaiting indictment in Providence." I was fully prepared to be indicted in Providence, where I had made a conscious, deliberate decision to surface publicly for the Action. But I had equally deliberately decided *not* to surface in Rochester and had for that precise reason not gone into the draft boards there.

On the phone, my mother reported to me that she had told the FBI agents who had come with the warrant that I was not there. The agents asked whether they might search the house anyway.

"You don't know my son," my mother had replied. "If he were hiding here and heard me tell you that he was not here, he'd come running out saying, 'Yes I am!'"

The FBI agents did not search the house. It was only toward the end of the conversation that I had the presence of mind to ask my mother where the indictment had been handed up.

"Providence," she said.

I heaved a sigh of relief that she could not have understood.

Now indicted in Providence, I had no interest in avoiding arrest, but I did want to use my arrest as an opportunity to make a public statement about our Action. I called a press conference for the following Monday morning on the steps of the Federal Building in Providence. The statement I distributed to the press on this occasion was longer and more personal than the very brief joint statement Bug and I had prepared for our surfacing in June. Since this was not a joint statement with Bug, I did not have to worry about whether or not he agreed with what I said. Part of the statement said:

> We must not be like the "good Germans" who were silent in the face of unspeakable atrocities. We must act boldly against the machineries of death, lest we be accounted accomplices in the crimes that are being committed.
>
> I feel that our action is in the best tradition of our nation. Our nation was founded by outlaws, by revolutionaries such as George Washington, Tom Paine, Thomas Jefferson. These men, like Christ, knew that when laws are unjust and do not serve the needs of people, it is the responsibility of conscientious people to violate those laws, to take conscientious actions on behalf of the community. . . .

The press were waiting when I arrived on Monday but I did not get to read much of my statement. Also waiting for me were FBI agent Tom Lardner (who had appeared the previous August in newspapers from New York to California after arresting Dan Berrigan on Block Island) and Chief Deputy U.S. Marshal George Douglas. They served the arrest warrant on me almost as soon as I arrived.

I was held in the marshal's lockup on the third floor of the Federal Building until I could be arraigned that afternoon before Chief Judge Edward Day. An amusing thing happened while I awaited arraignment. I asked whether I could be visited by my "fiancee," Carol Bragg. Marshal Douglas had no objections and Carol and I were left alone in one of the marshal's offices for an hour or so to chat. Here I was, a presumably dangerous criminal accused of destroying government files and records, left alone for an hour in an office filled with more government files and records! At noon, Marshal Douglas came in and apologetically explained that he would have to lock me in the cell at one end of the office because he was going out to lunch. (He also kindly inquired whether he could get me a sandwich.) He put the key in the lock of the cell, opened the door, and I walked into the cell. Then he closed the door, locked it, accidentally left the key in the lock, and left to go out to lunch. Carol was permitted to remain in the room, but outside the cell. We discussed whether to play a practical joke on Marshal Douglas by switching positions with each other—so Carol would be inside the cell and I sitting outside when Douglas returned from lunch. We decided not to.

At my arraignment that afternoon, I was informed of the three charges against us: destruction of government property valued over $100 (a possible ten-year sentence), interfering with the administration of Selective Service "by force, violence, or otherwise" (a possible five-year sentence), and theft and destruction of government documents (a possible three-year sentence).

There was also a fourth count in the indictment, but it was not, despite Linc Almond's suggestion to the FBI at the time of our surfacing in Burnside Park, conspiracy (which would have carried an additional penalty of up to five years in prison). Instead, the fourth count was aiding and abetting, which did not carry with it any possible additional jail time. It did, however, make it much easier for the government to obtain convictions against us. In effect, this additional charge meant that the government need not actually prove that we had burglarized the draft boards, only that we were somehow involved in the act. This was similar to the murder charge that had been brought against Angela Davis, the black activist. Everyone knew that Davis had not actually killed anyone; she was accused of supplying the weapon with which someone else had killed someone. I guessed that we were charged with aiding and abetting because we had taken pains not to leave evidence at the draft boards.

I was always intrigued by the charge that we had interfered with Selective Service, as the statute said, "by force, violence, or otherwise." I believed that we had certainly used force, but not violence. "Otherwise," of course, could mean anything.

Bail was set at $2,000. My mother attended the arraignment. This was not unexpected, as I had informed my parents by phone of my press-conference plans. My mother posted the bail and I was released that afternoon.

On October 3, 1970, Carol and I moved together from Voluntown to Providence, to an apartment we rented at 88 Gordon Avenue. We were by then involved in a romantic relationship. Our plan was to use the draft-board Action as an organizing tool until I was tried and sent to prison.

Carol organized a so-called "1-A Project," using as a model a similar project she had been involved with in St. Paul, Minnesota. Each month, she would go to the four draft boards we had hit and copy the names of all the men newly classified 1-A. This time she went as herself, not as Mary Mulligan. The draft-board clerks were not happy about releasing the names, especially to a person who had so obviously been involved in destruction of files at that very office, but there was little they could do to stop us since by law the names had to be available to the public.

After obtaining the names from the draft boards, Carol organized volunteers to call each and every man on the 1-A list with information about draft counseling and alternatives to military service. This was a bigger job than it might at first appear. The only information we had on a man was his name and some idea of where he lived (based on which draft board he had). For men with common names—say, Smith or Jones—a volunteer might call fifty people from the telephone directory before dialing a correct number and reaching a home where there was an eighteen-year-old man who had just been classified 1-A by his draft board. The 1-A project, like the exquisitely careful packing of file cards she had done in the draft boards, was typical of Carol. It involved slow, careful, meticulous work; it required persistence and stick-to-itiveness that few people could match. Carol ran the project for several years, never tiring of the work. The 1-A Project reached hundreds of draft-eligible men.

Meanwhile, I was in demand as a speaker in local high schools and colleges and in front of church audiences. The Catholic Church was then running an adult study group as part of its Christian Family Movement (CFM). Rhode Island is the most predominantly Catholic state in the country and, because draft-board Actions were heavily associated with the Berrigans and the Catholic Left, Catholics seemed to have a special interest in or curiosity about the Actions. These CFM groups met in the homes of individuals one night a week. Once word got around among the groups that I was a good speaker on the war and the draft, I was out several nights a week speaking to CFM groups. I developed a standard speech that I used on such occasions.

I have a theory about how Americans view civil disobedience that dates back to my speaking engagements during this period. Americans seem to approve of civil disobedience as an inverse function of their own geographical or temporal proximity to the actions being considered. The further away in time or location, the more Americans are willing to be accepting of civil disobedience; the closer they are to civil disobedience, the more upset they become. In the 1950s, the United States put an image of Mahatma Gandhi on a postage stamp; that was okay, because by then Gandhi was dead and, anyway, he had lived on another continent. In the 1970s, we put Henry David Thoreau on a postage stamp. He was American, so we had had to wait an entire century after he was dead before he could be so honored (rather than a mere decade, as with Gandhi). During his lifetime, Martin Luther King Jr. was a viewed as a dangerous agitator. He was pursued by the FBI and imprisoned repeatedly. Even moderate white Northerners worried that this civil disobedience stuff, going to jail all the time, would alienate Southerners potentially sympathetic to the integrationist cause. But once King was safely dead, it was acceptable to have a national holiday for him.

The early 1970s was a time when many in the peace movement, including the Weather Underground, were turning to violence. One of the main points that I sought to convey in all of my speeches at this time was that nonviolence could be an extremely, even uniquely, effective tool for creating social change.

I have already considered the question of whether draft-board Actions were nonviolent (see chapter 4). But were they *effective*? I think the draft-board Actions were extremely effective in two separate, but related, ways.

First, draft-board Actions succeeded in rendering hundreds of draft boards, all across the country, incapable of drafting people for months or years at a time. The Chicago Fifteen destroyed files at thirty-four draft boards in Chicago; the Beaver Fifty-five hit a complex housing forty-four local boards in Indianapolis; dozens of boards were hit in St. Paul, New York, Philadelphia, Boston, New Haven, and so forth. We had a sophisticated understanding of how Selective Service records were kept and the function of each of the three parts of the cross-reference system, and we worked carefully to destroy all the files necessary to render draft boards wholly non-functioning.

When draft boards were made inoperable by draft-board Actions,

Selective Service attempted to redistribute draft quotas from the non-functioning draft boards to other draft boards in the same state. Almost without exception, however, those other draft boards were already not able to meet their own quotas. The inability of other draft boards to meet quotas was a result of a variety of factors: some men were openly resisting the draft; many others were evading the draft by faking reasons for medical or other deferments; still others were fleeing to Canada to escape conscription or quietly not registering. Thus, when we destroyed files at *some* draft boards, Selective Service tried but was ultimately unable to redistribute quotas to *other* draft boards. The bottom line was that some men did not get drafted, and other men were not drafted in their place.

For years after the RIPOFF Action, I ran into men who had been expecting draft notices from a Providence draft board in 1970 that had never come. This happened once when I was hitchhiking, often when I was delivering speeches to college audiences, and occasionally at potluck dinners or local peace meetings. These men were usually quite grateful, and would sometimes gush their thanks for saving them.

The second way in which draft-board Actions were effective is that they significantly contributed to the overall level of protest against the war that was sweeping the country. And, like the acts of individual draft resisters, draft-board Actions showed that, in order for the government to prosecute the war, it would also be necessary to prosecute and jail a significant number of respectable, middle-class people for their anti-war activities.

Bug Goes Underground, Surfaces, and Re-Surfaces

Between mid-September and early November 1970, people often asked me where Bug was. I generally answered evasively. "Oh, he's out west somewhere traveling. He probably doesn't even know we've been indicted."

At first this was true. Bug *was* traveling on the West Coast and did not know immediately that we had been indicted. He learned of our indictment soon enough, however, and decided not to return for arrest. Instead, he went underground, moving after a short time to Rochester, where he took the name Kelly.

Bug's decision to go underground angered me greatly. One reason was that he did it without discussing it with me. Another reason was that I believed his decision to go underground undermined the open and public nature of our Action and, consequently, its nonviolent nature and tone. "At no time was our action 'underground' or clandestine," I had said in my statement on September 14, when I had been arrested. Bug's going underground made a liar out of me and foreshadowed additional problems to come.

Going underground seemed to be a popular thing to do when Bug did it. The previous April 9, when Dan and Phil Berrigan had both been ordered to surrender themselves to begin serving their Catonsville sentences, they had gone underground instead. Phil was arrested a few days later, on April 21, in a church rectory in Manhattan, but Dan had managed to stay underground through mid-August, when he was arrested at Bill Stringfellow's home on Block Island.

I had disapproved of the Berrigans' decision to go underground. Throughout their trial, and in all of their public statements after the Catonsville Action, they had described their Action as fitting squarely within the mainstream of the history of civil disobedience in the United States. After all, they had said, their Action was public; the participants clearly showed their willingness to accept the legal consequences of their Action by standing by the burning draft files, waiting to be arrested. It was no coincidence that the Berrigans had always emphasized the point about the openness of their Action. Draft-file destruction was controversial, even on the Left; sensibly they had sought to make the Action more understandable and more acceptable by making it open. By going underground instead of surrendering, they undermined their own earlier arguments in favor of what they had done.

To be sure, Dan Berrigan's half year underground was not really underground in the traditional sense of the word because he kept popping up for anti-war events and media interviews. Dan attended a large anti-war convocation at Cornell, where he had briefly served as chaplain; he preached a Sunday morning sermon from a church pulpit in Philadelphia, was interviewed on national television (including the NBC evening news), gave interviews to several newspapers (including the *New York Times*, which published an interview on April 26), met with anti-war friends, and even had a movie made about him. Had Dan *really* been underground in the sense of seriously trying to avoid capture, he would have done none of these things. Moreover, in tweaking the governmental authorities in this way, he was certainly bringing additional publicity to the anti-war movement. Nevertheless, to me it seemed like the wrong kind of publicity, because he was emphasizing his faithlessness with what he himself had earlier proclaimed was an important part of his civil disobedience.

Bug's time underground turned out to be short-lived. He soon grew weary of his clandestine existence in Rochester and, together, he and I worked out a marvelous way for him to re-surface. In November, the eight people who had been arrested in the Rochester draft boards over the Labor Day weekend were tried in federal court there. Their trial provided the occasion and backdrop for our plan. This is what we did.

Bug and I, of course, were quite close to the Rochester group. Each night, during the trial of the Rochester defendants, there was a large support rally for them at a local church. These rallies featured guest speakers, music, and speeches by the defendants. On the first night of the trial, William Kunstler, the celebrated attorney of both the Catonsville Nine and the Chicago Seven, spoke and the large church sanctuary was absolutely packed.

After Kunstler's speech, I addressed the crowd. My speech was short and dull to the point of banality. I explained that I had been involved in a draft-board raid in Providence similar to the one in Rochester. I said that David Rosen and I had been indicted and that I had been arrested but David had not yet been arrested. I finished my short speech this way: "Actually, the FBI has been looking all over the country for two months for Dave without being able to find him. Dave Rosen is probably just traveling around, and unavailable to the FBI." Then I sat down. A few people tried to make some polite applause but most of the people in the audience were puzzled or bored. Only the Rochester defendants knew what was coming next.

After I left the speaker's podium, there was a momentary lull in the program. No one got up to introduce the next speaker. Then a tall, blond man got up from the front row of the church and walked slowly to the stage. "Hi," he said casually into the microphone. "My name is Dave

Rosen." There was complete silence for a moment while the meaning of his words sank in with the audience. Then complete pandemonium broke out. Bug got a standing ovation from the crowd. Several men sitting in the back of the church dashed for the exit. Wearing business suits and white shirts, they were obviously plainclothed police officers or FBI agents.

After things quieted down, Bug gave a short talk about our Action and his time underground. Unlike my talk a moment before, which had met with only a smattering of polite applause, Bug got another thunderous ovation. Our plan for Bug to have an exciting surfacing had worked perfectly.

Except for one thing. Much to our surprise, Bug was not arrested that evening. As a result, we were forced to plan a second surfacing for him in Providence a few days later. On that occasion he was arrested.

The FBI surveillance report of Bug's surfacing in Rochester was quite accurate:

> Information has been received from informants at Rochester, New York, that subject ROSEN appeared at a meeting the night of 11/17/70 at the Central Presbyterian Church, Plymouth Avenue North, Rochester, New York. This meeting was attended by approximately 400 persons and was held in connection with the trial presently in progress at Rochester, New York, involving eight persons charged with the break-in and destruction of records in the Federal Building, Rochester, New York. During this meeting, ROSEN identified himself to the audience and stated that he was being sought by the FBI for destruction of Selective Service files in Providence, Rhode Island. It is noted that during this same meeting WILLIAM KUNSTLER was also a speaker.

However, in a comic example of FBI bungling, the following report is dated the day *after* Bug surfaced in Rochester. The report, written by the FBI national office in Washington, DC, is directed to the Special Agent in Charge of the Boston office. In it, the FBI seems to be completely ignorant of Bug's whereabouts:

David Rosen has been a fugitive since 9/11/70. Review of this matter reflects Rosen was last seen during mid August of 1970, and last known to be "out west." Additionally, he has been described as a hippie type and may be living in a hippie colony. His parents have been uncooperative.

It is apparent that the usual fugitive investigation leads to locate Rosen may prove inadequate in this case. You should explore means of identifying hippie-type groups to which subject Rosen may associate in an effort to locate Rosen and effect his arrest as soon as possible. It is obvious new avenues of approach must be developed if a successful solution of this case is to be achieved. Insure [sic] logical informants are assigned in this regard, especially those familiar with New-Left and SDS activities. . . .

After his arrest in Providence in late November—after we had arranged his *second* re-surfacing—Bug remained in Providence to join the work that Carol and I had begun. At first, he moved in with us at 88 Gordon Avenue; later, he took his own apartment a block away.

With Bug's return, our political differences mounted. Because I was a pacifist, I consistently sought to portray the Action as an example of how effective nonviolent direct action could be. Bug was most emphatically not a pacifist and in his public talks he would not rule out the possibility or validity of violent actions. Another problem was that Bug was represented in court by a lawyer, but I had chosen to represent myself, over the strenuous objections of the judge. Bug feared that my not having a lawyer (and thereby antagonizing the judge) might jeopardize him as well as me.

Despite our differences, Bug, Carol and I spent the ensuing year on a variety of political organizing projects in Providence. Bug and I continued to speak about the war and the draft before school and church audiences. Carol continued the 1-A Project. Together we started the Rhode Island Bail Fund, a project to help indigent awaiting-trial defendants incarcerated at the state prison, the Adult Correctional Institution in Cranston. In May 1971, Bug went to Washington to participate in the May Day demonstrations against the war. We took in some money from speaking honoraria and used up some savings.

The Plea Bargain

During the summer of 1971, when we still had not been brought to trial, Bug's lawyer began exploring the possibility of a plea bargain with U.S. Attorney Lincoln Almond. Almond made an offer that Bug would plead guilty to one of the three charges against us, interfering with Selective Service, and make a statement to the court that he would not repeat the crime. In return, Almond would recommend that the other two counts of the indictment be dropped and that Bug receive a two-year suspended sentence. Bug's lawyer was told that the same deal was also open to me.

Bug quickly accepted the offer, but I spent weeks agonizing over what to do. On the one hand, I believed that I was not guilty of doing anything wrong and wanted an opportunity to explain why in court. Furthermore, we had planned to use the upcoming trial as an organizing forum against the war, something I was still eager to do. But my biggest objection concerned the statement we were to make as part of the proposed deal. I was adamantly opposed to making any statement, regardless of how carefully worded, that could be construed or misconstrued as rejecting the validity and value of what we had done. I supported and cherished what we had done; I would not betray our Action by making a statement of regret to the court.

On the other hand, I was frightened of going to prison. The combined charges against us carried a possible total of eighteen years in prison. The recent sentences for the Chicago Fifteen had run five years for some members of the group and ten years for others. I told myself that the statement Almond wanted us to make was not one of regret or apology; it was merely a statement that we would not do the same thing again.

I finally decided to accept the offer but felt guilty about my decision for many years afterward.

A final split with Bug occurred on the day we appeared before Judge Day to be sentenced. When the judge asked me whether I would do the Action again, I felt constrained to answer fully and honestly. No, I told the judge, I would not do it again. But I still believed that what I had done was right and the only reason I would not do it again is that those draft boards had already been hit. Next time I would consider raiding different draft boards, or perhaps an army induction center.

It was difficult to tell who was more upset by my remarks, Judge

Day or Bug: Judge Day at the insolence of the young defendant before him, Bug at the prospect that his deal would fall through because of what I had said. Bug was right to be upset. My comments could have landed him in prison, thereby violating one of the first precepts of civil disobedience: that one accepts the consequences of one's own actions rather than having those consequences fall on others. However, the plea bargain went through after all, and Bug and I were each given two-year suspended sentences. During that period we were placed on probation and were not supposed to be arrested again. After we walked out of court that day, Bug and I did not talk to each other again for several years.

As the years have passed, I have felt progressively less guilty about having accepted the plea bargain. I have come to see that what was important about our Action was the deed of destroying draft files, the fact of doing so publicly, and the organizing work we did in Rhode Island afterwards, not the specific plea we later entered in court.

During my brief time at Bard College in the spring of 1970—after my secret participation in the Boston Action and before my public surfacing for the Providence one—I took a course on the Old Testament taught by the college chaplain, an Episcopal priest, Frederick Shafer. I wrote a paper for the course on the book of Jonah. I thought that the book of Jonah, like much great literature, was written with me in mind. One of the sources I used in my research on Jonah was subtitled, "The Reluctant Prophet." Jonah is the only book of Old Testament prophecy in which the message of God is conveyed not *through* the prophet but *despite* him. Jonah knows just what he is expected to do; after all, God tells him directly. Jonah just does not think he has the courage to do what he knows he should and must do; in fact, when God tells Jonah to go to Ninevah to preach, Jonah sets off in the exact opposite direction.

That spring at Bard, after Boston and before Providence, I knew just how Jonah felt. Never in my life have I felt such an unequivocally clear calling to do something as I did then with public draft-file destruction. Yet, like Jonah, I feared that I lacked the requisite courage. I shall always be grateful that somehow I found the courage and grace to follow that calling.

In the years since 1970, the draft-board Action has become a part of me, of my identity, of who I am. It is, to be sure, only a part of a much more complex identity. I am the only son of European Jewish refugees from Nazism. I am the angry, rebellious child. I am the nonviolent peace activist, the Selective Service nonregistrant. I am the husband, then father. I am the lawyer. I am the cook. I am the amateur humorist and practical joker. And, yes, I am the public destroyer of draft files and convicted felon.

Even "convicted felon" has become a centrally important part of my self-identity. I am aware of the shock value of the term; it is fun to drop the fact casually when I am, say, lecturing in a high school class or church basement. I know the audience thinks that this articulate moralist in suit and tie who is speaking of strict adherence to lofty religious and ethical ideals is a considerable distance from their image of the unshaven, poorly dressed, marginally literate criminal.

That is frivolity, but there is a serious side to the matter too. The Action that led to my felony conviction sprang from the deepest wellsprings of my soul: the unutterable anguish about the Vietnam War and the urgent need I felt to do all I could to end it. That is why when, in the spring of 1987, a lawyer who heard my story suggested that I apply to the government to receive a pardon and have my record wiped clean, I recoiled in horror at the suggestion. I was, and always have been, very proud of what I did against the war, proud to have had the strength of mind and purpose to commit nonviolent civil disobedience in the course of opposing the war, proud, in effect, of the way in which I had become a convicted felon. In short, I was proud to be a felon. Having my record wiped "clean" was the last thing I wanted.

In 1970, I was a Jew who took part in what was widely perceived to be a "Catholic action." Yet it was precisely my Judaism—or, more precisely, my Jewish family's experience with the Holocaust—that stood at the very center of my motivation for participating in draft-file destruction. As was the case with my individual nonregistration, here, too, I acted because I felt I could not stand by silently when crimes against humanity were being committed in my name.

7
The American Friends
Service Committee

WORKING FOR THE AMERICAN FRIENDS Service Committee was the best job in the world.

For one thing, I was actually paid to work for peace. This was work that I would have wanted to do anyway, whether I was paid or not. Many people wanted to work full-time in the peace movement, but, because of lack of funds, there were always very few paid jobs. To have one of those jobs was an honor and a privilege.

For another thing, my particular job in AFSC, as a Field Secretary running a small statewide office for Rhode Island, involved a wonderful and rare combination of factors. On the one hand, we were a local peace group for Rhode Island, just as SPV had been a local peace group in Great Neck when I was in high school. We had the independence of a local peace group to decide what we wanted to do and how we wanted to do it. But our local office was also part of a national (and international) organization: AFSC had about 400 paid, full-time staff people at a national headquarters in Philadelphia and forty offices throughout the United States. We received money, program ideas, literature, access to visiting speakers on national tours, and other resources from a large and well-funded organization. It was a perfect combination.

AFSC is the Quaker service and educational organization. It was founded in 1917 in order to give conscientious objectors to World War I a means of performing alternative service. Those World War I COs went to Europe as ambulance drivers and medics. Since then, AFSC has always provided medical aid to civilian war victims on all sides of the battle lines, without regard to the politics or affiliations of the recipients. During World War II, AFSC provided aid to Allied *and* German civilians. During the Vietnam War, AFSC provided aid to North Vietnamese civilians *and* to South Vietnamese civilians living in areas controlled by the Saigon government and in areas controlled by the liberation forces.

After World War II, AFSC began also doing peace movement organizing in the United States. Part of AFSC's reasoning was that, while it is no doubt a good thing to bind the wounds of those hurt in war, it may be even better to prevent war from occurring in the first place. AFSC began working against United States involvement in Vietnam in 1956, long before most Americans knew where Vietnam was. AFSC had separate program divisions carrying out its international relief efforts and its domestic peace programs. I always worked in the so-called "peace education" division, the one doing peace movement organizing in the United States. The transition from doing peace work in Rhode Island independently under the rubric of RIPOFF to being the co-director, with Carol Bragg, of the Rhode Island AFSC office was a smooth and natural one. After the draft-board Action in June 1970 (or, more precisely, after the California trip with Steve Dreisin), Carol and I continued doing peace movement work in Providence. Carol ran the 1-A project. I organized draft resistance and was a frequent anti-war speaker in schools and churches. Over time, we built up a mailing list of people interested in peace activities.

Bug and I were indicted for the RIPOFF Action in September 1970 and pleaded guilty in October 1971. About the same time, the New England Regional Office of AFSC (the unfortunate acronym in AFSC parlance was "NERO") was looking for so-called "field staff" in each of the six New England states. The impetus for this came primarily from the then-director of AFSC peace programs in New England, Ed Lazar. Ed had worked with the Gandhian movement in India and was a great believer in decentralization. He thought it was absurd that AFSC had an office that purported to be a "New England Regional Office" with forty staff people in Cambridge, Massachusetts, but no staff at all in the rest of New England.

The "field secretaries" Ed was looking for were people already doing peace work in their local areas who, in return for modest stipends, were willing to be loosely affiliated with AFSC. In the autumn of 1971, Ed approached Carol about being the AFSC Field Secretary for Rhode Island. Carol was interested, but hesitant about taking the position alone. She

Rhode Island AFSC staff, circa 1979. *Left to right:* Carol Bragg, Jerry Elmer, and Sister Ann Welch. Photo courtesy of the American Friends Service Committee.

arranged to share the part-time position on a 50–50 basis with another woman, Carol Reagan, a Catholic nun active in peace work.

Carol (Bragg) and Carol (Reagan) were formally appointed the AFSC Field Secretaries for Rhode Island effective January 2, 1972. The combined stipend for the position was $100 per month; that is, AFSC paid each Carol $50 per month. They had no specific responsibilities for AFSC, but were merely expected to continue the local peace work they were already doing. During this period, I worked as a dish-washer from noon to 2:00 P.M. on weekdays at Louie's Restaurant, a luncheonette on Broad Street in South Providence a few blocks from our apartment on Gordon Avenue. I earned the minimum wage at the time, $1.75 per hour, or $17.50 per week. Carol and I subsisted on that income, together with her $50 per month from AFSC.

Our combined income during this period was about $120 per month, so we had to be frugal. Our rent on Gordon Avenue was $60 per month, and it was not an insignificant increase when it went up to $63 per month. When we went from our home to meetings downtown, we walked. This saved 35¢ for the bus, so we could stop at the Dunkin

Donuts shop en route for a real luxury, spending 10¢ on a donut. We bought a 100-pound bag of soy beans from a feed lot; the beans were intended for animal consumption, but if one boiled them for eight hours they were fit to mash up and make into soy burgers for our consumption. If we put enough cheese and catsup on the soy burgers, they were just barely palatable, but they did give us a lot of gas.

Within a few months of being hired, Carol Reagan left the AFSC job to marry Henry Shelton, a local priest. Carol Bragg inherited the entire (albeit part-time) position, together with the entire stipend of $100 per month. The AFSC program inherited the mailing list that Carol and I had built up over the two years of RIPOFF work, and we began sponsoring events and programs under the name and sponsorship of AFSC. Carol and I worked jointly on these AFSC projects and, although the $100 paychecks continued for a while coming in her name alone, the shared nature of the work soon became clear to AFSC and I was formally added to the NERO staff (and payroll). I ended up working for AFSC for almost sixteen years, until I left full-time peace work to attend law school in 1987.

One of the first events Carol and I organized in AFSC's name was the "Religious Convocation for Peace." It was held on January 19, 1973, the eve of President Nixon's second inauguration. Over 600 Rhode Islanders attended this program, which we held in Grace Episcopal Church in downtown Providence. It was a few short weeks after the Nixon administration's notorious "Christmas bombing" of North Vietnam, which had targeted civilian population centers; this was not only morally repellent to many Americans but was also a crime against humanity under international law. Anti-war sentiment in the country was running high.

The Religious Convocation for Peace was led by many of the state's religious leaders, including the Episcopal bishop, Frederick Belden, and the Reverend James Webb, General Secretary of the State Council of Churches. In part, the program followed a traditional religious format, with readings from Scripture, prayers, and hymns, but we also had as part of the service a speech delivered by Noam Chomsky, the MIT linguistics professor and left-wing scholar. A collection was taken for AFSC's medical relief programs in Vietnam. The Religious Convocation for Peace was a big success, and after the service, one older priest commented to me that it was the first time in twenty years he had seen Grace Church filled to capacity.

My FBI file reveals that the FBI was aware of the Religious Convocation in advance and conducted surveillance on the night of the service. The advance report stated:

> The American Friends Service [sic], Providence, Rhode Island will sponsor a candlelight service and protest march against the war and United States Air Force bombing in Vietnam on Friday night, January 19, 1973. . . . The candlelight service will take place at the Grace

One of the first activities sponsored by the newly established AFSC program in Rhode Island in 1973 was a Religious Convocation for Peace at Grace Episcopal Church in Providence. The event was held on January 19, 1973, the eve of President Nixon's second inauguration, and shortly after the notorious American "Christmas bombing" of North Vietnam in December 1972. This photo shows the dangerous anarchist radical Noam Chomsky (*second from right*) in the church, singing a hymn while standing between a bishop (Episcopal Bishop Frederick Belden, *far right*) and a theologian (William Stringfellow, *third from right*). Photo courtesy of the American Friends Service Committee.

Episcopal Church . . . and those participating will walk the approximately five blocks to the Federal Building . . . Jerry Elmer is involved in running the affair. Jerry Elmer pled guilty in United States District Court in Providence, Rhode Island, on October 19, 1971, to charges of destroying Selective Service records. . . .

The actual surveillance report of the event in my FBI file was basically quite accurate (except for understating the attendance at the event):

On January 19, 1973, [name redacted] advised that the Grace Church was filled with about 400–500 people for the candelight service. [Name redacted] stated that William Stringfellow, in speaking, asked for the "exorcism" of President Nixon, asking that the "temptation of death vanish from his soul." Noam Chomsky spoke with doubt about President Nixon's desire for a true peace settlement in Vietnam. The Reverend Frederick Belden, Episcopal Bishop of Rhode Island, read scripture and led the people in prayer. The services lasted from about 7:45 to 9:45 PM. The group then marched to the Federal Building, carrying candles and singing songs. . . . An Agent of the Federal Bureau of Investigation observed the march and arrival at the Federal Building at 10:30 PM.

The FBI's surveillance of the Religious Convocation for Peace raises interesting questions about government surveillance of legal activities protected by the First Amendment. The FBI's investigation of the RIPOFF Action by, say, attending our June surfacing in Burnside Park or by looking for Bug while he was underground, was certainly proper; indeed, the FBI would have been derelict in its duty had it *not* investigated the Action. But secretly spying on a religious service held in a church at which people legally prayed for peace was outrageous and improper. It was also not the least bit surprising.

More AFSC programs followed the Religious Convocation for Peace. Carol and I were both working full-time organizing AFSC programs in exchange for the one, very meager part-time stipend. As the work expanded, it became increasingly clear to us that the scope and magnitude of the AFSC work being done had outgrown the living room

After the Religious Convocation for Peace, the attendees participated in a candlelight procession to the federal building. According to FBI files that were later made public, both the peaceful, legal Religious Convocation and candlelight procession were the subjects of improper FBI surveillance. Photo courtesy of the American Friends Service Committee.

of our small Gordon Avenue apartment. I found the lack of separation between home and office troubling because I could never get away from the office; we were, in effect, "on duty" and available for calls and inquiries twenty-four hours a day, seven days a week. For me, the last straw came when a local priest called at 11:30 P.M. to inquire about the location of a meeting scheduled two weeks in the future. That call may have been the last straw but, in fact, many people routinely called us late at night or on weekends on matters that should have been handled on a weekday during regular business hours.

As a result, in the spring of 1973, Carol and I wrote and submitted a proposal to NERO that, instead of merely working out of our home, we open an actual AFSC office in Providence. Given the considerable size of the AFSC operation we were by then running, the idea made obvious sense. The proposal was greeted by the bureaucrats at NERO with some initial skepticism, but it was eventually approved. Carol and I found a small room to rent in Mathewson Street United Methodist Church in downtown Providence. The room was at the far end of a long, dark corridor in the basement of the church. The "office" had no natural light, but we could have it for only $30 a month. We put in phone lines, shelving, and desks and, on October 1, 1973, the first day of AFSC's new fiscal year, we opened the new Rhode Island AFSC office.

Once the office was up and running, our work expanded rapidly. Many volunteers with diverse skills helped with the work. We started a newsletter, our mailing list expanded, and we organized statewide conferences on a wide range of peace issues. From year to year, our office budget grew quickly.

Our salaries, which were always paid by NERO, also increased significantly during this period. Under Ed Lazar's direction, AFSC now had field staff in each of the New England states. One by one, they opened statewide offices. There was a metamorphosis in the role of the NERO field staff: we were no longer part-time people paid $100 per month to maintain some loose affiliation with AFSC. We became full-time, salaried AFSC staff running actual AFSC offices. To be sure, our salaries were modest, but salaries—as opposed to stipends—they were.

Much of what I did working for AFSC was routine, mundane office work such as bookkeeping, maintaining a mailing list, stuffing envelopes. Even much of what counted as program work (as opposed to office maintenance) was routine. I presented films or slideshows on peace topics and spoke at schools, colleges, and churches, and to Rotary Clubs and other community groups. I booked local engagements for visiting speakers. Some of the work I did for AFSC undoubtedly counted as being glamorous; I was, for example, a frequent guest on local TV programs and radio talk shows. But most of the work was distinctly unglamorous, like spending eight hours a day stuffing envelopes or working for days to arrange the minutiæ of a small bakesale.

As a result of my generous exposure to the realities of scut work during my tenure with AFSC, when I arrived at law school at the age of thirty-six, I had a more realistic understanding than most of my classmates about the amount of routine work associated with even a desirable job. Many of my classmates were twenty-two years old and fresh out of college. Their only idea of what it meant to be a lawyer came from a TV show popular at the time, *L.A. Law*, on which every case was a landmark case, every lawyer was glamorous, and every client was sexy. I knew from my years with AFSC that even attractive, desirable jobs with some legitimately glamorous aspects could still consist of 80% scut work. When my classmates got their first jobs at prestigious Wall Street law firms and found themselves locked in a room ten hours a day reviewing boring documents, they were shocked; this was not like *L.A. Law* at all! When I got my first law job, I was delighted that there was relatively less scut work to be done than I had become used to in the peace movement.

The Tiger Cage Vigil and Fast

In 1973 and 1974 we had excellent results dramatizing the plight of South Vietnamese political prisoners by displaying a full-sized replica of a South Vietnamese "tiger cage" prison cell. A bit of background may be needed about how the conduct of the war had changed in 1969, after President Nixon took office.

On November 3, 1969, during his first year in office (and less than a week before the Boston draft-board Action) Nixon had made a major televised speech to the nation. The speech has come to be known as Nixon's "silent majority" speech for, in it, he first used that famous phrase referring to Americans who supported the war. In fact, what was important about the speech was the announcement of Nixon's so-called plan to end the war—"Vietnamization." Under Nixon the war continued unabated and, in fact, escalated significantly, both in intensity and geographically, into Laos and Cambodia. By "Vietnamization," Nixon meant withdrawing American ground forces while dramatically escalating the air war. (By "air war" I refer to American bombing of Indochina; the Communist forces of Vietnam, Cambodia, and Laos had no air forces and no planes, and never conducted ærial bombardment.)

Nixon's plan was brilliant. He sought to reduce domestic opposition to the war by reducing its visibility to Americans by reducing the number of American casualties. As peace activists pointed out at the time, Nixon was merely changing the nationality and color of the corpses. Still, with peace talks under way in Paris, and American troop levels in Vietnam and American combat casualties both dropping, the plan worked in part and some Americans were fooled. (In the wars since Vietnam—Colombia, Serbia/Kosovo, Afghanistan, Iraq, for example—American war planners have been careful to follow Nixon's "Vietnamization" paradigm and have sought to reduce domestic American opposition to our military adventures by relying heavily on ærial bombardment as a means of keeping American casualties low.)

As Nixon steadily withdrew American ground forces from Vietnam, the peace movement needed to come up with new handles for our antiwar efforts. The issue of the 200,000 political prisoners being held by the U.S. puppet government in Saigon became a major organizing tool. This occurred largely through the efforts of one person, Don Luce, a remarkable man.

Don had gone to Vietnam in 1958, long before the commitment of American troops to the war, as an agriculturalist with International Voluntary Services. Don lived in Ban Me Thuot and traveled from village to village in the Central Highlands helping the local peasants grow sweet potatoes. Typically, he would come into a village and persuade the head man to permit an experiment, planting different varieties of sweet potatoes to see which kind did best in the soil and climate of that particular village. As Don liked to recount later, he had never given any thought to the politics of the war until American planes defoliated his sweet potato plants. That made him angry, and he was turned against the war by seeing its awful effects on the people of Vietnam.

Don was fluent in Vietnamese, a language that virtually no one in the American peace movement spoke with any degree of fluency. He gained notoriety in July 1970 as a guide and translator for a delegation of American congressmen visiting Vietnam. One of the congressmen was Augustus Hawkins of California; one of the aides in the delegation was Tom Harkin, who was later elected to both the House and the Senate from Iowa. (Harkin also ran unsuccessfully for the Democratic presidential nomination in 1992.)

Don had received information about the notorious tiger cage prison cells on Con Son Island used for the torture of political prisoners. The cages were open only at the top, where the bars were. The cages were not tall enough to stand in, and prisoners sat shackled to bars for so long that they became permanently crippled. There were no sanitary facilities in the cages. Guards walking overhead would throw lime down on the prisoners below, sometimes blinding them.

The existence of the tiger cages had, of course, been routinely denied by the United States, and the cages themselves were segregated on Con Son from the main body of the prison as a way of hiding them from visiting press and others. Nevertheless, Don had learned from ex-prisoners the exact location of the cages and he was determined to reveal their existence both to the visiting congressmen and to the rest of the world. It was a difficult business, but speaking in Vietnamese, Don tricked one of the prison guards into admitting the delegation into the hidden wing of the prison that housed the tiger cages. There was much sputtering and fulminating by the prison warden, and by the minder from the U.S. Embassy as well, but once the delegation had been admitted to the secret wing of the prison, there was little that could be done. A spread of photographs of the tiger cages taken by a member of the delegation appeared prominently in *Life* magazine in July 1970. One classic photograph, taken from above a tiger cage looking down at a prisoner, bore the caption: "I am a Buddhist monk. I spoke for peace in 1966. I am here for no other reason except wanting peace. I have been beaten. I have been shackled. But I still speak out for peace." After the years of official denials, the revelation about the tiger cages was highly sensational.

Carol and I booked Don in Providence as a visiting speaker on the war in 1972 and 1973, and we became close personal friends with him. (Later, when our son Jonathan was born, we named Don as a godfather.) In his own quiet and gentle way, Don was a wonderfully effective speaker. He was the very antithesis of a firebrand. Don always started by talking about how he was an agriculturalist by training and had gone to Vietnam to grow sweet potatoes. Then he regaled his audience with a comic tale about Father Hoa, the local Catholic priest in Ban Me Thuot. Father Hoa was an elderly gentleman in his mid-eighties who went zooming around town and countryside on a Vespa, with his full, traditional black robes flowing out behind him. Early one morning, on his way to a wedding, Father Hoa ran into a cow. The collision hurt neither the cow nor

Don Luce, speaking in Providence in October 1973. Don is holding a bag handwoven by Vietnamese out of the multicolored wires of what had been "McNamara's Line." Named for the U.S. Secretary of Defense, McNamara's Line was an electronic barrier constructed across the demilitarized zone in Vietnam which was supposed to stop Communist infiltration across the DMZ. Of course, it never worked, but the Vietnamese who tore it up were able to fashion wonderful handicrafts out of it. Photo by Jerry Elmer.

the priest but badly damaged the Vespa. Father Hoa woke Don up and commandeered both Don and his jeep to take him to the wedding.

Next, Don would recount the story of Secretary of Defense McNamara's ill-fated trip to Saigon in 1963. This was shortly after President Kennedy had visited the Berlin Wall and had said, "Ich bin ein Berliner" (I am a jelly doughnut). Not to be outdone, on the plane ride from Washington to Saigon, McNamara had tried to learn a sentence in Vietnamese: *Viet Nam muon nam* (long live Vietnam). What McNamara did not know was that Vietnamese, like Mandarin, is a tonal language, and that one word will have a variety of meanings depending on the intonation used by the speaker. Meanwhile, in Saigon, the strongman General Khanh had given tens of thousands of high school students the day off from school; they were to come greet the American Secretary of Defense. The students had been given instructions to cheer for the U.S. official.

McNamara and Khanh appeared at a rally before the throng of students. Proud of his newly acquired linguistic skills, McNamara announced into the microphones, "*Viet Nam muon nam!*" He had the words mostly right, but the inflections were all wrong. Instead of saying "Long live Vietnam," McNamara had shouted, "The southern duck wants to lie down!"

The students dutifully cheered, and McNamara, misunderstanding, thought he was doing splendidly. He grabbed General Khanh's arm and waved it in the air, shouting over and over to the cheering students: "The southern duck wants to lie down! The southern duck wants to lie down!"

Don, having thus warmed up his audience, would then segue into talking about the war by explaining that, in fact, the United States had never had an ambassador in Saigon who could say "hello" in Vietnamese. Then he would talk about other ways in which Americans did not understand the Vietnamese: defoliating sweet potatoes and other crops turned the peasantry against the U.S. Widespread use of napalm and other anti-personnel weapons had devastating effects on infants, the elderly, and other civilians, and did not win hearts and minds. To the Vietnamese, the United States was just another foreign colonial power.

Like Jim Peck, Don was a tireless and selfless peace worker. But unlike Jim, Don was not independently wealthy. Don came from a poor family in rural East Calais, Vermont. After revealing the tiger cages in 1970, his life was threatened in Vietnam and he returned to the United States to work for the peace movement. He helped found the Indochina Resource Center and then the Indochina Mobile Education Project. IMEP was essentially a one-man show, in which Don toured the country speaking about the war and the tiger cages. Both Jim Peck and Don Luce were people who seemed largely indifferent to creature comforts; however, unlike Jim Peck, whose inherited family wealth permitted him to have a comfortable apartment on Riverside Drive in Manhattan (despite not drawing a peace movement paycheck), when Don was not touring, he slept on a mattress on the floor in a corner of the IMEP office in Washington, DC. Like Jim, Don seemed also to have a melancholy streak in him. Away from the lectern, Don was quiet and reserved—even shy, I would say.

Don was allergic to organizational bureaucracy. All organizations have some bureaucracy (and AFSC has probably the most intricate and arcane bureaucracy in the peace movement; see below). One of the big advantages of IMEP was that there was no bureaucracy at all. It was just Don and his office manager. Decisions could be made quickly and plans could be put into action without delay.

When Don spoke in Providence, we would book him on local television and radio talk shows, have him do interviews with print journalists, and speak at local colleges. I used to get into arguments with Don about the content of his talks. "You should be more political," I urged him. "Focus on war crimes, talk about resistance. The elderly priest on the Vespa makes a very funny story, but it is not as important as radicalizing your listeners with gory tales of civilian casualties."

Don disagreed. "You win more converts with pictures of smiling children than of maimed children," he said.

In retrospect, I would always prefer the more ostensibly political approach myself. Still, there is no gainsaying the fact that, in his years touring the United States, Don was both a uniquely powerful speaker and a uniquely effective organizer at the national level.

In 1973, AFSC staff in New England started using a full-size replica of a tiger cage prison cell as a way of dramatizing the plight of the South Vietnamese political prisoners. Our display emphasized that the real tiger cages on Con Son had been built by an American corporation, Raymond Morrison Knudson-Brown Root & Jones, under a contract with the U.S. government, using U.S. taxpayer dollars, and were being used by our client régime for the torture of political prisoners. Our tiger cage replica came complete with bars across the top (just as in the real tiger cages) and bars and shackles inside. Typically, when we used it, one or more peace demonstrators sat shackled inside the cage for emphasis. We mounted signs on the outside of our display, including an enlargement of the *Life* photograph of the Buddhist monk who had spoken for peace, with his words next to the photograph.

We tried to place our display on Westminster Mall in downtown

Providence, but were denied permission by the police department. An ACLU attorney, Steve Fortunato, took our case to federal court where, in very short order, we won. (Steve had been the first U.S. Marine in history to be discharged as a conscientious objector; later he became a state court judge. As a judge, Steve always kept a photograph of himself with Bill Kunstler in his judicial chambers. When I first went to chat with Steve after he became a judge (and I was a relatively new lawyer), he marveled at how two old radicals like us had become respected establishment types.)

After displaying the tiger cage replica in downtown Providence, we tried to take it to Eisenhower Park in downtown Newport. Again, the city fathers banned us. Again we went to federal court. Again we won. Next, we tried to take the tiger cage to Main Street, Woonsocket. One would think that the Rhode Island municipal authorities would have learned their lesson by then (but, if so, one would be wrong). We were, yet again, banned. We took the matter yet again to federal court (and won).

Aside from the obvious futility of the effort, there was something ironic in these efforts by the authorities to ban our display. The authorities were no doubt trying to prevent our public display of opposition to U.S. policies in Vietnam. But their failed attempts at suppression served only to increase tremendously the publicity we ultimately received. In each case, the city's refusal to permit our display received news coverage. Our subsequent court victories received more coverage. By the time the tiger cage was finally displayed in each city, media and public attention were both very high.

In April 1974, Carol conceived the idea of taking the tiger cage replica to Washington, DC, and displaying it on the steps of the U.S. Capitol. As a way of dramatizing the display, Carol planned to fast and sit each day inside the tiger cage replica. We agreed that I would go to New York, Philadelphia, Baltimore, and Washington, DC, to meet with the major national peace groups to see if some of them would sponsor such a project. There was strong interest, but the idea of the project evolved considerably from Carol's initial idea of an individual, personal witness by one or a very few people into a nationally coordinated project.

Thus was born the Tiger Cage Vigil and Fast, cosponsored by sixteen national peace groups. The project ran during the summer of 1974, from

Monday, June 24 through Friday, August 23, and involved hundreds of participants. Each week a new group of between twenty and fifty people from a different part of the country came to Washington to participate. While in Washington, project participants would fast for one week and conduct a vigil on the main steps of the East Front of the Capitol, displaying the tiger cage replica. The Capitol is a major tourist attraction during the summer months, and we distributed tens of thousands of our flyers to visiting tourists each week. Once we realized that many of the tourists were foreign visitors, we had our flyer translated into French, German, and Spanish.

Except for the first week of the Tiger Cage Vigil and Fast, our tiger cage replica was mounted on the top of the main, central steps on the East Front of the Capitol, leading directly into the Rotunda. This was the main route of entry into the Capitol for the tens of thousands of tourists that visited weekly. However, getting permission from the Capitol authorities to have our display there was not easy.

I began the necessary negotiations a couple of weeks before the project was scheduled to start. This involved lengthy discussions not only with the Capitol Police but with the Architect of the Capitol and the staffs of the Speaker of the House (then Representative Carl Albert of Oklahoma) and the President of the Senate (then Vice President Gerald Ford, who had been appointed by President Nixon following the indictment and resignation of Nixon's original vice president, Spiro Agnew). Each office put me off, sending me to one of the other offices. I found myself in a dizzying application process in which each office I dealt with told me to consult with someone else.

On the first day of the Tiger Cage Project, with about fifty participants in Washington from New England, we had still not received the required approvals to have our tiger cage replica where we wanted it, directly at the entrance to the Rotunda. We were forced to place the cage on the lawn nearly a block away from the Rotunda entrance. This was not nearly as desirable a location. For example, later in the summer we noticed that, with the tiger cage display directly at the main entrance to the Rotunda, at the top of the main, central steps of the Capitol, a great many tourists thought that we were somehow connected with or a part of the Capitol. By the time they realized that we were there protesting *against* U.S. government policy (rather than being a part of a

The Tiger Cage Vigil and Fast lasted from June 24 to August 23, 1974. Each week a group of twenty to fifty people from a different geographic area of the country took part. Participants mounted a full-sized replica of a tiger cage prison cell at the main entrance of the East Front of the U.S. Capitol. Some demonstrators sat shackled in the tiger cage replica for effect, while others explained the display to passers-by. Here, tourists from Ohio and North Dakota listen to Wendy Bomberg of New York explain the display. Photo by Karl Bissinger, courtesy of the American Friends Service Committee.

governmental display) many were already listening sympathetically to our pitch.

But during the first week of the project we did not yet have that very desirable location. In frustration, I contacted the Washington, DC, chapter of the ACLU and we began discussing filing a federal lawsuit seeking an injunction that would permit our display directly at the Rotunda entrance. We had, after all, prevailed in three similar cases in Providence.

On the other hand, we knew that, in addition to the considerable financial cost of bringing a lawsuit, there was no guarantee that we would win such a case. A court could reasonably rule that, while we had a right to protest at or near the U.S. Capitol, the authorities need not permit us to be almost inside the Rotunda. In addition, any lawsuit would inevitably involve considerable delay, and our project had already started.

At this point, Mitch Snyder, of the Community for Creative Non-violence (CCNV), became interested in the Tiger Cage Project. CCNV was a small Washington group much given to civil disobedience and other forms of direct action. Mitch decided that if the authorities would not permit placement of our tiger cage replica at the main entrance to the Capitol Rotunda, we should put it there anyway. Mitch tried hard to persuade us, in effect, to "just do it."

But it was not that easy for us to "just do it." For one thing, we were still hopeful that either our negotiations or a possible lawsuit might have the desired result. We were concerned that civil disobedience at the Capitol over the placement of the tiger cage replica would be so off-putting to the authorities that we would never get the required approval to place the cage directly at the Rotunda. For another thing, we were running the project on behalf of sixteen separate, national cosponsoring organizations. All of those organizations had signed up to participate in a legal project. Suddenly turning the project into an illegal one, involving civil disobedience, would have required consultation with all of our sponsors. Most would have withdrawn their sponsorship and participation if the project turned out to involve civil disobedience.

Clearly, Mitch's idea of what he wanted to see happen was different from ours. Mitch wanted to hold a one-time demonstration in which a few people could feel good by getting arrested. In contrast, we were trying to organize a nine-week project involving hundreds of participants from all over the United States, one that might succeed in bringing real pressure on Congress to cut funding for the war.

I met with Mitch and the CCNV crowd several times about this issue. When they were unable to persuade *us* to "just do it," they became frustrated and discussed whether to just do it themselves. I tried urgently to dissuade them. We had spent months organizing the project; we had sixteen national organizations sponsoring it; hundreds of people from all over the United States were scheduled to come to Washington during the course of the summer to participate. It seemed terribly unfair for an outside organization (CCNV), itself not even a sponsor, to take an action that could well preclude us from going ahead with a long-planned project. At the very least, peace movement solidarity might have suggested that CCNV have more respect for their colleagues who, after all, had very much the same goals as they did.

Mitch Snyder has been widely considered something of a hero in the peace movement. He had been a prisoner at Danbury Federal Prison (as a common criminal, not for civil disobedience) in the early 1970s when he met fellow-prisoner Phil Berrigan and became a convinced peace movement activist. When a movie was released in 1986 called *The Mitch Snyder Story*, Martin Sheen played Mitch. Mitch's stock went up again following his untimely death (by suicide) in 1990. But, in 1974, I saw a Mitch Snyder that was very different from his public persona. I found Mitch to be not only stubborn (arguably a desirable quality in a movement activist) but also difficult, self-absorbed, and egocentric in the extreme.

In all my discussions with Mitch about the placement of the tiger cage, I never once got the impression that Mitch heard what I was saying. The organizations sponsoring the Tiger Cage Vigil and Fast could either do what Mitch wanted them to do, or they could be damned and Mitch would do what he wanted to do himself. The idea of peace movement solidarity—of allowing others to organize a project without it being hijacked by Mitch—seemed quite beyond his contemplation.

The group dynamics at CCNV were disturbing as well. During our meetings, Mitch sat on a chair surrounded by sycophants and acolytes, many of them younger women, many of them sitting on the floor (that is, at Mitch's feet). Mitch did most of the talking for the group, and when others dared to speak many of their sentences began, "Mitch thinks we ought to. . . ." or "Mitch says that. . . ." It seemed a most unwholesome situation to me.

On Monday, July 1, the first day of the second week of the Tiger Cage Vigil and Fast, CCNV carried out their civil disobedience by placing their own tiger cage replica where we wanted ours to be—at the top of the main, central steps on the East Front of the Capitol, directly at the entrance to the Rotunda. They were not arrested. Having carried out their one-day demonstration, CCNV was satisfied. Now emboldened by

CCNV's success (and despite the fact that that success had come over our objections), the very next day and, indeed, for the rest of the summer, we placed our tiger cage in the same location without incident.

The irony of the situation was that Mitch, through his stubborn pigheadedness, may have gotten something for the Tiger Cage Vigil and Fast that we ourselves, on account of our timidity and organizational obligations, could not or would not have gotten ourselves. I thought about this irony often during the rest of the summer, and so my anger with Mitch became attenuated.

Carol's original idea, of an individual, highly personal witness, was not entirely lost even as the Tiger Cage Vigil and Fast became a much more ambitious project. Carol herself fasted the entire sixty-two days of the project, adding an important dimension to the project. When her 100-hour-a-week job coordinating the project permitted, she sat in the tiger cage replica herself.

During the ninth and final week of the project, Carol decided to

Shackled in the tiger cage replica on the Capitol steps are Michael DeGregory of New York (*left*) and veteran peace and civil rights activist Jim Peck. Photo by Karl Bissinger, courtesy of the American Friends Service Committee.

Nguyen Thi Thoa (*left*) and Joan Baez sit shackled in the tiger cage replica during the Tiger Cage Vigil and Fast in Washington, DC, during the summer of 1974. Photo courtesy of the American Friends Service Committee.

spend the entire week shackled inside the cage on the Capitol steps. She was joined by Mitch and a third person, Jill Arace, a high school student from New Jersey. Carol, Mitch, and Jill remained shackled in the tiger cage on the Capitol steps twenty-four hours a day. The authorities would not allow the three to sleep in the tiger cage, even at night, saying that no "structures" were permitted to be erected on the Capitol grounds and that, by Carol, Mitch, and Jill sleeping in it, the cage would somehow magically be converted into a "structure." This reasoning was silly, but nevertheless during the ninth and final week of the project, Carol, Mitch, and Jill stayed manacled in the tiger cage, fasting and going without sleep. (This was a simple, one-week fast for Mitch and Jill, but it was the ninth week of Carol's fast.)

A major part of the Tiger Cage Vigil and Fast was having participants visit with members of Congress while they were in Washington, urging an end to U.S. funding of the war and the Saigon régime. In addition, our leaflet and display urged tourists to visit *their* members of Congress while they were in Washington, and many did, returning later to the Capitol steps to tell us about their visits. During the course of the summer, we lobbied most of the Senate and House of Representatives. Partly as a result of our efforts, as well as other similar efforts taking place at the time, Congress cut by a full third U.S. funding for the war that summer. We all considered the Tiger Cage Vigil and Fast a big success. That cutback made it impossible for the U.S./Saigon side to respond as it wished to the final offensive of the liberation forces the following spring.

Many factors led to the victory of the liberation forces in Vietnam in April 1975. Obviously, their victory was largely a military one, a result of the liberation forces winning and the Saigon government forces losing on the battlefield. But one important factor that contributed significantly to the downfall of the Saigon régime and the end of the war was the huge cutback in U.S. support for the Saigon government that we had helped to effect the previous summer through the Tiger Cage Vigil and Fast. (See further discussion of this point in chapter 11.)

Carol and I, together with our friend Marj Swann, ran the Tiger Cage Vigil and Fast from a small office in the Methodist Building directly across the street from the Capitol and the Supreme Court. The summer of 1974 was when the House Judiciary Committee approved

Mitch Snyder (*left*) and Carol Bragg in the tiger cage replica during the last week of the project. Mitch, Carol, and Jill Arace spent the entire week in the tiger cage, in which they were prohibited by the Capitol Police from sleeping at any time. Carol, who had served as one of the coordinators of the Project, was in the ninth week of her fast. Photo by Jerry Elmer.

articles of impeachment against President Nixon, so this was an exciting time to be in Washington. Senator Sam Ervin, who had been the chairman of the Senate Watergate Committee, made his home in the Methodist Building where our office was located and we occasionally ran into him in the hallways. On Thursday, August 8, 1974, President Nixon resigned (effective the next day), and we joined the crowds of people dancing in the streets outside the White House and in Lafayette Park.

In some ways, the Tiger Cage Vigil and Fast might be viewed as being at the opposite end of the political spectrum from the draft-board Actions I had been involved with only four years earlier. Draft-board Actions were an extreme form of illegal civil disobedience. They were controversial and viewed by some, even in the peace movement, as not being nonviolent. In contrast, the Tiger Cage Vigil and Fast, although it did have a direct action component (vigiling and fasting), was largely oriented toward visiting members of Congress and urging support for a then-pending bill, the so-called Roybal Amendment (named for its main sponsor in the House) that cut $494 million from U.S. support for the Saigon régime and for the war. One does not get much more mainstream than lobbying members of Congress in support of a specific piece of legislation.

I did not see any contradiction. I always thought that a strong peace movement had to be multifaceted. There was room in the peace movement both for letter-writing campaigns to members of Congress and for draft resistance, for silent Quaker vigils on village greens and for raids on draft boards. What ultimately repelled me about Joe O'Rourke's comments at the WRI Triennial in Haverford in August 1969 was the suggestion that there was only one right way to end the war and that, if only people would all do just this one thing, the war would soon be over. I certainly believed in nonviolent civil disobedience. Yet when I refused to register for the draft, my public statement explained that one reason I was refusing to register was that I believed that such acts would give impetus to efforts in Congress to repeal the draft. I viewed different parts of the peace movement as acting synergistically, each helping and giving strength to the others.

Famine in Cambodia

On September 29, 1979, an AFSC delegation arrived in Phnom Penh, Cambodia, and found the entire country on the brink of starvation. The delegation members were the first Westerners admitted to Cambodia since the change of government in January 1979, when the Khmer Rouge had been driven from power by the Vietnamese. (The Khmer Rouge had ruled Cambodia since April 17, 1975, the date of the ouster of the U.S.-backed Lon Nol government.)

The reasons for the famine at that particular time were multiple. First, American bombing during the war had destroyed many fertile fields; rice paddies were still littered with unexploded U.S. land mines, making farming extremely dangerous. Second, Cambodia had experienced two years of severe drought after the war had ended, during the Khmer Rouge era. A third calamity was the Pol Pot government itself, which had brought massive social upheaval, large-scale repression, and the wholesale massacre of the Khmer people. The entire infrastructure of the country had been destroyed during the years of Khmer Rouge rule. Money had been abolished. There were few roads left and only about a dozen functioning motor vehicles in the entire country.

It was a crisis of immense proportions. Jim Matlack, then on the AFSC Board, was a member of the AFSC delegation to Cambodia in September 1979. His article about what they found in Cambodia was published on the front page of the *Washington Post*.

AFSC nationally immediately committed a million dollars to famine-relief efforts in Cambodia. This was something of an act of faith, because AFSC did not have that million dollars in hand. Eventually, UNICEF and the International Committee of the Red Cross stepped in with a $110 million famine-relief effort, but it took UNICEF and the ICRC months to gear up. There would have been few Cambodians left alive by then if it had not been for the much smaller interim efforts of AFSC, working with Oxfam.

AFSC asked Carol and me to set aside our regular work that autumn to coordinate AFSC's special fundraising drive for the Cambodia famine-relief effort. We agreed to do so, but we did not want to see this work be merely an apolitical effort focusing on starving babies. The Khmer Rouge could never have come to power had it not been for U.S. sponsorship of the Lon Nol coup in Phnom Penh in March 1970, the U.S. "incursion" into Cambodia later that spring (which had led to the campus uprisings that spring and the shooting of student protesters at Kent State University in May 1970), and the years of secret bombing by the United States. (The secret bombing was later the subject of a proposed article of impeachment against Nixon, but the article was not approved by the House Judiciary Committee. Apparently the cover-up of a third-rate burglary in which no one was hurt was an impeachable offense, but secretly bombing a neutral country and killing and maiming tens of thousands of its citizens was not.)

Incredibly, in 1979, the United States actually opposed the international relief efforts to aid starving Cambodia, because Cambodia was then ruled by a new government backed by our Vietnamese enemies. Worse still, the Carter White House put out false stories about the Cambodian government diverting humanitarian aid for military purposes. At the United Nations, the United States (virtually alone, except for the People's Republic of China) backed the continued seating of the ousted

Khmer Rouge government as the sole legitimate representative of the Cambodian people rather than permitting the current, Vietnamese-backed government to take Cambodia's seat in the General Assembly.

Carol and I were willing to coordinate AFSC's fundraising efforts for Cambodia, but we insisted on combining the fundraising with political education about the historical roots of U.S. responsibility for the current crisis and the unhelpful (and dishonest) posture of the Carter administration in opposing humanitarian food aid for the country. We created a petition addressed to the administration, urging a change in U.S. policy toward Cambodia that would permit humanitarian aid for the people of the country, despite the administration's hostility toward the Vietnamese-backed government in Phnom Penh. Then, using our contacts at AFSC offices and other local peace groups across the country, we developed a network of hundreds of volunteers nationwide who would simultaneously circulate the petition and seek contributions to AFSC famine relief efforts in Cambodia. We quickly wrote resource pieces for the campaign that, unlike reports then appearing in the mainstream press, discussed not only the humanitarian dimensions of the crisis in Cambodia, but also the political and historical causes of that crisis, with particular emphasis on the United States' responsibility through years of unnecessary war. (For further discussion on the issue of U.S. responsibility, see chapter 10.) The campaign we put together raised several hundred thousand dollars that autumn, a large percentage of AFSC's total commitment to Cambodia, and generated thousands of petition signatures.

It is true that during this campaign we used the petition as a means of raising money for AFSC's famine-relief efforts in Cambodia. But the petition was not just a trick, or ruse, in what was "really" just a fundraising effort. At the same time we were raising funds for famine relief we were organizing a nationwide campaign aimed at changing U.S. policy toward Cambodia. In addition to the petition campaign, we organized speaking tours and letter-writing efforts to members of Congress and the administration.

In December 1979, we sought, and obtained, a meeting at the White House with administration officials to present our petition urging a change in U.S. policy toward Cambodia.

The Cambodia project that Carol and I ran in 1979 was a mixed success. On the one hand, we did raise a lot of money in a very short time for AFSC's famine-relief efforts in Cambodia. As I indicated, this was a critical factor in saving at least hundreds of thousands of lives while the larger international aid effort was gearing up all too slowly. In addition, we were able to publicize widely a political message about Cambodia that was at odds with the message that the Carter White House was promoting. On the other hand, we were completely and totally unsuccessful in effecting even the slightest change in the adminstration's policy of unremitting hostility toward the government and people of Cambodia.

For me personally, the project was difficult and stressful work. Carol and I worked sixteen or more hours a day, seven days a week—well over a hundred hours per week. I felt intensely the burden that was on us. The lives of millions of people depended, very directly and in the very short term, on the work that we were doing. How hard we worked during those weeks and months, and how successful we were, would spell life or death for the people of Cambodia. Each time I took time off from

At the White House in December 1979, presenting AFSC petitions seeking a change in U.S. policy toward Cambodia at the time of the famine. AFSC explicitly tied its fundraising for its Cambodia famine-relief efforts to domestic political work aimed at effecting a change in U.S. policy toward Cambodia. *Left to right:* Dr. James Matlack, Jerry Elmer, and Sharon Bauer Breakstone, all of AFSC; and Henry Owen and Lincoln Bloomfield, members of the National Security Council. Photo courtesy of the American Friends Service Committee.

work to sleep or eat I felt that I was killing people by my action. I became constipated because I begrudged myself time to go to the bathroom. The work was at once exhilarating, because of the importance of the issues we were addressing, and exhausting—a quintessential exemplar of much of the labors one performs when working in the peace movement.

The Draft—Again!

There are cycles to work in the peace movement, just as there are cycles in the wider economy, and there is nothing like a war (or the imminent threat of war) to remind liberals of the importance of peace organizations and peace activism.

In 1980, in the aftermath of the Soviet invasion of Afghanistan, President Carter reinstated draft registration, which had been discontinued in the waning days of the Nixon administration. This was an issue just made for AFSC and for me. AFSC had been founded in order to provide World War I conscientious objectors with alternative service, and (amidst much controversy among pacifists) AFSC had actually run some of the Civilian Public Service Camps for COs during World War II. I had been involved with anti-draft work for as long as I had been active in the peace movement.

Our AFSC office geared up immediately in response to the reinstatement of draft registration. We held several day-long training sessions for draft counselors at the Friends Meeting House, training about fifty draft counselors in all. We set up and publicized widely a telephone hotline, staffed with these draft counselors, which young men of draft age could call for information about the new registration law, conscientious objection, and outright resistance. We were suddenly flooded with requests from schools and colleges to send speakers about the draft and conscientious objection. I spoke to classes and assemblies at many local high schools and colleges, and I appeared almost nightly as a guest on the local television news, commenting both on President Carter's reinstatement of draft registration in particular and U.S. foreign policy more generally.

There was also significant backlash against our work. Although hundreds of people were taking part, I was the person most publicly visible in connection with our anti-draft work, largely because I was appearing on television so frequently. At the height of our anti-draft-registration activities, I started receiving a series of increasingly graphic death threats, both at the office and on our home telephone. It was clear from these messages that the callers were quite familiar with the locations of both the AFSC office and Carol's and my home in Seekonk, Massachusetts, a few miles from Providence.

Because of these death threats, Carol and I went to the Providence Police, who told us that there was a small but very active group of neo-Nazis working in the area which, they believed, were responsible for these threatening calls. The police showed us photographs of an arms cache that they had seized from members of this group, and urged us to take the threats seriously. We also contacted the FBI which, not surprisingly, showed not the slightest interest in the situation, despite the likelihood that some of the threats were being transmitted across state lines, from Rhode Island to our home just over the state border, in Seekonk. The warnings and admonitions of the Providence Police left us shaken.

The threatening telephone calls continued and intensified. Soon, we were receiving these calls at all hours of the day and night—sometimes dozens over a single night. At the height of these threats, our office was vandalized, with swastikas and "Elmer Dies" spray-painted on the outside of our building. Tombstones at a Jewish cemetery were defaced, and shots were fired into a synagogue. The Providence Police told us that all of these actions were the work of the local neo-Nazis, and again urged us to be careful. Our fear grew.

After the AFSC office was vandalized, we went to the Seekonk Police with our concerns about our safety. They responded immediately and, for some time, we had a uniformed Seekonk police officer outside our house all night every night. At the same time, they urged us not to change our telephone number to an unlisted one because they wanted to try to trace the calls. For a couple of weeks, we were kept up most of every night by a barrage of threatening telephone calls, while the police were on guard outside our door. Our fear grew.

After the death threats subsided, and our lives (at least outwardly) returned more to normal, I continued to be unnerved and frightened by what we had gone through. The death threats from local neo-Nazis had rekindled in me old fears from the Minuteman attack in Voluntown twelve years earlier. Having been at the CNVA Farm during that epi-

At the time that President Carter reinstated draft registration in response
to the Soviet invasion of Afghanistan in December 1979 and early 1980, the
Rhode Island AFSC staff was very visible in opposing renewed registration. In
response, the office was vandalized (*above*), and staff members received a series
of death threats from a local group of neo-Nazis. Photo by Jerry Elmer.

sode, the possibility of heavily armed right-wingers launching an assault
upon peace activists in the middle of the night seemed to me only too
real. During the period when we were most directly under siege, Carol
was the more overtly upset of the two of us; I held things together with
an outward façade of stoicism. But *after* the threats seemed to recede,
Carol and I had a role reversal. She calmed down quickly, but I stayed
upset for some months.

In late 1980, I went to consult a psychologist about my anxieties. It
was an odd appointment. In effect, I said: My office has been vandalized
by a band of local neo-Nazis who are threatening my life. The police tell
me that this group is heavily armed and that I should take their threats
seriously. In fact, the police posted an armed guard outside my house at
night to prevent an attack. This makes me frightened and nervous.

The psychologist did not think that my reaction was indicative of
a psychological problem. "If these things did *not* upset you, that would

be something to worry about," he told me. I did not return for a second visit.

The death threats I received at that time were an understandable and perhaps inevitable result of the exposure I regularly had in the local media because of my peace work. I became quite used to being recognized by the teller in the bank ("Didn't I see you on TV last night?"), the waitress at the restaurant, the bus driver. Even now, years after leaving AFSC, I still run into people who recognize me from my work back then. In 2002, I dropped some letters off at the post office. The clerk remembered me from nonviolence training I had provided at his high school in Portsmouth, Rhode Island, twenty-five years earlier. In 2000, I met a parent of a friend of my son Joshua. The parent remembered me from a talk on draft resistance I had given at LaSalle Academy, a Catholic high school in Providence, in 1972.

The Nuclear Freeze

The nuclear-weapons Freeze burst on the public consciousness on June 12, 1982, when a million people participated in a (legal) Freeze demonstration in New York City. This was the largest peace demonstration in American history.

The Freeze campaign had been launched at a national conference in March 1981. I had been in Vietnam at the time (see next chapter), but Carol had attended the conference, which had been convened by our friend Randy Forsberg. Randy's idea behind the Freeze campaign was admirably simple: before you could effect *reductions* in the nuclear arsenals of the superpowers, you first had to effect a halt in development of new weapons systems. In the early 1980s, this was an especially urgent issue, because under President Reagan the United States was embarking on a huge nuclear-weapons build-up that included a host of new, highly accurate and destabilizing counterforce (that is, first-strike) weapons. The particular concern was that, because negotiations leading to an arms control treaty could take years (or decades), an entire, new generation of nuclear weapons could come on line while the negotiators talked. The goal of the Freeze campaign was stated in a single sentence: the United States and the Soviet Union should have an immediate, mutual, verifi-

Rhode Island AFSC and Women for a Non-Nuclear Future chartered twenty buses to bring Rhode Islanders to the million-person nuclear Freeze demonstration in New York City on June 12, 1982. Photo by Jerry Elmer.

able Freeze on the development, production, and deployment of new nuclear weapons and delivery systems. In this formulation, each adjective describing the Freeze was important. The Freeze had to be *immediate* in order to ensure that no new generation of first-strike weapons were built while arms control negotiators dithered. The Freeze had to be *mutual* on the part of the United States and the Soviet Union because, whatever pacifists thought, the United States was not about to undertake any unilateral initiatives to end the arms race at the very height of the Cold War. And the Freeze had to be *verifiable* by both sides, as the governments of both sides distrusted the other side.

Directly after the conference that launched the Freeze campaign, the AFSC staff person in Vermont, David McCauley, had started an unglamorous but phenomenally successful grassroots effort to get Vermonters to support the Freeze. Vermont has a kind of participatory democracy in the form of town meetings that occur in every city, town, and hamlet in the state on the first Tuesday of March. David had spent a year going from town to town organizing small local groups that put the nuclear Freeze on the agenda of town meetings all across the state. On Tuesday, March 2, 161 cities and towns in Vermont voted to approve the nuclear-weapons freeze. David's low-key but brilliant efforts put the nuclear Freeze issue on the national agenda over night.

Our Rhode Island AFSC office immediately picked up the idea of the new campaign directly when it was launched in 1981 and promoted it vigorously. We circulated petitions for a nuclear Freeze, and met with our senators and representatives urging them to support the bipartisan Freeze resolution that had been introduced into Congress by Senators Edward Kennedy, Mark Hatfield, and others. We chartered twenty buses to bring Rhode Islanders to the million-person disarmament and Freeze demonstration in New York City on June 12, 1982.

I served on the national board of the Freeze campaign, which met several times a year, each time in a different part of the country. Our role was to coordinate nuclear Freeze work nationwide. The Freeze campaign was an excellent example of a decentralized, grassroots movement at its best. The heart and soul of the Freeze campaign were the separate, individual efforts of thousands of local activists working in cities and towns across the country. Yet, the efforts of all the independent, disparate grassroots groups working on the Freeze nationwide were supported and coordinated by a national structure.

In our local work in Rhode Island, during the spring and summer of 1981, we collected thousands of signatures on petitions calling for a nuclear Freeze. We met with all four members of the Rhode Island congressional delegation (two senators and two representatives), urging them to support the Congressional Freeze resolution. That autumn, Representative Fernand J. St Germain became the first member of the delegation formally to endorse the concept of a Freeze, and to sign on as a cosponsor of a Freeze resolution in Congress. Shortly thereafter, Senator Claiborne Pell, chairman of the Senate Foreign Relations Committee, publicly endorsed the Freeze and became a cosponsor of the Senate bill. The other two members of Rhode Island's congressional delegation were both Republicans: Congresswoman Claudine Schneider and Senator John Chafee. (Chafee had been President Nixon's Secretary of the Navy during the height of the naval bombardment of Vietnam; under any reasonable definition, he was a war criminal.) Although they were moderate Republicans, they were Republicans nonetheless, and we were pessimistic about the chances of having them support the Freeze resolution in Congress.

Instead of giving up, Carol and I viewed it as a personal challenge to get them to cosponsor the bill. In addition to circulating petitions, we organized constituent visits to their offices in Rhode Island and Washington, DC, and a letter-writing campaign. We printed postcards addressed to the two Republicans that Freeze supporters could simply sign and mail. Both Senator Chafee and Representative Schneider soon endorsed the Freeze, and Rhode Island became the first (and, I believe, ultimately the only) state in the country to have 100% of its congressional delegation formally endorse the Freeze and cosponsor the congressional Freeze resolutions.

The national campaign reached its apogee in November 1982 when the Freeze appeared as a referendum question on the ballots in ten states and thirty-eight additional counties and cities nationwide. This was the largest, coordinated referendum on any public-policy question ever held at one time in American history. The Freeze passed in nine of the ten states (including California, Massachusetts, Michigan, Montana, and New Jersey) and in thirty-five of the thirty-eight counties and cities. In Rhode Island, the Freeze not only passed statewide with nearly 60% of the vote, but it was approved in thirty-six of the state's thirty-nine cities and towns.

The Rhode Island electoral campaign that we organized illustrates well both the advantages and disadvantages of a true grassroots movement.

In early May 1982, I received a phone call that a state legislator whom I had never heard of had written a bill, which was about to pass the state legislature, that would put the Freeze on the ballot in Rhode Island as a referendum question. I regret to report that my first response was that of a true peace movement bureaucrat: our committee had not decided to put this on the ballot; this was not necessarily our chosen program priority for local Freeze work; how dare this legislator whom I had never even heard of take this initiative on his own without even consulting the people who were coordinating and leading nuclear Freeze work in the state; didn't he know that I was on the national board of the Freeze campaign?

In November 1982, the nuclear weapons Freeze appeared on the ballot in ten states and thirty-eight counties nationwide, making it the largest public policy referendum in United States history. The Freeze was approved in nine out of the ten states, and in thirty-five out of the thirty-eight counties. Depicted here is the billboard bought during the campaign in Rhode Island by Women for a Non-Nuclear Future. Photo by Jerry Elmer.

When I saw the text of the actual question as it was supposed to appear on the ballot, I became even more upset. The legislator who had written the bill was someone completely outside of the peace movement. He had apparently read about the Freeze campaign in the mainstream press and liked what he had read, but he was so unconnected to the movement that the referendum question he had drafted was atrocious: so badly worded and so watered down that a vote *for* this referendum could fairly have been interpreted as a vote *against* the Freeze. The bill was about to pass the legislature, and I was aghast. Luckily, our office successfully sought the intervention of Rhode Island's senators and representatives (and also Senator Ted Kennedy's office), and we were able to get the state legislator to rewrite his referendum question so that it tracked much more closely with not only the language being used by the Freeze campaign nationally, but also the language of the referendum questions on the ballots elsewhere in the country.

In the end, this problem was worked out in a satisfactory manner, but it was a close thing. This near-fiasco illustrates one of the problems with a truly decentralized, grassroots movement: not all the local activists in a grassroots movement are as smart, competent, or politically sophisticated as the national leaders and key organizers are. An inevitable consequence is that in a truly grassroots movement, the quality of the work is debased from what it would be if only the national leaders organized everything: meetings are not as well-planned, press releases are not as carefully written, demonstrations are more shoddily organized. A small group of highly skilled, politically sophisticated activists will almost always do work of higher quality than is possible in a mass movement.

On the other hand, real social change—especially in areas as intractable as ending war and injustice in the world—unequivocally requires mass movements. The Freeze campaign also illustrated the *advantages* of a mass movement. Most statewide political campaigns costs large sums of money. Even back in 1982, and even in a small state like Rhode Island, a statewide campaign on a referendum question would normally have cost at least many hundreds of thousands of dollars. We ran our campaign for well under $100,000. Recruiting and training hundreds of volunteers—every city and town in the state had a local Freeze chapter—we substituted human labor and energy for our lack of financial capital.

The centerpiece of the campaign was a door-to-door canvassing effort in which nearly every home in the state was visited during the electoral campaign by a local canvasser from that town. I designed and wrote the basic campaign brochure (in the format of a tabloid-sized newspaper) used by the canvassers. The grassroots movement, by utilizing so many volunteers, accomplished something that a couple of peace bureaucrats sitting alone in an office could never have done.

Problems with AFSC

I cannot leave the subject of working for AFSC without acknowledging some of the problems the organization had. Everything I have said in this chapter about the benefits of working for AFSC is true. I say additional good things about AFSC in the next chapter, as all of my travels to

Southeast Asia were sponsored by AFSC. Working for AFSC really *was* the best job in the world, largely because it permitted me to work for peace, which I would have wanted to do anyway, and still get paid for it. But AFSC was not an organization without its difficulties.

One problem was the almost unbelievably complicated, snail-paced, and inefficient bureaucracy. Change and innovation were nearly impossible. An example from early in my tenure will illustrate the point.

In 1974, Carol and I proposed that our office create a new staff position for a peace intern. Our reasoning was simple. Peace movement organizations are always strapped for funds. When money is available, a peace group understandably wants to hire an experienced, competent person. In this circumstance, it is very difficult for smart and dedicated but inexperienced young people to "break into" working for the movement and gain the experience necessary eventually to become qualified for a paid job. Our proposal was to create a one-year internship, a kind of intensive training program. We would hire a young person who wanted a career in social change work, pay him or her a minimal stipend ($50 per week), and give the person a room to live in free of charge in the home of a local AFSC supporter.

The proposal was greeted favorably by NERO, but it nevertheless took *two years* to be approved. AFSC is run by lay (that is, non-staff) committees. NERO has an Executive Committee, which functions much like the board of directors of any organization. But then there is an endless list of *additional* committees, each with its own small, yet important, fiefdom. The Personnel Committee makes decisions about staff matters, including hiring, firing, and setting salary levels. The Program Priorities Committee, as the name suggests, decides what work should be done. And so forth. When my friend Doug Hostetter was the Executive Director of NERO, he counted nineteen such committees whose meetings he was required to attend.

Our proposal for a peace intern first went to the Peace Committee that oversees all of NERO's peace programs. The Peace Committee met quarterly, so there was a considerable wait before the committee could consider the proposal. The Peace Committee approved the proposal and sent it to the Personnel Committee (because this was a staff issue) that also met quarterly; hence, there was another delay. This committee approved it and sent it to the Program Priorities Committee, which approved it and sent it to the Budget Review Committee, which approved it and sent it to the Affirmative Action Committee, which approved it and sent it to the Executive Committee. The Executive Committee was favorably inclined, but had a question which it referred to the Peace Committee again . . . and so it went. Every separate committee considered a different nuance of this very, very small proposal. Every separate committee took some months to reach its (invariably favorable) decision. Although, in the end, the proposal was approved and implemented (and we ran the program for some years with great success), we had to attend innumerable meetings over a period of two years in order to win approval of a small, inexpensive, simple idea.

This is madness. For one thing, this is a terribly inefficient way to run an organization. It means that salaried staff spend much of their time on pointlessly duplicative and unnecessarily bureaucratic administrative tasks rather than spending their time on program work. It means that contributors' money is being misspent, too. AFSC runs on money received from the public. Those people give their money to AFSC so that AFSC will work to end war and injustice in the world, not squander time just spinning its wheels uselessly. Finally, this is a ridiculous system because it creates a screen whereby only those people with an unusually high threshold for bureaucratic nonsense will be willing to take AFSC jobs.

AFSC was also inordinately given to the worst excesses of political correctness. Appropriate nomenclature for minority groups changed with the tides of political fashion. Black people one year were African Americans the next and persons of color the next. The changes were taken *very* seriously, and woe betide the innocent who inadvertently used the term that was correct last week or last month but is no longer! Once I sat through half a day of an Executive Committee meeting, the sole purpose of which was for an albino staff person from Philadelphia to harangue us that she was not to be referred to as an albino, but rather as a "person with albinism." This sounds like a self-parody; sadly, it was not.

Naturally, race relations at NERO were a sore and sensitive subject. AFSC, like much of the peace movement in the United States, has historically been mostly white. North American Quakers are predominately white, so it is no surprise that, in its early decades, AFSC was a mostly white organization. AFSC devised and adopted an affirmative action plan in the 1970s that, although reasonable on paper, was applied by NERO in absurd ways. For years, NERO took "affirmative action" to mean hiring blacks for positions for which they were manifestly unqualified. A series of incompetent clerical workers was hired for the sole reason that they were black. Of course, when it turned out that they were unable to perform their job responsibilities, each one was fired in turn. When it came to firing the third, there was much hand-wringing and soul searching: *how will it look that of the three people we have fired in the last two years, each one has been a woman of color? It will look like we are racist!* Not one person had the gumption to say that NERO had brought the situation on itself by hiring unqualified applicants merely because they were not white.

NERO had a bookkeeper who embezzled money. He was not fired (*how would it look if we fired another black?*); instead, he was given a glowing job recommendation and kept on the staff until he had found a job at another non-profit agency.

NERO had a black staff person in New Bedford, Massachusetts. He explained how he does peace organizing: "I buy a bottle of cheap wine, put it in a brown paper bag, and hang out on a street corner rapping with the brothers." I was aghast, and argued that drinking wine on street corners was not a responsible use of contributors' money, but it was clear that this was not the politically correct position and I got nowhere.

Shortly after I left the staff, there was a terrible episode involving my friend, Doug Hostetter. A black staff person, Muhammed Kenyatta (he had changed his name from Donald Jackson), accused Doug, a white man, of making a racist remark. The accusation was not merely wrong; it was absolutely ludicrous to anyone who knew Doug. However, because the accuser was black, the accusation had to be treated with great respect. NERO appointed a special committee (as if there were not already a surfeit of committees!) to investigate the allegation. The committee worked slowly, and program work at the Cambridge AFSC office ground to a halt for months. The investigating committee concluded (correctly) that the allegations against Doug were wholly false. So what was NERO to do? It could not just sanction Muhammed for making a false accusation; after all, he was black. So NERO fired Muhammed *and* Doug; that way things would be racially balanced.

This result reminded me of the joke about two people arguing. One person says that two plus two equals four; the other one says that two plus two equals six. A Quaker comes along, hears the dispute, and decides to compromise. The Quaker announces that two plus two equals five.

During my time on the AFSC staff I dealt with these problems—the arcane bureaucracy and the devotion to a ludicrous political correctness—by staying as far away as possible from NERO. This was possible because we field staff were given a great amount of latitude and independence. I tried to do my work for peace and keep my nose out of the thicket of politics that poisoned the AFSC office in Cambridge. I was largely successful in keeping a safe distance from NERO, and thus was able to enjoy my work for the most part, and to find great satisfaction in it. But on those occasions when I got caught up in NERO politics, the result was always discouraging and dispiriting.

8
Travels in Southeast Asia

AFTER THE VIETNAM WAR ENDED in 1975, I continued to have an interest in Southeast Asia. AFSC had on its staff at that time an older gentleman, Russell Johnson, who had run an AFSC conference program for diplomats and other leaders in Southeast Asia between 1961 and 1965. Russ had maintained extensive contacts in the region and traveled there with some regularity. During the Vietnam War, Russ had been much in demand as a speaker and expert on Southeast Asia. He had been to Indochina often and knew many of the key players personally, including Cambodia's Prince Sihanouk. Russ had also been one of the very first Americans to travel extensively in China in the early 1970s, and was a popular speaker on that topic as well.

In 1977, Russ was planning another trip, to last from May until September. The purposes of Russ's trip were to investigate the status of human rights in the countries visited, and to examine the impact of Western aid programs, especially military aid. Human rights was a key issue in Southeast Asia, with more or less despotic governments in power in all of the countries that were U.S. allies in the region at the time. Ferdinand Marcos was at the height of his powers in the Philippines, having declared martial law in September 1972. In Indonesia, Suharto was the dictator; with the active encouragement, backing, and support of the United States, he was waging a genocidal war in East Timor.

I remembered that when I had been on the staff of WRL in 1969, some Executive Committee members had suggested that Dave McReynolds, who was usually the WRL representative to international peace meetings, take with him some younger people in order to introduce them to these international gatherings. The reasoning was to let the younger people learn from the older, more experienced staff, so that, in time, the younger ones would be in a position to step into more responsible positions. I now suggested that AFSC do much the same thing, and send some younger people along with Russ on his forthcoming trip. I was, in part, hoping that I would be selected to go; but, even if I was not selected, the idea of older staff members showing the ropes to younger ones still made good sense.

My idea of sending some younger staff people along with Russ was approved by AFSC. When it came time to select them, no one was interested but Carol Bragg and me. We were selected by default.

The trip was absolutely wonderful. Russ was an exemplary mentor, generous with sharing background knowledge and information, and easy to travel with. We spent several weeks each in India, Burma, Thailand, Malaysia, Singapore, Indonesia, and the Philippines. Russ's contacts in Asia were incredible. In India, we met with the newly elected prime minister, Moraji Desai, an old Gandhian activist, even before the American ambassador (whom we also met) had presented his credentials. In Thailand we met on the same day (but at different times!) with underground urban guerrillas and with the top Thai military officials who were trying to capture them. In every country we visited, we had access to senior government ministers, journalists, religious leaders, opposition figures, and human rights activists. Russ, although in his sixties, was tireless. He scheduled meetings and appointments each day from early morning until late in the evening.

Before leaving on this trip, I had approached editors at the *Providence Journal* about whether they would publish articles I sent them from Southeast Asia. They had occasionally used my pieces before, and I was hopeful that they would use more now. The editors had been very cagey—send us the articles, they said, but we will not commit ourselves to using any of them. This was in the days before e-mail and faxes. As we travelled through Southeast Asia, I carried with me from country to country a small, manual typewriter and a ream of onion-skin paper. At the end of the day (and, with Russ's schedules, these were often 12- or 15-hour work days, ending close to midnight) I wrote out articles in long-hand and then typed them onto onion-skin, sending the original by mail to the *Journal* and a carbon copy (a *real* carbon copy, made with old-fashioned carbon paper) to the AFSC office in Providence. The mail took a week or two to be delivered. In all, I sent seventeen articles to the *Journal*, several each from India, Thailand, Malaysia, Singapore, and the Philippines. The newspaper published all of them. The payment I received from these articles, together with honoraria I received from speaking engagements upon my return, paid for the trip.

Some of the articles I published were not terribly original. For example, President Marcos's human rights abuses in the Philippines—political prisoners, torture, lack of free speech and assembly—were well known in the West and had been extensively documented by others, including Amnesty International. In my articles on the Philippines, I tried to tell the stories of particular prisoners, to add some human interest to the rather drier statistics found in Amnesty International reports. I think my work may have been useful as part of the wider human rights movement focusing on the Philippines.

In other respects, I think my work was quite original; an example of this is the case of Thailand. In 1976, the democratic government of Thailand had been overthrown. The current dictator, who had strong American backing, was Tanin Kraivixien. I found striking similarities between Thailand in 1977 and Vietnam in the pre-1963 period: there was a right-wing dictator who lacked the support of his own people, but who was propped up with massive aid from the United States; there was an indigenous Communist insurgency opposing the dictator; and there was a growing American military presence in response to the Communist threat. I discussed these similarities in my articles. I also discussed the economic injustices in Thailand that helped fuel the growth of the guerrilla movement. For example, the government's five-year plan for economic development, published while we were in Thailand, called for rapid development of production of luxury items for the rich, urban elite—soft drinks, air conditioning, expensive cars—but had little or nothing for the rural poor, who needed irrigation systems and local health care facilities.

In addition to the money I received, there was another, longer-term term benefit from the *Journal* having used so many of my articles during this trip: I had established myself as a credible writer with its editors. From the time I got back, until I left AFSC in 1987, the *Journal* published almost every article I sent them—dozens in all over the years—on a wide range of issues, including nuclear weapons and disarmament, human rights, and nuclear power.

I loved the time I spent in Southeast Asia in 1977. I found the research, especially on human rights issues, fascinating, and I liked publishing and doing speaking tours on the subject after I returned to the United States. But I also loved the countries themselves, the cultures of the people, and the food. I returned to the United States in the autumn eager for an opportunity to go back to Southeast Asia.

An opportunity to return to Southeast Asia came in 1981 when Don Luce and I organized a trip to Vietnam for representatives of American and Canadian peace groups and religious organizations, most of which had active aid programs in Vietnam. My old mentor, Dave McReynolds, participated on behalf of WRL. In addition to Vietnam, we visited Cambodia, and were among the early groups of Westerners admitted to that country in the aftermath of the famine. After the other members of this delegation returned home, I went on to Laos on my own and visited there with the AFSC staff in Vientiane.

In both Vietnam and Cambodia, we were the guests of the Viet-My (Vietnam-America friendship committee), a quasi-governmental agency that coordinated relations with American peace groups. The committee took care of all the logistical arrangements for our trip, including hotel reservations and in-country travel. In addition, the Viet-My also arranged our schedule and set up meetings for us, including with such luminaries as Nguyen Co Thach, the Foreign Minister of Vietnam.

The 1981 trip to Indochina had several purposes. Many of the delegation members came from organizations that had aid programs in Indochina—medical aid, famine relief and reconstruction programs. These were highly controversial at the time, because the U.S. administration, as part of its overall campaign against the Communist governments in Hanoi and Phnom Penh, was saying that aid was being misused by the recipients and was being improperly diverted from humanitarian to military purposes. These reports were untrue, and it was important for the organizations running these aid projects to have accurate, firsthand information from Indochina to refute the administration's propaganda.

The trip also was part of our overall political organizing strategy. In addition to running relief programs, many of the organizations represented in our delegation were working to change U.S. policy toward the governments of Indochina. Specifically, we wanted the United States to turn away from its post-war hostility toward the Communist governments of Indochina, and normalize diplomatic, trade, and cultural relations with those countries. Having people who could publish articles and do speaking tours in the United States based on their own recent, direct observations was an important part of our overall political efforts.

I had been involved in the national controversy over alleged diversion of aid supplies from the time the controversy started. On December 6, 1979, just before our meeting at the White House with National Security Council members Lincoln Bloomfield and Henry Owen, President Carter had personally charged that international relief shipments to Cambodia were not reaching civilians and had been deliberately obstructed for political reasons by Vietnamese soldiers in Cambodia. A few days later, *New York Times* columnist James Reston made a similar charge in an Op-Ed article entitled "Is There No Mercy?". I submitted to the *Times* an Op-Ed article rebutting the Reston piece, citing the experiences of AFSC and other humanitarian organizations in Cambodia that showed that relief supplies were not being obstructed or diverted. To be sure, there were distribution problems with the international relief effort, but these were mostly due to the lack of infrastructure in Cambodia, not to diversion by the Vietnamese. The *Times* did not accept my piece, so on December 20, I published it in the *Providence Journal*. On December 17, 1979, just after our meeting with Bloomfield and Owen, nationally syndicated columnist Mary McGrory ran a column challenging the Carter/Reston assertions of diversion. She pointed out that the administration was making charges of diversion without any evidence whatsoever, since the United States had no personnel on the ground in Cambodia; and that all the relief agencies that did have people working in Cambodia asserted that the charges of diversion were untrue. McGrory used our just-concluded meeting at the White House with Bloomfield and Owen as the centerpiece of her column, juxtaposing our lobbying of the administration in favor of U.S. humanitarian and food aid to Cambodia with the administration's own policy of unrelenting

In Vietnam in 1981. Photo by Jerry Elmer.

hostility toward Cambodia. "Attacking Vietnam is politically popular. It's a Communist country and it defeated us," McGrory quoted me in her column as saying after our White House meeting.

For me personally, the 1981 trip to Indochina was a highlight of many years of working in the peace movement. I had devoted years of my life to ending the war in Indochina, work that had involved considerable inconvenience and risk, and I felt a special affinity with the country and its people. It was a deeply moving experience finally to go to Vietnam and see the country and meet the people with whom my life had become so intricately entwined.

Our delegation of ten white people stood out in Vietnam. Everywhere we went, and especially in the countryside, groups of children would gather around us. They would greet us with "Lien Xo, Lien Xo," which meant "Russian." When the children learned that we were not Russian, but American, they were fascinated, and always had especially warm greetings for us. Given what the United States had done to their country, this might seem odd, but there was a simple explanation. For all the years of the war, the party line of the Communist Party of Vietnam had been that the American *government* was the enemy of the Vietnamese people, but the American *people* were their friends. The American *government* was making war on Vietnam, but the American *people* were working and demonstrating for peace. These ordinary Vietnamese had been fed this line for years, but had never met a real American. When they finally met us, the first actual Americans they had ever seen, they were well prepared to like us.

The party line of the Communist Party of Vietnam was, of course, utter nonsense. The United States is a reasonably democratic country. The fact is that, for much of the war, the war continued because the American people supported it. As I noted, as late as 1968, near the end of his presidency, President Johnson enjoyed the support of a majority of the public for his war policies. Later, President Nixon succeeded in fooling much of the public into supporting his policy of "Vietnamization."

In addition, even when public polling showed that a clear majority of the American people opposed the war, the war continued because people who *said* they opposed the war were unwilling to do what was necessary to stop it: refuse to register for the draft; refuse to be inducted into the Army; sit in at draft boards to close them down; destroy draft files; refuse to vote for any congressional candidate who voted to appropriate any funds, regardless of how small an amount, for the war; and so forth. If every American who *said* that he or she opposed the war had engaged in some form of direct action to actually stop the war, the war would have been over in a matter of days. Imagine the impact on the American body politic if, say, tens of millions of Americans had engaged in a general strike or refused to pay their federal taxes until the war ended.

That is why, except for the Stanley Millet congressional campaign in 1966, I never thought it was useful to engage in electoral politics (such as working for presidential peace candidate Gene McCarthy in 1968) as a means of ending the war. Political change in the United States doesn't start at the top and filter down; rather, political change starts at the bottom and percolates up. The war was not going to be ended by electing this or that particular person to the presidency. Rather, regardless of who was president, the war would end when the American people created so irresistible a political force that *whoever* was president at the time would be forced to end the war.

Another reason for my aversion to electoral politics is that, for too many people, a focus on electoral politics is an excuse to do nothing except vote once every four years, an action that might take thirty minutes if there is a line at the polling place. As I have tried to show in this book, my view is that voting every four years is not nearly enough, and that one accomplishes much more by being politically active day in and day out, election year or not.

To be sure, my aversion to electoral politics may sensibly be challenged. In the early 1960s, a debate was carried on within the civil rights movement about how much effort should be put into getting civil rights bills passed in Congress. The side that advocated direct action, rather than legislative action, argued much as I do above: changing hearts and minds is the *sine qua non* of social change; once people's *minds* are changed, legislation will fall into place naturally. There is much to recommend this point of view. To take but a single example, as I argue elsewhere in this book, Nixon did not end the draft because he had one grandparent who had been a Quaker; Nixon ended the draft because of the irresistible pressure put on him by the peace movement, and the draft would probably have ended more or less when it did regardless of what individual of which political party sat in the White House.

In the civil rights movement debate of the early 1960s, the opposite point of view went something like this: *we don't care a whit about what is in people's hearts; we care about their* actions. *Let the Southern bigots harbor all the secret prejudices they want, so long as civil rights* laws *make discrimination in employment, housing, and all other public spheres illegal and impossible.* History shows that this latter view is not nearly as misguided as I (for one) would probably have argued at the time. Civil rights laws *were* passed in 1964 and 1965, over stiff opposition from Southern members of Congress, and over the next forty years, as new generations of young people grew up, people's attitudes actually did change over time as a result of a different legal landscape. To be sure, attitudes did not change either as quickly or as completely as civil rights activists would have wished. Still, there is no denying that throughout the South (and elsewhere) today there are cross-racial friendships and even marriages with a frequency that would have been unthinkable in the 1950s. The racial integration that was at first forced by law has over time come to be reflected in the attitudes of many ordinary people.

And even my (admitted) aversion to electoral politics is not single-minded. In chapter 7, I explained how an important element of the Tiger Cage Vigil and Fast was congressional visitation and lobbying. In chapter 11, I discuss further how the lobbying associated with the Tiger Cage Vigil and Fast was part of a much wider and highly effective lobbying effort at the time, an effort in which I was an active participant. Nevertheless, the fact remains that my basic philosophical belief is that which individuals are elected to office is nearly always less important than what the overall climate in the country is, and that in a democratic society such as ours politicians will respond to the climate created by activists (and others).

When I say that the war would have ended in a matter of days if all the Americans who *believed* the war was wrong had actually engaged in direct action to stop the war, political moderates who fancy themselves "realists" object that my view is naïve because it fails to take into account bureaucratic inertia and how hard it is to change governmental policy, particularly long-standing governmental policy like a war that had been going on for years. In fact, I think it is I who am the realist here. I am positing what would have happened if *millions* of people had engaged in direct action and civil disobedience to stop the war. Such a thing has never happened in U.S. history and the effects of such an outpouring of sentiment *and action* would, likewise, have been unprecedented.

A more intriguing question is why that did not happen. Why were there only thousands of draft resisters in prison instead of millions? Why did only a few score of people publicly destroy draft files, instead scores of thousands? (Remember that there only were 4,100 draft boards in the entire country. Allowing ten people per draft board, it would have taken only 41,000 people to raid them all, thereby entirely shutting down the nation's entire draft apparatus *regardless* of what the president and Congress might choose to do or not do. Yet obviously nothing approaching such numbers took part in draft-file destruction.) Why, for that matter, were there fifty or a hundred Americans who believed the war was wrong for every one who ever took part in a legal peace demonstration? There are, no doubt, many answers to this puzzle, but I think I can suggest a few of them.

The astute reader of this book may well find a streak of self-importance in some of what I have written. I have, after all, spoken highly of the work that many peace activists, including me, engaged in and, perhaps worse, I have dared to say that I thought that some of these activities were quite effective. (An equally astute but less charitable reader might call me arrogant.) These readers would be correct. It *is* a bit arrogant to think that one can pit oneself against the entire might of the U.S. government and have an important effect. This is not so much a conscious belief (because if we activists really thought about it we would realize how implausible it all is) as it is a *Weltanschauung*, an underlying attitude toward everything in life. One of the fundamental differences in attitude between a committed activist and a non-activist is that the activist proceeds from the unspoken (and perhaps even unconscious) assumption that his or her actions can and do make an important difference in the world.

I have seen this attitude in other activists I have known. After the Rochester draft-board Action, I visited Suzi Williams at her new home at the Federal Prison for Women in Alderson, West Virginia. Suzi told me that she had recently had an interview with the prison psychiatrist. After hearing Suzi tell about the beliefs that had led her to her second incarceration in Alderson for draft-file destruction, the doctor commented, "You seem to believe that the cosmic state of the entire universe depends on *your* actions." It struck me then (and I still believe now) that the doctor was onto something important. One of the things that made Suzi such an attractive figure—that allowed her to accomplish so much for peace—was precisely her underlying attitude that what she did (or did not do) counted for something.

Here is another example of the same underlying attitude: DeCourcy Squire's younger brother, Ralph, was a draft resister. As a child, DeCourcy and Ralph's parents used to take them to classical music concerts. Ralph hated classical music. At the end of each concert, Ralph tried to organize his family and those sitting near him not to clap—because sustained applause might lead to an encore, and Ralph, who hated the music, wanted less, not more. Again, the necessary predicate to Ralph's actions was that his clapping or non-clapping would (or could) make a difference. His action or non-action would affect the world in a noticeable way.

This perhaps arrogant, certainly fundamental, confidence in the efficacy (or at least the importance) of our own actions is a crucial factor that sets the activist apart from the non-activist. This is true in all social change movements, from the Abolitionists in the antebellum period to the women's suffrage advocates, to the leaders of the civil rights movement in the 1950s and 1960s. One of the beliefs that allowed James Meredith to risk life and limb by enrolling in the University of Mississippi in 1962 was that by doing so he could help to change the world. When Martin Luther King Jr. led the Montgomery bus boycott in 1955 and 1956, he no doubt was motivated, in part, by the attitude, to quote the Alderson Prison psychiatrist, that his actions could affect the cosmic state of the universe (and so they did). The non-activist lacks this arrogant outlook on life.

Another factor that deterred many people from participating in direct action or civil disobedience was fear. I spent years organizing draft resistance in high schools and colleges, encouraging young people to resist the draft, destroy draft files, and so forth. One of the main things that deterred more people from taking such actions—one of the objections I heard over and over and over—was the realistic fear that breaking the law would result in imprisonment. One of the things that all organizers of civil disobedience must contend with is the fear that all sensible people have to the consequences of civil disobedience. It was this fear that Gandhi was attempting to address when he demanded that judges give him a maximum sentence in connection with his civil disobedience campaigns. By his demand, Gandhi was trying to demonstrate the power that could be had if people were able to overcome their fear of imprisonment or other consequences that might result from joining his campaign. Similarly, it was this fear that I was trying to address in my public statement on September 15, 1970, when I was arrested in Providence for the RIPOFF Action:

At no time was our action underground or clandestine. After the action, we held a press conference here in Providence to explain ourselves and what we hoped to accomplish. I speak now, as we did then, about fear and responsibility.

Fear is used by the government to make the Selective Service System work, and to stifle dissent. The threat of incarceration is used against many who work for social change: draft resisters, draft board liberators, Black Panthers, etc. We acted publicly, and I am here today, to say that we will no longer let fear of government threats rule our lives . . .

I speak of responsibility–the need for people to accept responsibility for their lives and actions. We must not be like the "good Germans". . . .

Yet another factor that prevented or interfered with more people taking part in serious political action was the counter-culture that grew up in the 1960s and 1970s. The guru of LSD, Timothy Leary (who was successfully freed from a California state prison by the Weather Underground), famously urged people to "Tune in, turn on, and drop out." The three parts of his admonition hung together coherently, and to me the most damning part of the trilogy was the third and last part. While I was busy trying to get young (and other) people *engaged* in serious political activity, direct action, and civil disobedience, the siren song of the counter-culture was that politics was a drag. Don't waste your life going to prison for your beliefs when you can have much more fun with drugs, sex, and rock and roll. To be sure, there were significant overlaps between the peace movement and the counter-culture. Some activists grew their hair long and smoked marijuana. Plenty of people at Woodstock also participated in protest activities. Yet those who truly dropped out were lost to political agitation.

All of these factors played a role in keeping the number of people engaged in direct action and committing civil disobedience smaller than it might otherwise have been.

But I must return to the story of my trip to Indochina. Despite my political disagreement with the aspect of the Vietnamese Communist Party line that said that the American *people* are the friends of the Vietnamese, it was nevertheless a pleasure to be greeted with so much spontaneous and obviously genuine warmth everywhere we went in Vietnam.

The time we spent in Cambodia was moving as well. It was extremely gratifying to see in Cambodia the tangible results of the work I had done eighteen months earlier, back in the autumn of 1979. The country was obviously still very poor. In our interview with the Foreign Minister, for example, he actually cadged some pages from my notebook from me because the Ministry could not afford to buy paper even for senior officials! Nevertheless the entire people were no longer on the brink of starvation as they had been a year earlier. Commerce was even beginning to return to Phnom Penh.

At the same time, there was just no escaping the fact that we were visiting a country that had but recently experienced a holocaust. When we arrived at the Phnom Penh airport, we were met by Eva Mysliviec, the director of the AFSC relief effort in Cambodia. On the drive into town from the airport, Eva said, "There is not one person in this country who did not have family members killed by Pol Pot." I was skeptical; I thought the statement rather sweeping, so during my stay in the country I asked nearly every Cambodian I met whether he or she had seen family members killed by Pol Pot cadres. I did find one who did not have family members murdered; Peap, one of our interpreters, told us that his parents and siblings had all *starved* to death in the Pol Pot years.

Typical of the Cambodians I interviewed was a young woman who worked at a pharmaceutical factory in Phnom Penh. She had been ordered out of the city in 1975 and forced to live on a collective farm, where she worked sixteen-hour days. She had seen her husband and both parents murdered by Pol Pot soldiers and dumped into a mass grave. She and one sibling were the only survivors of her family.

One middle-aged woman I talked with tearfully recounted how her husband had died. They were living in a forced-labor camp when her husband became ill and asked to see the camp medic. The medic injected lethal poison into the man's veins.

After a time, we became embarrassed asking Cambodians what had happened to them under Pol Pot, for the answers we received were predictable, grim, and heart-rending. One middle-aged man wept through much of our discussion. He had lost his wife, all four children, and his mother, he said, and he was too old to start another family. He now worked as the head of an orphanage in Phnom Penh.

Such stories about Cambodia under Pol Pot are now familiar in the

West, but at the time were only just beginning to emerge. These stories cast the United States government position of support for the Pol Pot government in a very unfavorable light.

One morning our guides took us to visit Rolous village, about thirty minutes from Phnom Penh via a very dusty dirt road. This was then the site of the latest mass-grave excavation. There were an estimated 129 separate mass graves in the village. When we visited, thirty-three had been excavated, covering an area the size of a football field. At each grave were piles of human skeletons, victims of Pol Pot's mass murders. Each excavated grave contained 80–100 skulls, perhaps 12,000–15,000 for the entire complex. The stench from thousands of rotting human bodies was overwhelming, and the sight of human skeletons, stacked in macabre piles as far as the eye could see, was staggering. Walking between the piles, my footsteps were occasionally punctuated by the cracking sound of a human leg or arm bone that I had not seen. In one

At Rolous Village, outside Phnom Penh, there were 129 separate mass graves in the process of being excavated. These were the notorious "killing fields" of Cambodia. Some of the rotting skulls still had blindfolds on them. Photo by Jerry Elmer.

Toul Sleng had been a girl's *lycee* in Phnom Penh, but under the Khmer Rouge regime (April 17, 1975 to January 7, 1979) it was turned into an extermination center. Thousands of people perished in Toul Sleng, and there were only a handful of survivors. Like their Nazi predecessors, the Khmer Rouge kept meticulous records of their victims. Many of the dead, like the ones in this photo, were children. Photo by Jerry Elmer.

corner of the field, I discovered a group of whitened skulls with their blindfolds still on.

Later the same day, our guides took us to the Toul Sleng prison, which had been used during the Pol Pot years as a torture house and extermination camp. Toul Sleng is now reasonably well known in the West, because it has since been made into a kind of holocaust museum of the Khmer Rouge years and many Westerners have visited it. But we were among the first Westerners to visit. It had not yet been made into a permanent museum, and the place was very much as it had been found in January 1979 by the Khmer and Vietnamese forces that had driven the Khmer Rouge from power.

Over 16,000 people died at Toul Sleng during the three-and-a-half years of Pol Pot's rule. There were only a handful of survivors. Like the Nazis before them, Pol Pot's men had kept meticulous records of those who perished there, including photographs of the victims. Several hundred of those photographs were on display on the walls when we visited. The torture rooms were still intact, with their ghastly implements on full display; and, in one room, there was a ceiling-high pile of clothing that had belonged to the dead. I was reminded of the visit I had made in July 1975 with my father to the memorial that now stands at the site of the former concentration camp at Dachau, and I felt, once again, very, very glad that I had worked as hard as I had to end the war.

In January 1981, two months before I left on this trip to Indochina, there had been a change in Washington: the Carter administration left power and the Reagan administration arrived. In March, just before leaving for Indochina, I met at the White House with James Lilley, a new member of the National Security Council under President Reagan. Lilley had responsibility on the NSC for Indochina affairs. I went to the White House in order to urge a change in the official U.S. attitude toward Cambodia that had prevailed under President Carter, a position that included diplomatic support at the UN for the ousted Khmer Rouge and no humanitarian aid for the current government in Phnom Penh. Lilley told me that a major review of U.S. policy toward Cambodia was under way within the administration. During the 1980 presidential campaign, candidate Reagan had castigated President Carter because, as Reagan charged, Carter "supported the Pol Pot Communist régime, which had slaughtered millions of its own people, in the United Nations." Lilley told me that the new administration was concerned about the implications of seeming to support one of the most brutal and murderous régimes of the century.

On my way home from Indochina, I stopped at the U.S. Embassy in Bangkok, Thailand, to discuss the trip with the embassy staff. There I was informed of the results of policy review: the Reagan administration would continue the previous administration's policy of support for the ousted Pol Pot régime at the United Nations. I heard this only a few days after I had been to Rolous Village and Toul Sleng. I was stunned.

When I returned to the U.S., I arranged another meeting at the White House with Lilley; I would again try to lobby for a change in U.S. policy toward Cambodia. A few days before the meeting was to take place, Lilley called me to make sure I had no objection to his inviting a CIA officer to the meeting.

At the time, it was not immediately clear to me that objecting to the CIA's presence was the correct thing to do. For one thing, Lilley was himself a former CIA officer; it would have been naïve to think that anything told to Lilley at the White House would not make it back to the CIA. In addition, nothing about our trip was secret; we were, at all times, eager to share our insights based on the trip with all who would listen. However, Doug Hostetter persuaded me to object, more for reasons of appearances than substance. "You don't want it to look like you are reporting to the CIA as soon as you came back," Doug explained. I did object, and Lilley cancelled our meeting.

My work trying to change the U.S. policy of hostility toward Cambodia went on for years. I did speaking tours, published articles, organized visits to members of Congress—all notably without success. The official U.S. policy was that we could not recognize a government in Phnom Penh that had been installed by means of a foreign invasion. To be sure, the government in Phnom Penh *had* been installed by the Vietnamese after they had driven Pol Pot from power. (On the other hand, to a person, every Cambodian I had spoken to on my trip there described the Vietnamese invasion that had toppled Pol Pot as a "liberation." It was easy to understand why.)

The official U.S. government position on why we could not recognize the Vietnamese-backed government in Phnom Penh was fatuous. The United States frequently backs governments that come to power through military means. At that time, the most recent example was that the United States had immediately extended diplomatic recognition to the Tanzanian-backed government of Uganda that had ousted dictator Idi Amin following a Tanzanian-backed invasion. In recent times, to take but a single example, the United States did not merely back, but actually installed, the Afghan government of Hamid Karzai after the United States toppled, by military means, the prior Afghan government.

The real reason for Washington's hostility toward the Phnom Penh government and support for the ousted Khmer Rouge was that Washington viewed Vietnam as a puppet of the Soviet Union. This was, after all, at the very height of the Cold War. By opposing a Vietnamese-installed government in Phnom Penh, Washington believed it was striking a blow against the Soviet Union. The policy was unfortunate on many levels. On a moral level, it put us in the position of backing a genocidal government. On a practical level, it precluded United States participation in desperately needed famine-relief and post-war reconstruction efforts in Cambodia, and made the relief efforts of voluntary organizations like AFSC, UNICEF, and the International Committee of the Red Cross much harder to carry out. The policy also put the United States in the absurd position of backing a government, the Khmer Rouge, long after it had ceased to exist.

My route back to the United States from Indochina in 1981 was via Bangkok and Tokyo. At Tokyo's Narita Airport, I changed planes for a Boeing 747 that flew directly to New York's Kennedy airport. At Kennedy, I had a scary experience.

Because my flight from Narita to Kennedy was nonstop, I came through U.S. Customs in New York. The jumbo jet I was on landed at about the same time as four or five other jumbo jets. Thus, when I disembarked there were several thousand passengers milling around the baggage carousels. It took some time for my bag to arrive. Finally, I saw my bag, and I went to pick it up. As soon as I touched my bag, there were two customs officers, one on either side of me. "Please come this way with us, Mr. Elmer," one of them said.

The odd thing was that I had not yet presented my passport or other identification to anybody. That is, I was greeted by name, in a milling crowd of thousands of people, before I had identified myself to any official.

I was led to a back room, where another customs officer was already filling out a narcotics search form in my name. I was thoroughly searched, as was my baggage. The officers were especially curious about a jar of over-the-counter skin cream that my doctor had suggested I use. They put probes through the cream to see what lay beneath the surface; they poked through it and ran the cream between their fingers to test the texture.

"What's this?" one of the agents asked me suspiciously.

"Skin cream from my doctor," I answered, truthfully.

"Oh, yeah? What do you need it for?" he asked.

"I have dry skin on my legs," I said.

"Let's see," the agent demanded.

Nothing would do but I had to take my pants off and show them my legs.

"Your skin doesn't look dry to me," the agent said suspiciously.

I just couldn't resist the temptation. "See how well the cream is working," I replied.

During this trip, I again published a series of articles in the *Providence Journal*. When I returned, I again did a speaking tour arranged by AFSC offices across the country. In Denver, I was booked as the guest of a radio talk show hosted by Gary Tessler. This was before nationally syndicated radio talk shows became popular. During a commercial, Tessler told me that he had four million listeners in twenty-three states. I did not believe him, so he asked subsequent callers to say where they were calling from. It turned out that he actually *was* broadcast in twenty-three states!

My time in Cambodia, however, left me badly shaken—perhaps depressed—and with a deep pessimism about what lies at the core of the human soul. It is very different knowing intellectually about the depravity of which human beings are capable, reading about it in the newspaper or in a history book or novel, and actually walking through a charnel house—Toul Sleng, Rolous Village—and having the reek of thousands of freshly dug up, rotting corpses fill your nostrils and overcome your senses. Even my earlier visit to Dachau had not prepared me for Cambodia. When I visited the memorial at Dachau in 1975, the crematoria had been cold for three decades. In Cambodia, everything was still fresh and new.

The memorial at Dachau has a stone monument on which are written the German words "Nie Wieder" (Never Again) and the quotation of George Santayana to the effect that those who cannot learn from history are doomed to repeat past mistakes. What did it say about the human soul that it did happen again, and so soon, too?

At the core of every pacifist's beliefs is an appreciation of how wonderful our species is—capable of rapturous devotion, immeasurable wisdom, wondrous art. We look at our children, our parents, our friends, and our breasts are filled with an overweening love; we look at

With Cory Aquino in Manila in May 1984. In the background are portraits of her slain husband, Senator Benigno (Ninoy) Aquino, a leader of the non-Communist opposition to dictator Ferdinand Marcos. Aquino later became the first elected president of the Philippines in the post-Marcos era. Photo courtesy of the American Friends Service Committee.

our neighbors, those in other countries, of other races or religions, and we see our brothers and sisters. Like the Quakers perceiving that of God in every man and woman, we pacifists see a wonderful, divine spark in every person. That is why we find it impossible to kill, even in time of war. Cambodia showed me with a terrible, inescapable clarity what a scurvy, debased, and depraved lot we human beings are, and so it shook my pacifism to its foundation.

And yet, and yet, I remain a pacifist. It may be a slender reed but, in the end, I think that there may be little else than this refusal to countenance the killing of other human beings, even in war, that sets us pacifists apart from the perpetrators of Dachau and Toul Sleng.

In 1984, I again returned to Southeast Asia, this time on my own, this time only to the Philippines. I went at the time of the National Assembly elections, shortly before Corazon Aquino became president. I had met with Aquino during my 1977 visit to the Philippines—she was an old friend of Russ Johnson's—and I did again on this occasion. This time I published my articles through Pacific News Service, so they were picked up by newspapers all across the country. Once again, I did speaking tours upon my return to pay the costs of the trip.

My trips to Southeast Asia in 1981 and 1984 were, in a way, applications of a lesson I had learned as a child from my mom: if you want something badly enough, you should work to make it happen, organize it, create the future you want. In 1981, the State Department did not permit travel to Vietnam, the Vietnamese did not grant visas to Americans, and I did not have a spare $5,000 to travel to Vietnam. Yet I found a way to go because I wanted to, by organizing a delegation and coordinating the visit with the Vietnamese, and I figured out ways to pay for the trip as well. Nobody told me to go to the Philippines in 1984, but I wanted to very much and I found a way, through my work, to make it happen.

9

Mass Civil Disobedience

MASS CIVIL DISOBEDIENCE is almost (but not quite) an oxymoron. I realize that there are some historical examples of large-scale civil disobedience: Gandhi's salt march to the sea, some of the lunch-counter and other integration sit-ins during the civil rights movement. Still, to me, the quintessential civil disobedience is the action of an individual or of a small group: A. J. Muste and a few others climbing over the fence at Mead Missile Base near Omaha, Nebraska on July 1, 1959, to protest against nuclear weapons; Dave Miller publicly burning his draft card at an anti-draft rally in Manhattan in October 1965; Phil Berrigan and three friends pouring blood on draft files in Baltimore in October 1967.

There are several reasons for my view of civil disobedience as mainly an individual or small-scale action. Most obviously, throughout history most civil disobedience *has* been small-scale. For every one salt march to the sea, there have been a great many individual acts of nonviolent civil disobedience that few people ever hear of. Another factor contributing to my view probably has to do with the kind of person likely to engage in civil disobedience. In order to be able to violate the law openly, one must truly be a dissenter at heart, and it is perhaps that oddball quality about us that makes us more likely to make our protests in individual and individualistic ways rather than as part of mass movements.

But probably the single biggest reason that I think of civil disobedience as being quintessentially small-scale in nature rather than a mass movement is that, having participated in and organized civil disobedience actions over a period of years, I am acutely aware of how *all* civil disobedience, including what ends up as large-scale actions with thousands of participants, exists as a result of highly personal, separate decisions of conscience, made by individuals one at a time. The large-scale draft-card turn-ins on April 15 and October 16, 1967, were successful because scores of men took part. Yet when I view these actions in my mind's eye I see not a large group participating in a mass action; instead, I see individual after solitary individual who each came to a separate, personal choice for highly personal (and often idiosyncratic) reasons.

Having said this, however, I have nevertheless participated in mass civil disobedience on two separate occasions. One was Act For Friendship With Vietnam in 1975; the other was the occupation of the proposed site of a nuclear power plant in Seabrook, New Hampshire, in 1977.

Act For Friendship With Vietnam

Throughout much of the Vietnam War, AFSC had provided medical aid and other relief supplies to civilian war victims in all three parts of Vietnam: North Vietnam, South Vietnam in territory controlled by the Saigon government, and South Vietnam in territory controlled by the liberation forces. AFSC had always applied for U.S. government licenses for this aid from the appropriate agencies, generally the Treasury and Commerce Departments. During the war, AFSC had always received the licenses to provide the aid, and it was always something of an open question what AFSC might be led to do if, at some point, these licenses were denied.

Of course, we got the usual criticism from conservatives about giving aid and comfort to the enemy; we were, after all, providing aid to the North Vietnamese "enemy," and to the liberation forces in South Vietnam. On the other hand, AFSC's provision of non-military relief aid to civilian war victims had a long and cherished history. We had provided such aid on all sides of the battle lines during World Wars I and II and had been the co-recipient of the Nobel Peace Prize for our efforts in Europe during and after World War II. It was easy to show how providing such relief sprang from the Quaker belief that there is that of God in every man and woman. And, after all, how could we be committing treason if we were acting at all times with U.S. governmental licenses?

During the early years of my tenure with AFSC, the largest portion of my job was anti-war organizing, but I also did some fundraising for AFSC's medical aid programs in Vietnam. For example, Carol and I worked with the artist Fritz Eichenberg, who lived in Rhode Island, on organizing an art show to benefit AFSC's medical aid programs in Vietnam. Fritz solicited donations from his artist friends and put together a wonderful collection. Carol and I organized the show itself, publicizing it in the peace community so that the works would ultimately be sold. We held the sale over a weekend at the Friends Meeting House in Providence. We sold thousands of dollars worth of artwork (at a fraction of its actual worth on the open market, as Fritz pointed out to us more than once), and then sent the remaining unsold pieces on to AFSC offices in other states, where similar sales were held, raising additional funds.

In March 1975, just weeks before the war ended, during the final offensive by the liberation forces, AFSC increased its relief efforts in Vietnam in response to the suddenly increasing number of civilian war casualties. In Rhode Island, Carol and I stepped up our local fundraising efforts in support of those aid programs. One thing we did was to ask Episcopal bishop Frederick Belden to have the churches in his diocese take up a special collection for AFSC's Vietnam relief programs on a designated Sunday. Bishop Belden agreed.

After the war ended, for the first time in history, AFSC was denied U.S. governmental licenses for sending medical relief and reconstruction supplies to Vietnam. Since these same licenses had always been granted before, even when there was a shooting war going on, we assumed that the license denial was somehow a puerile form of retribution by an administration that felt humiliated because the United States had been defeated by the liberation forces of a supposedly backward, third world, agrarian country.

Whatever the reason for the license denial, AFSC now faced for the first time the dilemma of what to do. Would AFSC violate the law and ship the supplies anyway (with the concomitant risk of losing its IRS-approved tax-exempt status as a religious or charitable organization)? Would it buckle under and not ship the supplies for which licenses had been denied? Would it reapply for licenses and, if so, would it ship or not ship in the interim? There was a lively debate within AFSC on these issues.

That summer, there was a gathering of AFSC peace staff from all over the country at Estes Park, Colorado. All of us had been working against the war for so long that, with the war now over, it was time to do some serious thinking about future directions for our peace work. Many of the AFSC staff had, like me, come into the peace movement during (and because of) the Vietnam War. Unlike some of the older or longer-term AFSC staff, we relative newcomers could never remember a time working in the movement when there had not been a Vietnam War on which to focus our energies. One of the topics we discussed at Estes Park was the appropriate response of AFSC to the recent, unprecedented license denial. I came up with a proposal that was accepted and implemented.

I remembered back to the time in high school when I was co-chairman of SPV. On January 5, 1968, Dr. Benjamin Spock, the famous pediatrician; Bill Coffin, the chaplain of Yale; and three others were indicted for conspiracy to counsel young men to resist the draft. The indictment of such prominent Americans—half of the country at that time had been raised on Dr. Spock's book on child care—proved to be a major political blunder in many respects. (Among other things, some of the defendants who were alleged to have "conspired" with each other had, in fact, never even met each other.) One of the things that peace activists did in response to the indictments was to circulate statements of solidarity with Spock, Coffin, and the three others. These were petitions in which the signers said, in effect, if Spock and Coffin are guilty of counseling and encouraging draft resistance, then so am I; indict me, too, because, like Spock and Coffin, I, too, urge young men to resist the draft.

In 1975, at the AFSC meeting in Estes Park, I remembered those earlier solidarity statements well. I remembered how long and hard I had thought before I signed a petition myself. And I remembered circulating the petition at SPV meetings in the spring of 1968, always with the admonition to potential signers that they could possibly be prosecuted for signing. And I especially remembered what a wonderful boost to draft resistance organizing the Spock-Coffin indictment had provided. Why not turn the current license denial to our advantage in a similar way?

With the memory of the organizing that followed the Spock indictment very much in mind, I conceived of a project that AFSC named "Act For Friendship With Vietnam." The idea of the project was very simple: we would publicize the fact that, after the war had ended, AFSC had been denied licenses to ship humanitarian relief supplies to Vietnam for the first time ever—specifically penicillin, fishnets, and rototillers. We would invite people to contribute funds to AFSC earmarked for the now-illegal shipments. In addition, we would have donors sign "confessions," acknowledging that they had contributed for the illegal shipments and that they knew they were violating the Trading With the Enemy Act and could be prosecuted. My idea was that on a single, coordinated day during the autumn, project participants would "turn themselves in" to local FBI offices, together with their signed confessions, and invite the government to arrest them.

I ended up coordinating the project nationwide. I drafted, and AFSC produced, a background manual for prospective participants, which provided information on the history of AFSC's relief efforts in Vietnam, the current license denial, and a detailed discussion of civil disobedience in general and, more specifically, the possible consequences of violating the Trading With the Enemy Act. I helped local AFSC offices all over the country with organizing ideas and advice for the project. We selected Tuesday, November 2, 1975, as the day people would turn themselves in to the government. We suggested that if a local FBI office was not available, people could turn themselves in to the local United States Attorney or even a municipal police department.

Participants were instructed to send their checks and "confessions" to AFSC well in advance of November 2. They were to keep photocopies of both the confession and the check to present to the authorities, the check being "evidence" with which the government might prosecute the civil disobedience. The organizing manual I wrote explained how to arrange the appointments on November 2 with the FBI or other governmental agency (call and say you want to report evidence of violation of federal law) and how to arrange for press coverage.

In his book *Confronting the War Machine: Draft Resistance During the Vietnam War* (2003), historian Michael Foley describes the tremendous organizing boost given to the draft resistance movement by the indictments of Dr. Spock, Rev. Coffin and the three others:

> The groundswell of support for the five defendants and the draft resistance movement surprised even the most experienced political organizers. One week after the indictments came down, Resist

organized an event in New York City's Town Hall with the idea that individuals could line up and sign the group's complicity statement on stage in a very public, dramatic fashion. As the day approached, Louis Kampf and other movement leaders worried that the turnout might be too small. But when the time came, people packed Town Hall and overflowed onto the streets. The meeting never opened formally since people spontaneously began signing the statement and speaking into the microphone one at a time. "We couldn't keep people off the stage," Kampf recalled. "People just rushed up there wanting to sign up and made a lot of very heartfelt statements about overcoming fear." Even more significant, the money began pouring into Resist. Instead of scaring the draft resistance movement, and the larger antiwar movement, the government opened the financial floodgates.

Something very similar happened nearly a decade later with AFSC's Act for Friendship With Vietnam. At the outset of the project, I had hoped that we might get several hundred people to participate but I did not dare to hope for more. This was, after all, civil disobedience, and I thought it doubtful that more than a few hundred would want to take part. Participants were signing confessions acknowledging that they had violated the law, and were presenting to the government sufficient evidence of the crime to permit prosecution. But I was mistaken about the level of participation we would get.

The promotional materials for the project were distributed soon after Labor Day. By early October, it was clear that the project was going to garner far broader participation than I had at first anticipated. At first hundreds, then thousands, of responses came in, many with substantial contributions. I had viewed the project as a potentially useful organizing tool, but never as a serious fundraiser. I was, however, mistaken about the money we would raise, too. In the end, hundreds of thousands of dollars for AFSC's Vietnam relief projects were raised in the space of only a few weeks.

On Tuesday, November 2, demonstrations or "surrenders" occurred in fifty-two cities nationwide. A total of approximately 6,000 people participated. In addition to coverage in the national news media, each of the fifty-two local events drew local press coverage, much of it featur-

After the Vietnam War ended in 1975, AFSC organized a civil disobedience project called Act for Friendship With Vietnam. Participants contributed money to AFSC for Vietnam relief and signed confessions stating that they knew they were violating the Trading With the Enemy Act. On Tuesday, November 2, 1975, 6,000 people in fifty-two cities nationwide turned themselves in to local FBI offices with signed confessions and copies of their checks, demanding to be arrested. Jerry Elmer, who initiated the project and coordinated it nationally, is shown at the microphone at a press conference in Providence. Photo courtesy of the American Friends Service Committee.

ing people turning themselves in to police and FBI offices, insisting that they be immediately arrested and prosecuted for violating the Trading With the Enemy Act.

On Friday, November 5, Secretary of State Henry Kissinger announced that AFSC would receive all of the contested licenses. Act for Friendship With Vietnam turned out to be far more successful far more quickly than any of us had anticipated. Like the government's 1968 indictment of Dr. Spock and the four others, the government's 1975 license denial showed how good political organizing can sometimes turn government efforts to hurt or undermine our movement into powerfully effective organizing tools.

Since then, when giving talks on civil disobedience, I have frequently pointed to the Act For Friendship With Vietnam project as an example of how nonviolent civil disobedience can be an effective tool in changing government policy. Because of the close connection in time between the public event (on Tuesday) and the reversal of government policy (on Friday of the same week), it is an example that is unusually easy to explain and to understand.

On a more personal level, I have always been proud of my idea in initiating the Act For Friendship With Vietnam project because, in general, I do not view myself as being a very creative thinker. I was a draft resister, but I did not invent draft resistance; I just participated in a form of protest that had been around for decades. I participated in draft-file destruction, but I did not invent that, either. My skills lay not in developing creative new organizing ideas or models; rather, my skills lay in the careful, well-planned execution of programs and projects conceived or initiated by others.

I do not mean here to denigrate my work. All of us have strengths and weaknesses. I was a careful, thorough organizer who carried off many successful projects. But I was not much of a creative thinker, and rarely developed new ideas on my own. Act For Friendship With Vietnam was an exception to that rule; and, as a result, I have always been quite pleased with my role in the project.

Seabrook

I am naturally a skeptic, and when I first learned of activists opposing civilian nuclear power plants I was deeply skeptical. Nuclear *weapons* must be opposed, but the peaceful atom generating electricity for civilian use sounded like a fine idea to me. I was at a peace conference around 1974 when I first heard the anti-nuclear-power position articulated and I asked the speaker a series of questions. The more I heard, the more skeptical of the speaker's position I became.

The speaker said that as civilian reactors split uranium atoms they would necessarily generate free neutrons to sustain their nuclear chain reaction, and that such neutrons could be released into the environment constituting dangerous radiation. But I had learned in high school that boron control rods are used in reactors to absorb neutrons (and are thus used to control the chain reaction); why not insulate civilian reactors with boron and thereby prevent the escape of dangerous neutron radiation? I asked. The speaker had no response; he apparently did not know much about how civilian reactors worked and was not able to respond to even this basic technical question.

Instead, the speaker changed the subject and discussed how civilian reactors inevitably produce plutonium, a dangerous emitter of alpha particles. But this made no sense to me either. Alpha particles, I argued, are big and heavy (an alpha particle is essentially a helium nucleus, two protons and two neutrons) and they have little penetrating power. An ordinary piece of paper is enough to stop an alpha particle; how could they not be stopped by the reinforced concrete of a containment vessel? Again, the speaker had no response.

My interest was piqued, and I started doing research on civilian nuclear power plants. It turned out that the research was not easy. The Left was starting to oppose construction of civilian reactors, but there was a real dearth of accurate, scientifically sound information on precisely *why* civilian reactors were not a good idea. I was eventually persuaded, but I remained painfully conscious that the Left had failed to make the argument against nuclear power carefully or persuasively.

In 1978, Carol and I organized a project called the "Walk for a Non-Nuclear Future." The idea of the project was publicly to draw an explicit connection between nuclear weapons and nuclear power. Participants would take part in a three-day walk across the state of Rhode Island. The Walk would start on August 6, the anniversary of the bombing of Hiroshima, with a demonstration at the Electric Boat facility at Quonset Point, Rhode Island, where the Trident nuclear submarine was manufactured. That would be the nuclear *weapons* part of the Walk. From Quonset Point, walkers would take three days traversing the state, ending up on August 9, the anniversary of the Nagasaki bombing, in Charlestown, Rhode Island, at the site of a proposed civilian nuclear power plant. That would be the nuclear *power* part of the Walk.

From an organizing standpoint, the Walk was very successful. At Quonset Point, the focus of the demonstration was the symbolic planting of spiderworts, a plant that changes color in response to elevated levels of radiation. Hundreds of people participated in the beginning and ending demonstrations, and scores took part in the Walk itself. The demonstrations and the Walk received a lot of media coverage. But our political message of linking the issues of nuclear weapons and nuclear power received some severe criticism. "There is no more relationship between Hiroshima and nuclear power than there is between electricity and the electric chair," a spokesman for the utility that wanted to build the civilian reactor was quoted in the *Providence Journal* as saying. One editorial in the *Providence Journal* ran under the headline "Demonstrations That Distort." "It's like comparing air travel with a B-52 bomber," sniffed another *Journal* editorial.

In response to this criticism, I wrote two Op-Ed articles that were published in the *Journal,* discussing specifically the connections between nuclear weapons and nuclear power. After they were published, I expanded the two articles into a single, longer piece that AFSC published as a brochure under the title *Power Plants and Weapons: The Nuclear Connection.* The brochure evidently filled a crying need in the anti-nuclear movement because it immediately became a best-seller. We received orders for thousands of copies from anti-nuclear activists all over the country. We kept printing and reprinting the brochure in ever-larger quantities, but no matter how many copies we printed at a time, we quickly sold out.

Then I received requests for permission to reprint *The Nuclear Connection* as part of anthologies. In 1979, the Environmental Action Foundation published an anthology called *Accidents Will Happen: The Case Against Nuclear Power.* My article was included, alongside articles by such anti-nuclear movement heavyweights as Ralph Nader and Helen Caldicott. The next year I got a request to reprint the article from Mark Reader, a college professor who was preparing an anthology to be used in college curricula. This time my co-authors included the likes of Lewis Mumford, E. F. Schumacher, Jacques Cousteau, and Dr. Caldicott (again).

As *The Nuclear Connection* became popular nationwide, I started getting requests for speaking engagements from local anti-nuclear groups that had used the brochure in their organizing work. I was at this time still in touch with Dan Berrigan, Phil Berrigan's older brother, from my days working with the Catholic Left. I proposed to Dan that he and I do a joint speaking tour about nuclear weapons and nuclear power. Local organizers could book the two of us as a package: Dan would speak on nuclear weapons, and I would discuss connections between nuclear weapons and civilian nuclear power plants. My idea was partly that it would be fun to tour that way with Dan, but also partly that I could raise some money for the Providence AFSC office. I guaranteed Dan $500 per day in honoraria from our talks, and AFSC would keep any money taken in beyond that guarantee.

Our joint speaking tour worked just as planned. By careful advance planning, and by scheduling talks at major colleges that were able to pay large lecture fees, we brought in over $1,000 per day during our tour. All of the "profits," of course, went to AFSC.

In August 1976, the U.S. Nuclear Regulatory Commission approved the license for construction of a nuclear power plant in the small Atlantic coastal town of Seabrook, New Hampshire. A few weeks later, eighteen demonstrators were arrested for nonviolently obstructing access to the site of the proposed plant. A few weeks after that, 188 demonstrators, more than ten times the earlier number, were arrested doing nonviolent civil disobedience at the Seabrook site. At that point, anti-Seabrook organizers started planning for an even larger demonstration at the site of the proposed plant the following spring.

The demonstration took place on April 30, 1977, by coincidence the anniversary of the end of the Vietnam War. (The demonstration was not planned with that date in mind.) One thousand four hundred fourteen people were arrested after nonviolently occupying the site of the proposed power plant for two days and nights. I participated in the demonstration, which was remarkable and memorable. Indeed, the 1977 civil disobedience at Seabrook marked a turning point in the nonviolent movement for several important reasons.

In the narrowest sense, the Seabrook occupation, and especially its aftermath, succeeded in putting the anti-nuclear-power movement on the map. That is, it was a turning point in public sentiment with regard to civilian nuclear power, in much the same way that the Tet Offensive in January through March 1968 was a key time in turning public opinion against American involvement in Vietnam. After the 1,414 of us were arrested, we all declined to post bail unless all of us, including the overwhelming majority of us who were from outside New Hampshire, were released on personal recognizance. Personal recognizance

"Nuclear connections" speaking tour with Dan Berrigan in 1979. Dan spoke on nuclear weapons, and Jerry spoke on the connections between nuclear weapons and nuclear power. Photo by Carol Bragg. Photo courtesy of the American Friends Service Committee.

is a form of pre-trial release in which the arrestee does not have to post any bail money with the court in order to ensure his or her return; the defendant is released "on his own recognizance," that is, simply on his or her promise to return later for trial. By engaging in this kind of "bail solidarity"—that is, by announcing that none of us would accept release on recognizance unless everyone was released that way—we hoped to pressure the authorities into releasing everyone.

In fact, the tactic worked perfectly. The State of New Hampshire had no jails to hold 1,414 extra prisoners, and so they opened National Guard Armories in Portsmouth, Concord, and Manchester to house us. They had no guards to guard us. They had no food to provide us, so the state hurriedly contracted with outside vendors to provide food for the sudden flood of prisoners. The tremendous expense of all of these accommodations quickly became a political issue in the state; New Hampshire prides itself on being the only state in the Union with neither an income tax nor a sales tax. After less than two weeks, everyone was released on personal recognizance.

But while we were in custody, we were big news. There were front-page articles about us in the *Boston Globe*. Other newspapers around the country also carried articles. We were on the national news on television several nights in a row. The result of all the news coverage stemming from our arrest and imprisonment was that the nuclear power issue became a national controversy in a way and with a force that the issue had not had before.

There is another sense in which I believe that the Seabrook demonstration and arrests in 1977 were an important turning point in the nonviolent movement in the United States. There had long been pacifist organizations in the United States. FOR was founded in 1915, AFSC was founded in 1917, and WRL in 1923. The Women's International League for Peace and Freedom was founded in 1919 (renaming the Woman's Peace Party, founded in 1915). Nevertheless, getting large numbers of peace activists to accept, consciously and deliberately, nonviolent discipline for their public demonstrations and actions was largely unknown outside the context of the civil rights movement. For years I had organized demonstrations, and for years I had always had an uphill battle persuading demonstrators that nonviolent discipline should be an important component of our events. At best, I might persuade people to adopt nonviolence as a sensible *tactic*, a way of not undermining our message with thoughtless acts of violence that might turn the public against us. Only rarely was it possible to persuade activists to adopt nonviolence as a principled *philosophy*, a moral necessity to undergird all of our work, and then only within the narrow confines of the pacifist wing of the larger peace movement.

All that changed at Seabrook. The organizers of the April 1977 occupation were deeply committed to nonviolence as both a tactic and a philosophy. The organizers decreed that no one would be *permitted* to participate in the occupation unless they were both personally committed to nonviolence *and* had participated in a full-day training session in nonviolence. To me, who had for years been frustrated in not being able to encourage wider acceptance of nonviolent discipline among those in the wider Left, the organizers' success with this was as astonishing as it was wonderful. The requirement to participate in a full-day nonviolence training session had several good results. Most obviously, this meant that all of the demonstrators had a deeper, more comprehensive understanding of nonviolence than they would have had otherwise. Less obviously, but not less importantly, it meant that the occupiers did not, and could not, include the usual cohort of scruffy hangers-on and hippie-dippies who might have shown up at the last moment for a demonstration but would have had, at best, a shallow understanding of the issues involved or the need for discipline. By requiring the occupiers actually to take part in a full-day training session well in advance of the occupation itself, the organizers ended up with a self-selected group of only the most committed, serious individuals. The requirement of advance training also permitted all the occupiers to develop a common and shared understanding of certain matters such as the bail solidarity issue.

Many matters were covered in the day-long preparation sessions. There were discussions of nonviolence as a philosophy and as a movement tactic. Participants were taught ways to respond nonviolently to possible police mistreatment or attacks by rowdy right-wingers (always a potential danger at demonstrations) or, in this case, by construction workers who may have felt their jobs threatened by the anti-nuclear activists. Participants were introduced to consensus decision-making.

There was time devoted to certain purely mechanical matters: dressing appropriately for what might turn into a multi-day-and-night campout (in fact, we were on the site for two days and nights before being arrested) and bringing food and camping gear with us. The matter of bringing food with us turned out to be unexpectedly important after we were arrested. The State of New Hampshire, apparently not expecting such a large bust, had made inadequate preparations for us. As a result, we were given no food at all by our jailers for the first two or three days we were in custody! Instead, we all had to fend for ourselves. Luckily, *we* had planned ahead, even if the state had not, and had brought lots of food with us, which we shared out while incarcerated in the various National Guard armories.

In addition, the mandatory nonviolence training and preparation sessions devoted time to other aspects of arrest: being arraigned, entering pleas in court, being represented by attorneys. Each of these are issues that have both a practical dimension and an ethical dimension. By this time, I had engaged in civil disobedience repeatedly, had been arrested several times, and was familiar with the practical and ethical issues presented, but for most of the participants this was all entirely new territory. Some of the issues we covered in these sessions were matters that were not immediately obvious to people not familiar with the process.

The matter of entering pleas in court is a case in point. There are at least four different options for how a criminal defendant who has been arrested for civil disobedience can plead. She can plead guilty. Gandhi always pled guilty in court, reasoning that he *was* guilty—that is, he *had* broken the law he was accused of violating (indeed, had violated the law proudly)—and that truthfulness obligated him to plead guilty. Many civil disobedients, however, myself included, generally plead not guilty. We reason that "guilt" implies wrongdoing, and we believe that we did not do anything morally culpable by committing civil disobedience. Thus, we plead not guilty. A person can also plead *nolo contendere*, a plea in which the charges are not contested, but no guilty plea is entered. This is sometimes viewed as splitting the difference between pleading guilty and not guilty. Civil disobedients sometimes also enter what are euphemistically called "creative pleas." Someone arrested for, say, sitting in at a draft board, when asked how she pleads, might respond, "I plead for an end to conscription." A demonstrator arrested at the site of a nuclear power plant might say, "I plead that the United States spend money on clean, renewable energy sources."

There is no one right answer to how people should plead. Although I always pled not guilty when being arraigned after civil disobedience, I would certainly never suggest that Gandhi was wrong because he always entered precisely the opposite plea.

In addition to the ethical dimensions of entering a plea, there are practical issues to be considered as well. If a demonstrator pleads guilty, there is no need for a trial to determine guilt or innocence, and the demonstrator will simply come before the judge to be sentenced. Only defendants who plead not guilty require, or receive, a trial. Thus, if one wishes to use one's trial as a means of gaining additional publicity for one's cause, one must plead not guilty. As a practical matter, also, prosecutors (or the courts) sometimes dismiss charges against demonstrators who plead not guilty. In the case of the Seabrook occupation, demonstrators who pled not guilty were convicted; but for those who appealed their convictions (as I did), the state simply dropped the charges rather than pursuing the appeals. Thus, Seabrook demonstrators who pled guilty may have had to serve additional time after their release from the armories, while their compatriots, like me, who pleaded not guilty, never had to serve any additional time. Such a situation is not uncommon.

The matter of being represented by an attorney in court is similarly one that different demonstrators approach differently and for which there is no single right answer. Some demonstrators do want to be represented by an attorney in court. They reason that the court procedure is arcane and unfamiliar to them; consequently, they need a lawyer to help them through the unfamiliar processes and procedures. On the other hand, I always took exactly the opposite view. (I had not attended law school at the time of my various arrests; thus, I was just as much a lay person as any other demonstrator.) I reasoned that if I were ever in court on something that was primarily a *legal* matter, I would be delighted to be represented by an attorney. Lawyers are, after all, trained experts in legal matters. But since I always viewed my arrests for civil disobedience as primarily a *moral* issue, I never wanted to be represented by a lawyer. My purpose in court was always to explain why I had acted as I had— that is, the underlying moral beliefs that led me to be arrested. Since I could explain my own actions and motivations better than someone else could, I had no need for a legal professional to represent me in court.

Interestingly, since becoming an attorney, my views on this matter have not only not changed but have actually become firmer. In 2001, I was asked to represent two peace activists who had been arrested when they had unfurled an anti-war banner on the grounds of the Naval War College in Newport. The first thing I did when I met with the demonstrators was to urge them to consider representing themselves. Judges are notoriously unwilling to allow demonstrators to explain in court their reasons or motivations for acting as they have. If a defendant is represented by an attorney, and the judge cuts off such a line of discussion in court, the attorney, who is an officer of the court, is honor-bound to follow the judge's ruling, even when that ruling inures to the detriment of his client. A defendant representing herself, on the other hand, can sometimes get away with saying and doing things in court that a lawyer would never be permitted to do. That is, as a practicing attorney, I can see important political and practical reasons why people in court for civil disobedience would not want to be represented by an attorney (precisely as I argued long before I became a lawyer myself).

One of the things I enjoyed about my work with AFSC was being able to be a resource person for other organizations and groups working for left-wing causes. Over the years, I provided nonviolence training to many organizations, including groups planning civil disobedience against apartheid in South Africa, against U.S. support for the contras in Nicaragua, against nuclear weapons, and, of course, against civilian nuclear power plants. On one occasion I was invited to give nonviolence training to a group of Brown University students planning to get arrested in an anti-apartheid demonstration. Everyone in the group introduced themselves to me, but by first name only. It was only several hours into the session that I realized that the slight blonde woman in the group who had introduced herself as "Amy" was Amy Carter, President Carter's daughter.

Shortly after getting out of jail after the Seabrook occupation, I left for Asia with Russ Johnson. Our first stop in Asia was Bombay, where we were the guests of Daniel Mazgaonkar, a Gandhian activist. Daniel arranged for me to deliver a lecture on the nonviolence movement in the United States at the Mani Bhavan, the Gandhi Museum in Bombay. The audience largely consisted of elderly Gandhian activists, many of whom had known the Mahatma during his lifetime. (This was not a good thing; it betokened the inability of the Gandhian movement in India to attract new people.) The focus of my talk was the importance of the Seabrook demonstration as a turning point in the nonviolent movement in the United States. Seabrook, I said, was the first time outside of the civil rights movement that we had succeeded in having large numbers of demonstrators both accept nonviolence philosophically and, as a practical matter, actually engage in a significant degree of nonviolence preparation before participating in an action.

10

After the War:
Human Rights in Vietnam

AS THE LIBERATION FORCES opened their final offensive in the central highlands of Vietnam in March 1975, and refugees started streaming south, President Ford said that the people of Vietnam were "voting with their feet," fleeing Communism. The president's subtext was clear: the Vietnamese fear and hate the Communist tyrants, and the United States had been right in Vietnam all along. The war would be over in a matter of weeks, but Ford's comments were the opening salvo in a new battle, the battle to interpret the lessons of Vietnam for Americans.

In fact, there were at that time multiple factors accounting for the flood of refugees that filled the screens of American televisions and the front pages of American newspapers. Some refugees were in fact fleeing Communism. The first provinces and cities to be liberated—Pleiku, Kontum, Ban Me Thuot—were all in the Central Highlands, the part of Vietnam where many Catholic refugees from the north had settled in 1954. They had come south at the time of the Geneva Agreement that had ended the French-Indochina War (1945–1954) in response to a massive propaganda effort that had emphasized the alleged anti-Catholic sentiment of the Communists. "The Virgin Mary has gone south" was one of the slogans from that time. These Catholics were deeply anti-Communist: they had fled Communism once twenty years earlier, and in the spring of 1975 they were genuinely frightened of what might happen to them under a new régime.

But many more of the refugees were fleeing because they feared American and South Vietnamese bombing. Throughout the long years of the war, whenever a city or province had "fallen" to the other side, the U.S. Air Force had devastated the city or province with ærial bombardment. The United States euphemistically called the policy "area denial"—the bombing was a means of denying territory to enemy forces. This had happened in Hue at the time of the Tet Offensive in 1968, in Quang Tri in 1972, and was happening already in Ban Me Thuot in 1975. In other words, the great bulk of the refugees were not fleeing from Communism, but rather from the perfectly predictable American-South Vietnamese bombing that inevitably followed closely on the heels of a Communist victory. In fact, AFSC medical aid staff in the Central Highlands at the time reported that many refugees were actually fleeing west rather than east—that is, away from Saigon forces, not toward them—despite the difficulty of the mountainous terrain in that direction. This fact went virtually unmentioned in the Western press.

But the real problem with President Ford's remarks was not that he misunderstood the ætiology and meaning of the refugee flow. The real problem was the implication that his remarks, if widely believed by Americans, could have for future American foreign policy.

When the final American evacuation from Vietnam occurred at the end of April, the only Americans to remain behind in Vietnam through the change in governments in southern Vietnam were the medical aid staff from AFSC and the Mennonite Central Committee (MCC). Thus, for a time, AFSC and the MCC had a monopoly on accurate, firsthand news from Vietnam at a time when there were no American soldiers, diplomats, CIA operatives, or journalists there. The firsthand insights provided by these staff would prove critical in the debates over Vietnam that broke out during the years that followed.

Things were relatively quiet for a bit over a year after the change in governments in southern Vietnam, and then a furious debate erupted— first just within the peace movement and then with the wider public— over the status of human rights in postwar Vietnam.

It started slowly. In the October 1976 issue of *Fellowship,* the magazine of FOR, editor Jim Forest published an article alleging that there were 300,000 political prisoners in Vietnam. Jim was a longtime peace activist. He had been chairman of the Catholic Peace Fellowship and had participated in the draft-board Action of the Milwaukee Fourteen in September 1968. "My time in prison," wrote Jim (referring to his sentence for the Milwaukee Fourteen Action) "was like a stay in a Hilton hotel compared to the post-liberation sufferings" of these Vietnamese political prisoners.

The next month, Jim organized eighty prominent peace activists to sign a letter addressed to the Vietnamese government. The signers included Joan Baez; Phil and Dan Berrigan; Dan Ellsberg; Sandy Gottlieb, director of SANE; Bishop Thomas Gumbleton; Jim Peck; Henry Schwarzschild of the American Civil Liberties Union; and Mitch Snyder. After discussing alleged human rights violations, the letter said:

> We call for a complete public accounting of those detained or imprisoned indicating, as well, the charges for which they are held. We call on the government of Vietnam to facilitate on-the-spot inspection by the United Nations, Amnesty International or other independent international agencies in order to assure that those in the government's charge are treated in accord with international covenants regarding human rights. We call on you to release any individuals who are held purely because of their religious or political convictions.

The letter was transmitted to the Vietnamese government, but no response was forthcoming.

In December, frustrated by the lack of a response, Jim and some of the other signers tried to deliver the letter to the office of the Vietnamese observer at the United Nations in New York. Rebuffed again, the signers released their letter at a press conference on December 28. Two days later, Vietnam's UN observer rejected the charges of the Forest group that Vietnam held between 200,000 and 300,000 political prisoners (Jim used different figures at different times).

A few months later, in April 1977, Jim circulated another appeal, this time addressed to Vietnamese Prime Minister Pham Van Dong concerning "a crisis between the Unified Buddhist Church of Vietnam and the state authorities." Again there were charges of religious repression, political prisoners, and opposition newspapers being closed down.

The debate over human rights in Vietnam escalated further. On May 30, 1979, Joan Baez and eighty co-signers placed full page advertisements in the *New York Times, Washington Post, Los Angeles Times*, and other newspapers. Her "Open Letter to the Socialist Republic of

Vietnam" repeated many of the same charges that Jim Forest had raised earlier. Baez used the figure of 150,000 to 200,000 political prisoners and charged widespread torture and starvation of government opponents. Dan Berrigan, Sandy Gottlieb, Bishop Gumbleton, Staughton Lynd, and Brad Lyttle were among the prominent peace activists who signed the Baez appeal.

As with the earlier remarks by President Ford about the Vietnamese "voting with their feet," there were problems with the Forest-Baez charges on several different levels.

At one level, many of the specific charges made were just wrong. Jim charged that the Buddhist monk Thich (Venerable) Tri Quang, a leader of the An Quang pagoda, was one of the prominent Vietnamese political prisoners, and that his arrest was part of a more generalized repression against the Buddhists. But AFSC staff in Vietnam had met repeatedly with Buddhist monks who reported that neither Thich Tri Quang, nor any of the An Quang leaders, had been arrested. Moreover, in their postwar travels in Vietnam, AFSC staff found no evidence of the generalized repression against the Buddhists that so exercised Jim. Jim charged that the School of Youth for Social Services had been closed down, and that the director and his assistant had been badly beaten. But at the time these events were supposedly happening, AFSC staff in Vietnam, Julie Forsythe and Sophie Quinn-Judge, had been at the school (which was not closed) and met with the director (who had been neither arrested nor beaten). Jim spoke of repression against Protestants, but the MCC staff in Vietnam, Jim Klassen and Max Ediger, reported no such repression—they continued teaching Bible classes, holding church services, and baptizing people. Where the Baez letter charged widespread torture of political dissidents, the Amnesty International country reports on Vietnam for 1977 and 1978 did not list a single verified incident of torture.

Factual accuracy is important, and the many falsehoods in the Forest and Baez charges did matter. But the wider context was important, too.

Many Americans believed that the exodus of the boat people refugees after 1975 was evidence of the brutality of the new Vietnam under Communism. But the reasons for the exodus, like the reasons for the refugee flow from the Central Highlands in March 1975, were multiple. Some Vietnamese, especially those who had collaborated with the American invaders, were no doubt ideological refugees fleeing Communism. But AFSC staff interviewed and worked with boat people refugees in Hong Kong and Malaysia, and found that most were economic, not political, refugees, fleeing deprivation at home wrought largely by a decade of war and, especially, American bombing that had devastated the agricultural economy of the country. Some of these economic refugees were ethnic Chinese who had been part of a merchant class in southern Vietnam and stood to lose their relatively privileged position under the rigors of the new socialist règime.

At the very heart of the human rights controversy was the sensitive issue of political prisoners. After the war, there were, in fact, thousands of Vietnamese held in what Forest and Baez called "re-education camps." (Actually, the word used by the Vietnamese to describe the camps, *hoc-tap*, translates as "study-practice.") As Jim pointed out accurately, these people were held against their will and were not free to go home if they wished. However, contrary to Forest and Baez's charges, most were held for days, weeks or months, not years; nevertheless, some were held for longer periods. Here, once again, context was important.

The crucial question the Vietnamese re-education camps posed for pacifists and others with humanitarian leanings was this: how can a deeply divided society effect a reconciliation after years of bitter internal division and war? Let us remember two critical points here. First, the years of war of which I speak were caused by the United States; the Vietnam War was *not* primarily a civil war between Vietnamese, but rather a conflict between a foreign invading power (the United States) and Vietnamese fighting for independence. Second, many of the Vietnamese in re-education camps were, by any fair definition, war criminals.

There are many models of what societies can do to heal such wounds of war, many models of how to deal with war criminals. After World War II, at Nuremberg (and other lesser-known trials), the United States gave accused Nazi war criminals lots of due process: we brought formal criminal charges (although without worrying about such niceties as *ex post facto* law), permitted legal representation for the accused, held public trials, and then hanged the bastards. In France after liberation, there was less of the due process and more of the hanging. Few war crimes trials were held, but a great many Vichy collaborators were strung up on trees and lampposts by their outraged neighbors.

As a pacifist, I oppose capital punishment, even for convicted war criminals, even if they are afforded lots of procedural rights before they are executed. The idea of re-educating people for a few weeks and then attempting to re-integrate them into society is much more to my liking.

To be sure, the Vietnamese model was not a perfect one. Nevertheless, the comparison with what the United States and others did after World War II is a useful one, because it highlights the difficulty of the issue. Since 1975, the world has seen yet a newer model for postwar reconciliation, the Truth and Reconciliation Commission set up in South Africa after the toppling of the apartheid government in 1994. In the truth-commission model, former war criminals are offered amnesty in exchange for full confessions about their wartime misdeeds. The hope is that two separate needs will be served—a truth about a shameful past will be exposed, and a reconciliation for the future may be hastened. As a pacifist, I like the truth-commission model better than the Vietnamese model of re-education. On the other hand, I must acknowledge that the truth-commission model was only first invented twenty years after the Vietnam War ended. As an American, I must also consider the extent to which it is my job to attack the Vietnamese model when it was, after all, my country's actions that created the occasion for re-education in Vietnam in the first place.

Aside from the specifics, it was the wider context of the human rights debate that was important as Americans grappled with the lessons of Vietnam. If the Communist government of Vietnam tortured and starved its political opponents, maybe the anti-war movement had been wrong all along. Maybe the lesson of Vietnam was, after all, the lesson of Munich: it is dangerous to appease ruthless totalitarians. On the other hand, the lesson I wanted Americans to learn from Vietnam was that our country was an imperialist aggressor—that, as I had said when I had refused to register for the draft in August 1969, Vietnam was just another example of the same disease that had led us into Guatemala in 1954 and into the Dominican Republic in 1965—and that we must work hard not to repeat these mistakes in the future.

The Forest-Baez charges provoked an angry response from many segments of the peace movement. In what must have been an exquisitely embarrassing moment for Jim Forest, FOR's Executive Secretary, Barton Hunter, in the March 1977 issue of *Fellowship*, expressly disavowed Jim's actions and even went so far as to say that Jim had misused FOR letterhead to circulate his appeal. Said Hunter: "Most members of the FOR. and its staff were not aware of [Forest's] project until it was well along and, in this connection, it must be clearly understood that the American Fellowship of Reconciliation is in no way responsible for letters or statements directed to the Vietnamese government or its UN Permanent Observer's office." Scholars like Noam Chomsky and activists like Dave McReynolds denounced Forest and Baez, both because of the many inaccuracies in their charges, and more broadly because of the political impact their campaigns could have. Forest and Baez may have represented a minority viewpoint in the peace community, but their charges received extensive publicity in the mainstream media.

The human rights debate degenerated into an unseemly mess of name-calling. Critics of Forest and Baez called them liars (and worse), and the Forest-Baez camp charged their critics with being hypocrites (and worse). At the height of the controversy, Carol Bragg and I stepped in and tried to effect a reconciliation. In January 1980, we wrote a long "Public Statement on Vietnam" and sought endorsements and signatures from people on *both* sides of the by-then acrimonious and bitter debate. Together with Carol and me, the signers of our initial letter to peace activists seeking endorsements were Dan Berrigan, who had signed both the Forest and Baez appeals, and Noam Chomsky and Dave McReynolds, who were among Forest and Baez's strongest critics. In that letter, we explained that we had several purposes in circulating the Public Statement. One was that we sought to examine some of the underlying causes of recent events in Vietnam, including the exodus of refugees by boat. Another was that we wanted to reaffirm points of agreement that united former peace activists on both sides of the human rights debate—that the war had been wrong and immoral, that the United States had a continuing obligation to provide humanitarian and reconstruction assistance to the people of Vietnam, and that efforts by our government to justify the war by reference to the refugees were dangerously off target. Finally, we said that we wanted to be a reconciling force within the peace movement, which was sorely divided by the debate.

The heart of the Public Statement on Vietnam was this:

> Those of us signing this statement have differing opinions on whether or not there are significant violations of human rights in Vietnam. We are united, however, in our support for the full range of human rights guaranteed by the Universal Declaration of Human Rights—civil and political, economic, social and cultural. We believe that human rights in Vietnam cannot be understood apart from events and circumstances shaped by the war and its aftermath. Historical events have produced conditions in Vietnam which would sorely test any government, whatever its political ideology. As advocates of human rights, we should seek to understand what obstacles exist to the fulfillment of human rights and what we can do to help eliminate those obstacles.

The Public Statement on Vietnam went on to make three concrete proposals for U.S. governmental policy to help Vietnam: normalize diplomatic and trade relations with Vietnam, provide emergency (short-term) food aid, and provide long-term development assistance.

Our immediate hope for the Public Statement on Vietnam was to take some of the sting out of the Forest-Baez attacks. Our wider purpose was to have an impact on the ongoing debate about the lessons of the war.

We were partly, but only partly, successful. Four hundred prominent anti-war activists signed the Public Statement on Vietnam. These included Bella Abzug, Julian Bond, Malcolm Boyd, Helen Caldicott, Rev. William Sloane Coffin Jr., Dave Dellinger, Howard Fast, Jules Feiffer, Tom Hayden, Jonathan Kozol, Bill Kunstler, Benjamin Spock, and Studs Terkel. Three Nobel Prize laureates signed: George Wald, Salvadore Luria, and Albert Szent-Gyorgyi. As we had hoped, some of the signers of our Public Statement on Vietnam had signed the Forest or Baez statements, including Dan Berrigan, Robert Bly, Robert McAfee Brown, Richard Deats, Lawrence Ferlinghetti, Allen Ginsberg, Bishop Gumbleton, Scott Kennedy, Staughton Lynd, and Jim Peck. Also, as we had hoped, some of Forest and Baez's harshest critics signed the Public

Statement, including Jane Fonda, Noam Chomsky, John McAuliff, Dave McReynolds, and Paul and Sophie Quinn-Judge.

But we failed to get either Joan Baez or Jim Forest to sign.

In addition, our release of the Public Statement on Vietnam at a press conference in Washington on April 18, 1980, received almost no coverage in the mainstream press. We did, however, receive some favorable coverage in the peace movement press.

We presented the Public Statement, with its call for normalized relations and food aid for Vietnam, to the White House. Carol and I put together a group of prominent signers, including Nobel laureate George Wald, to participate in this meeting. Of course, our pleas had little or no effect on U.S. policy, although there was some interesting publicity as a result of the meeting. We met at the White House with National Security Council member Lincoln Bloomfield and NSC staffer Roger Sullivan. Dr. Bloomfield, a political scientist on leave from MIT, made some intemperate remarks during the meeting. Apparently provoked by some frank talk by Dr. Wald, Bloomfield blurted out that he could think of no reason to provide humanitarian assistance to Vietnam other than "liberal, neurotic guilt." Shortly thereafter, I was quoted in the *New York Times* about what Bloomfield had said, and Bloomfield had a letter to the editor published in the *Times* taking me to task. In turn, I published a letter in the *Times* rebuking Bloomfield (by name) and outlining the humanitarian and political reasons for such aid.

The controversy surrounding the status of human rights in post-war Vietnam was part of a wider issue that had vexed much of the peace movement throughout the war (and has continued since then). This was the question of how the American peace movement in general, and pacifists in particular, viewed the Vietnamese Communists, the Hanoi government and the Provision Revolutionary Government (PRG) of southern Vietnam. During the war, just as after it, some anti-Communists in the peace movement accused AFSC and other pacifist groups of hyprocrisy and willful blindness with regard to atrocities committed by the Communists in Vietnam. We were accused of inappropriately criticizing the United States only, while viewing the Vietnamese Communists through rose-colored glasses. One of the most outspoken of these critics was the late Professor Guenther Lewy of the University of Massachusetts at Amherst. His 1988 book, *Peace & Revolution: The Moral Crisis of American Pacifism*, may be the most extensive, detailed, and passionately articulated rendering of one side of this debate. Dr. Lewy's thesis is succinctly stated in the opening sentences of the preface: "Over the past twenty years, American pacifism has undergone a remarkable transformation. While at one time pacifists were single-mindedly devoted to the principles of nonviolence and reconciliation, today most pacifist groups defend the moral legitimacy of armed struggle and guerrilla warfare, and they praise and support the communist régimes emerging from such conflicts." About Vietnam, Dr. Lewy wrote:

> The extent to which, by the early 1970s, the AFSC had positioned itself on the side of the PRG [Provisional Revolutionary Government] and North Vietnam was brought out by the AFSC's reaction to the North Vietnamese Easter offensive in 1972. In response to this full-scale invasion of South Vietnam by heavily armed North Vietnamese divisions, President Nixon on 6 April had ordered the resumption of the bombing of North Vietnam, suspended since 1968, as well as air strikes and naval gunfire support for the beleaguered South Vietnamese. On 3 May the AFSC held a vigil in front of the White House, and a statement, drafted by the board of directors, was delivered to the president. The statement made no mention of the North Vietnamese invasion, which had prompted the new American involvement, but instead denounced Nixon for calling off the Paris talks and for ordering the resumption of the bombing of Hanoi and Haiphong.

The problems with Lewy's analysis are both small and large. I start with two of the smaller problems. Lewy speaks of the "invasion of South Vietnam by heavily armed North Vietnamese divisions. . . ." This betrays a lack of understanding of Vietnamese history. Article I Paragraph 1 of the 1954 Geneva Agreement, which ended the French attempt to retake its Vietnam colony after World War II, said that there was only one Vietnam, not two. The 17th parallel was to be only a *temporary, military* demarcation line, a ceasefire line, *not* a political boundary between countries. Because there was only one Vietnam, it was profoundly wrong to talk about "North Vietnam" and "South Vietnam." So-called North Vietnamese troops in so-called South Vietnam was no more an "invasion" than U.S. troops in Ft. Bragg are an "invasion." There *was*, in fact, an invasion of Vietnam; it was the invasion by 500,000 *foreign* troops. Vietnamese troops in Vietnam were not foreign troops; American troops were.

Another one of the smaller problems with Lewy's analysis is the portrayal of Nixon's actions as having been "prompted" by the Vietnamese, of somehow being an appropriate response to the offensive by the liberation forces. The United States was the aggressor in Vietnam. There *was* an action-reaction cycle at work in Vietnam, but it was not the innocent, beset Americans responding reasonably to the wrongful invasion by the North Vietnamese. It was the Vietnamese responding to the invasion of their country by foreign troops.

The deeper issue that Lewy highlights, however, is something about which he is absolutely correct. Most of the pacifists in AFSC, WRL, and FOR did *not* view the violence used by the Vietnamese as identical to the violence used by the Americans. As pacifists, we deplore *all* violence regardless of by whom committed and regardless of the noble statements of purpose that accompany it. If we were in Vietnam, we would refuse to bear arms for the liberation forces, even as we refused to bear arms for the United States. Nevertheless, most pacifists recognized the differences between the two sides in this war. While we deplored the means, we did support the *goal* for which the Vietnamese liberation forces were fighting, freedom and independence for their country. And we equally opposed the *goal* for which the United States was fighting, the neocolonial subjugation of a foreign land.

An analogy here might be helpful. Some pacifists might urge women to try to avoid the use of violence even in resisting sexual assault. But everyone, including those pacifists, would recognize the important differences between the actions of a man who rapes a woman at knifepoint and the woman who resists the attack by kicking and scratching. It is not that anyone here is endorsing violence; but no one I know, pacifist or nonpacifist, would equate the actions of those two people.

Even pacifists who refuse to bear arms can understand and appreciate the fact that not all sides in a war are morally identical. All the pacifist war resisters I know who were imprisoned during World War II have told me that they wanted the Allies to win and the Axis to lose. None cheered when news came over the prison radio of Nazi victories.

Lewy is also correct that the issue is wider than just Vietnam; the broader issue is how American pacifists relate in general to human rights abuses committed by U.S. allies or client states and how we relate to such abuses committed by other countries. Lewy writes: "Pacifist groups decry the imperfect human rights record of American allies like Israel and South Korea but find few words of condemnation for the far worse record of Communist-ruled states like North Korea and Ethiopia."

To be sure, there is something attractive, for pacifists especially, about taking what Lewy would probably call an evenhanded approach— criticizing alike governments of the left and the right where criticism is warranted. It is easy to see why such an approach would be attractive to pacifists in particular, for it is uniquely the pacifist insight that violence is wrong regardless of who commits it. It is the pacifists who say, we don't care if your violence is committed in the name of free enterprise or the workers' revolution; violence is violence, and we oppose all violence. One of the reasons why Amnesty International, recipient of the Nobel Peace Prize in 1977, is so well regarded is precisely that it takes an evenhanded approach to prisoners of conscience, torture, and capital punishment regardless of the politics of the perpetrators or the victims.

And yet, the issue is complicated, and I disagree with Lewy's approach. Although I am a pacifist, I am not only a pacifist. I am an *American* pacifist. As an American pacifist, I must recognize two things.

First, it is my country that is the major purveyor of violence in the world today. It is my country that most frequently and most recklessly invades other countries. It is my country that is also responsible for so much of the violence of the status quo that keeps hundreds of millions in the Third World in desperate poverty. An early, classic exposition of the concept of the "violence of the status quo" comes from Jim Bristol's article, published in the October 1972 issue of *Gandhi Marg*, a pacifist journal. The article was entitled "Nonviolence: Not First for Export."

Bristol was a lifelong pacifist. As a Lutheran minister, he was entitled to a ministerial deferment to the draft during World War II. Instead, he resisted the draft and went to prison. Bristol devotes the first half of his essay to contrasting violence and nonviolence as means of social change, concluding that nonviolence is morally and practically superior. Only toward the end of the essay does Bristol introduce the concept of the violence of the status quo:

> This violence is expressed in the agony of millions of men, women and children who in varying degrees suffer hunger, poverty, ill-health, lack of education, non-acceptance by their fellowmen. It is compounded by the slights and insults of rampant injustice, of exploitation, of police brutality, of a thousand indignities from dawn to dusk and through the night.

Then, with truly startling prescience, Bristol writes: "While two wrongs never make a right, before we deplore terrorism it is essential for us to recognize fully and clearly whose 'terrorism' came first, so that we can assess what is cause and what is effect."

The second important thing I must recognize is that the United States is, as I have said before, a reasonably democratic country. As a politically active American, I can realistically hope to influence the policies of my country.

These two factors, when viewed together, show why I, as an *American* pacifist, have a special, unique responsibility to try to influence and affect the policies of my own government. I deplore the Cuban government's arrest of dissidents and its discrimination against gays. But I am not a Cuban. I am an American, and while I cannot hope to have much influence on Fidel Castro, I can and should expect to have an influence on my own country.

It is also worth mentioning that the term "human rights" is a broad one. We in the United States valorize one type of human rights, civil and political: the rights of free speech, free press, and freedom of assembly and dissent. Yet as Carol and I pointed out in the Public Statement on Vietnam, the United Nations' Universal Declaration of Human Rights also protects economic and social rights: the rights to food, shelter, medical care and education. There is no excuse for Cuba to hold those who criticize the government as political prisoners, but it is also true that Cuba has lower infant mortality than the United States, lower illiteracy than the United States, and a far better doctor-patient ratio than the United States. While the civil liberties that we so cherish in the

United States are extremely important, Americans must also broaden their view of human rights to include economic and social rights as well. When we do, we will come to see that American foreign policy is one of the greatest violators of human rights in the world today.

Our moral obligation as *American* pacifists to pay particularly close and careful attention to the uniquely important role of our country in driving international affairs may be illustrated by the case of the Communist Khmer Rouge. The government of Pol Pot came to power in Cambodia on April 17, 1975, with the defeat of the United States and the Lon Nol government, and remained in power until January 7, 1979. There can be no excuse for the monstrous crimes against humanity committed by the Khmer Rouge, and I take a back seat to nobody in criticizing them. I saw the killing fields myself; the awful stench of thousands of rotting corpses filled my nostrils. Unlike many Americans, I devoted years of my life to ending United States diplomatic support for the Khmer Rouge after they had been deposed by the Vietnamese invasion. I worked tirelessly to raise funds in the United States to help heal the wounds in Cambodia that had been inflicted by the Khmer Rouge, and I worked (unsuccessfully) to get my government to provide such humanitarian aid.

Yet there is a terrible irony here. The Khmer Rouge would never have come to power had it not been for the actions of the United States between 1970 and 1975. For most of the 1960s, while war consumed Vietnam and then Laos, Cambodia was an island at peace. The head of state, Prince Sihanouk, was a neutralist, and part of the reason for his overwhelming popularity with the Cambodian people was that he had kept his country out of the war then engulfing the rest of Indochina. The Khmer Rouge were a presence in the Cambodian jungles during the 1960s but they had little support from the Khmer people. Prince Sihanouk was an esteemed and popular leader, the country was stable, and Sihanouk had kept Cambodia out of war. In this context, Cambodians were not inclined to support the bizarre and extreme form of Maoist agrarian revolution that had always been espoused by the Khmer Rouge.

Then Nixon expanded the war into Cambodia. First came the bombing. Then, as I discussed in chapter 5, in March 1970 the United States helped to overthrow Sihanouk and put a Cambodian puppet, Lon

Nol, into his place. The United States invaded Cambodia. Thousands of Cambodians were killed, and fully one third of the population was made refugees by U.S. bombing. The Khmer Rouge, which had before been an insignificant factor in the life of the country, were transformed into the primary opposition to the United States presence. The United States did for Pol Pot what he had never been able to do for himself—we made him a more popular figure who could fairly be seen to be opposing the United States' invasion of his country.

In short, while there is no excuse for the atrocities committed by the Khmer Rouge, it is also important to understand that the Khmer Rouge would have had not one chance in a thousand of coming to power in Cambodia had it not been for the actions of Nixon and Kissinger. If not for Nixon and Kissinger, there would have been no killing fields in Cambodia. In this context, it is not enough for Americans merely to decry the atrocities of the Khmer Rouge. Americans must also understand the unique and crucially important role played by our country in bringing the Khmer Rouge to power.

We pacifists are right to oppose all violence, regardless of who commits it or what excuses are given for it. But we American pacifists are also right to recognize that we have an especially important role to play in bringing about a world of peace because we are well situated to have an effect on the world's greatest purveyor of violence, our own government.

11

After the War: Was the Peace Movement Effective?

I HAVE ARGUED IN THIS BOOK that destroying draft files was an effective anti-war tactic, and in the previous chapter, I began to consider some of the lessons of the Vietnam War, specifically those arising from the human rights debate that erupted among peace activists after the war ended. But I have not yet addressed the wider question of whether the multifaceted anti-war movement as whole was a success. Did we end the war? Did we even help to end the war? Were we successful in achieving our goals? If so, what goals did we achieve?

Professional historians and peace-studies scholars have chronicled the Vietnam era from a variety of perspectives, but their conclusions about the efficacy of the peace movement as an undifferentiated whole, or of specific, narrower tactics within the wider movement, are elusive. Professor Lawrence S. Wittner's rather vague conclusion in *Rebels Against War: The American Peace Movement, 1933–1983* is typical of the problem: "Beginning in the 1960s, the peace movement emerged as a powerful force in American life . . . the peace movement was no longer a marginal force in American politics, but an important participant, a serious contender for power."

A reader who looks for specific peace movement tactics being tied to specific (positive) responses by the government will not find much in the extant literature (with two notable exceptions that I discuss below, one of which was attested to by a remarkable and unexpected source).

It is easy to see why the historians and scholars are reluctant to posit cause and effect between actions of the peace movement and governmental responses. Causation in world affairs—what specific event led to what specific result—is almost always impossible to prove with any degree of certainty. To be sure, on some narrow issues it is sometimes possible to draw such a link. We know that the picture of Chris Kearns burning his draft card, printed in the August 20, 1965, issue of *Life* magazine, led to the swift passage of the draft-card burning bill in the Senate the following week, because the senators who took to the Senate floor told us so. But such obvious correlations are rare. Moreover, part of the reason that the question of the Vietnam peace movement's overall effectiveness is such a difficult one is that the natural concomitant of the question "Were we effective?" is "Were we effective *at doing what?*" Depending on what one thinks we were trying to accomplish, we were more or less effective. At least for those of us in the pacifist wing of the wider peace movement, our interest in peace activity during the Vietnam War was always in part wider than only affecting this or that specific American policy.

I do not pretend to be a historian; to the extent that I can bring a useful perspective to such questions, it is as an activist, not as a scholar.

Certainly, the Vietnam peace movement accomplished a number of very specific goals. The government used Selective Service to conscript hundreds of thousands of men to fight, kill, and die in an undeclared war. At the same time, the government provided draft-age men with little or no help in negotiating the arcane maze of sixteen separate classifications, exemptions, and deferments that existed under Selective Service law. The peace movement—most notably AFSC and Women Strike for Peace at the national level, but also hundreds of unaffiliated local peace organizations and centers—stepped in and provided thousands of draft counselors at hundreds of locations nationwide who gave vital, often life-saving information to millions of men. I was never involved in draft counseling because I did not see my role as providing objective information about deferments to draft-age men; I was more interested in organizing total resistance to the draft. Still, to the millions of men that were helped, the creation of this nationwide network of draft counselors was not a small accomplishment.

Later in the war, peace activists set up coffeehouses outside military bases to provide information on conscientious objection and desertion to soldiers. An underground railroad was established to help spirit deserters (as well as draft evaders) to Canada. A stream of such deserters passed through my apartment when I lived in Manhattan, and

I was only one tiny cog in a large and sprawling operation. (Professor Wittner puts the number of military deserters at 40,000 in 1968 and 53,000 in 1969.) Again, for the many men we helped, this was not a small accomplishment.

But what about changing American policy in Vietnam? Did the peace movement ever have an effect on changing U.S. policy? One of the clearest examples of the direct effect of the peace movement on U.S. Vietnam policy was the eleventh-hour aborting of Operation Duck Hook by President Nixon in response to the Moratorium activities of autumn 1969.

Shortly after taking office in January 1969, Nixon, who had won the election in large part based on his promise that he had a "secret plan" to end the war, directed his aides to prepare a major escalation of the war, Operation Duck Hook. Nixon gave the Vietnamese until November 1 to capitulate at the Paris negotiations. If Nixon's ultimatum were not met, the United States would mine Haiphong Harbor, bomb Hanoi, and destroy North Vietnam's agricultural dikes. These actions were to be followed by a United States ground invasion of North Vietnam and the use of nuclear weapons. The specific plans called for the use of two atomic bombs. As activist-scholar Joseph Gerson recounts in his book, *With Hiroshima Eyes* (1995), Nixon's threats were conveyed to the Vietnamese in July through a French diplomat in Hanoi, and in August by Henry Kissinger on one of his secret trips to the Paris negotiations. The threat of American use of nuclear weapons in Vietnam at that time was confirmed by Dan Ellsberg, writing in the March 1975 issue of *Fellowship*. On October 1, Nixon signaled the seriousness of his intentions by raising the alert status of U.S. military forces worldwide.

A range of scholars agree that it was the autumn Moratorium demonstrations that year that stayed Nixon's hand. On October 15, literally millions of Americans participated in hundreds of separate events in cities and towns across the country. On November 15, 500,000 people rallied in Washington, DC. (This was the demonstration at which the Boston Eight surfaced, over my objections, with stolen draft files.) The huge demonstration was preceded by a three-day March Against Death, conceived and organized by Ron Young. For three days and nights, 45,000 demonstrators walked in single file from Arlington National Cemetery, past the White House, to the steps of the Capitol. Each demonstrator carried a candle and a placard bearing the name of an American or Vietnamese who had been killed in the war. At the Capitol, the placards were placed into coffins. To many participants and observers, the power and quiet dignity of the March Against Death made this the most moving demonstration of the entire war.

Those of us who participated in these events were frustrated at the time. Nixon, in a show of bravado, let it be known that his administration would not be swayed by protests and that he had spent November 15 watching a football game on television rather than meeting with a delegation from the anti-war movement. Only later did we learn of the effect that those demonstrations had. Professor Melvin Small, in *Johnson, Nixon, and the Doves,* concludes that "The Moratorium helped to convince Nixon that Americans would not accept the savage blows envisioned in Operation Duck Hook." Nixon himself substantially corroborates this account in his own writing after leaving office. Both Ellsberg and Joseph Gerson go further, concluding that the autumn 1970 demonstrations led *directly* to the abandonment of the plan by the Nixon administration. Ellsberg concludes:

> Those who demonstrated against the war saved hundreds of thousands of lives, certainly. But we are in their debt for having avoided a probable nuclear war. The benefits to humanity of having avoided nuclear war are simply incalculable.

Yet, in other important ways, the peace movement surely failed. Between 1967 and 1968, the slogan of the umbrella National Mobilization Committee to End the War was "From Dissent to Resistance." During this period, huge demonstrations were held, individual draft resistance soared, acts of draft-file destruction multiplied, there was a nationally coordinated academic strike, and the Columbia uprising occurred. There was lots of both dissent *and* resistance. Meanwhile, U.S. troop levels in Vietnam increased from 485,000 to 536,000.

Some of the worst and most fundamental attitudes of Americans—attitudes that allowed the war to happen in the first place—were not changed by the long efforts of the peace movement either. I discussed in chapter 2 how the change of American attitude that came about at the time of the Tet Offensive in 1968 was a shallow one. To many Americans, the problem with the war after Tet was not that it was wrong and immoral, but that it didn't seem to be working. Much the same attitude can be seen in the public's response to the U.S. invasion of Iraq in 2003. Most of those who did dissent raised superficial issues: the cost of post-war reconstruction is too steep, Bush may have lied about the presence of weapons of mass destruction, it is impractical to think that we can pacify Iraq. Writing in the *New York Times* of April 2, 2004, liberal columnist Bob Herbert said, "We are mired in a savage mess in Iraq, and no ones knows how to get out of it." I wonder if he was aware of how closely his remarks tracked the *Times* editorial of March 24, 1968, written in the wake of the Tet Offensive, to the effect that "the search for a military solution [in Vietnam] is futile . . ." Immediately after the U.S. invasion of Iraq, President Bush's war policy was wildly popular with the American people. As had been the case with Vietnam, it was only later, when it seemed that the war policy was not really working, that the American public soured on the war in Iraq. Back in 2003, the very few who dared to say the truth about the U.S. invasion of Iraq were viewed by the mainstream as a kooky fringe, but the simple truth was that for the United States to invade Iraq was a crime against humanity. Indeed, waging a "war of aggression"—that is, attacking another country that had not attacked you first—was the heart of the Nuremberg indictment.

Other attitudes have similarly not changed. Americans still do not seem to understand that actions have consequences. In the previous chapter, I discussed the catastrophic consequences of Nixon and Kissinger's actions in Cambodia between 1970 and 1975, consequences that are very much still present for the people of Cambodia today. Other examples from recent history abound. For instance, in 1953, the United States, through the CIA, overthrew the democratically elected government of Dr. Mohammad Mossadegh in Iran; we installed a brutal dictator, the Shah, in his place. (For a fine hour-by-hour and minute-by-minute account of the coup, see Steven Kinzer's wonderful *All the Shah's Men.*) Twenty-six years later, in 1979, the people of Iran rose up and ousted the U.S.-installed despot. Americans were shocked—shocked!—that Iranian students would then, in their fury, turn on the American embassy and take hostages. There may have been multiple causes that contributed to the overthrow of the Shah, but the takeover of the American embassy in 1979 can be directly traced to the U.S.-organized coup in

1953 and of the twenty-six years of U.S. support thereafter for the hated Shah. No one should have been surprised. Actions have consequences.

But Americans did not learn, and in 2003 the United States invaded Iraq and toppled Saddam Hussein. Aside from a few people in the Bush administration, the person in the world who was most hoping for such a stupid move by the United States was Osama bin Laden, for the U.S. invasion of Iraq will surely send a new generation of eager young recruits into his arms. What was especially distressing about the tiger cages in Vietnam when Don Luce revealed their existence to the world was that the abuse and torture of political prisoners on Con Son was neither an aberration nor a mistake but rather part of conscious, deliberate policy by the U.S.-Saigon forces. A generation later in Iraq we have American abuses of prisoners at Abu Ghraib. When the next terrorist attack against Americans occurs, we will, once again, be surprised and shocked because, for the most part, we Americans have still not grasped that our actions have consequences. The failure of the peace movement to teach this simple lesson to Americans must surely be counted as a major failure.

For better or for worse, activists like me seem to have a different perspective on events than the scholars do. For example, in *Johnson, Nixon, and the Doves*, Professor Small describes at some length the demise of the anti-war movement after protests in the spring of 1970:

> The nationwide response to the Cambodian invasion and the Kent State killings was the last success for the anti-war movement during the Nixon administration, at least in terms of the quantity, quality, and impact of mass demonstrations . . .
>
> When the North Vietnamese launched a major offensive in the spring of [1972] and Nixon responded with stepped-up bombing and the mining of the Haiphong harbor, he met little serious opposition. The boys were almost all home, the movement was in disarray, radicals and hippies were discredited. . . .
>
> The life had gone out of the movement.

In fact, from the perspective of one who was involved in the movement in 1972 and thereafter, very much the opposite appears to have been true. More than forty national organizations joined together to form the Coalition to Stop Funding the War. These included the traditional pacifist organizations like AFSC, WRL, and FOR that had been in the Fifth Avenue Vietnam Peace Parade Committee in 1965, then the Mobilization Committee to End the War, then the New Mobilization Committee—the successive coalitions that had sponsored the mass demonstrations—but the Coalition to Stop Funding the War also included mainline religious denominations such as the United Methodist Church, the Union of American Hebrew Congregations, and the United Presbyterian Church in the USA, and liberal groups such as Americans for Democratic Action. Professor Small is correct that peace movement strategy shifted away from mass demonstrations after 1972, but visibility in the press by means of mass demonstrations is not the only way to measure the strength of a movement. The forty national organizations that made up the Coalition mounted a nationwide lobbying effort aimed at cutting funding for the ongoing American war effort. The effort was both sophisticated and, more to the point, successful. For fiscal year 1975 (beginning October 1, 1974), the effort succeeded in getting Congress to cut the administration's request for aid to Saigon by over 50%, from $1.6 billion to $700 million.

As I discussed in chapter 7, the Tiger Cage Vigil and Fast in Washington during the summer of 1974 was coordinated closely with the Coalition to Stop Funding the War. The Tiger Cage Project was a centralized project in which participants came to Washington, DC, and lobbied members of Congress there. Immediately after the conclusion of the Tiger Cage Project, many of its sponsors participated in a decentralized effort called the "Week of Concern," September 29 through October 6, 1974. In Rhode Island, during the Week of Concern, we took the tiger cage display to a different city in the state each day. On Thursday evening, October 3, we sponsored a Religious Convocation for Peace at a local church, and on Friday evening, October 4, we sponsored a Vietnamese dinner with guest speaker Marj Nelson, a physician recently returned from service at the AFSC medical facility at Quang Ngai, Vietnam.

Similar events were held in about fifty cities nationwide. In Pasadena, California, a tiger cage was erected on the City Hall steps during the city art fair. In Holly Spring, Mississippi, signatures were collected on anti-war petitions addressed to members of Congress. In Connecticut, tiger cage displays appeared in New Britain, Bristol, Waterbury, New London, Storrs, Winsted, New Haven, Fairfield, Hartford, and Middletown. In Denver, Colorado, Joan Baez sat chained inside a tiger cage replica before singing at an anti-war event. An anti-war vigil in Chapel Hill, North Carolina, received front-page coverage in the local newspaper. In Davenport, Iowa, John Young, a former Vietnam prisoner of war, and Peg Mullen, a Gold Star mother, spoke at an anti-war program. Press conferences, public meetings, and church services were held in Indiana and Kentucky. A centerpiece for all of these events was lobbying members of Congress to cut off funds for the war. Where the Tiger Cage Project had brought participants to Washington to lobby members of Congress on the war, the Week of Concern brought lobbyists to senators' and representatives' home offices.

In December 1974, a Pastoral Letter signed by dozens of major religious leaders called peace activists to Washington, DC, in January 1975, for further action:

> We call the nation to action once again. We summon the members of religious communities of our nation to a National Assembly to Save the Peace Agreement in Washington, D.C. from January 25 to January 27, 1975, the second anniversary of the signing of the Agreement in Paris. We must communicate to our leaders an urgent demand that this nation live up to its pledged word at Paris, both by implementing its unkept promises and by ceasing current actions, such as massive military aid to the oppressive Thieu régime.

Thousands of activists attended the Assembly to Save the Peace Agreement. We chartered a bus to bring fifty Rhode Islanders to Washington for the event, and there was similar participation from all parts of the country. Over the weekend, a series of speakers including Don Luce trained participants in how to lobby Congress effectively. The climax of the Assembly was on Monday, January 27, when thousands of activists fanned out and visited nearly every senator and representative's office, urging a cutoff in funds for the war. The Tiger Cage Project, the Week of Concern, and the Assembly to Save the Peace Agreement were all complementary efforts. All focused on members of Congress, all involved extensive lobbying by constituents to cut American funds for Saigon.

The Assembly to Save the Peace Agreement was held in Washington, DC, in January 1975, on the second anniversary of the signing of the Paris Agreement on Vietnam. Photo courtesy of the American Friends Service Committee.

Lobbying members of Congress to cut off funds for the war was a major focus of the Assembly to Save the Peace Agreement. Shown here at a meeting with Rhode Island's senior senator, John O. Pastore (*far right*), are (*left to right*) William Barbour, Rosa Hodgson, Jerry Elmer, and the Reverend Richard Dannenfelser. Photo courtesy of the American Friends Service Committee.

Workshop during the Assembly to Save the Peace Agreement: Ngo Vinh Long (*far left*) and Ron Young (*second from right*). Photo courtesy of the American Friends Service Committee.

When the liberation forces launched their final offensive in the spring of 1975, the administration's hands were tied. That spring, the administration repeatedly, and with increasing desperation and then panic, sought supplemental spending authority to try to avert the coming defeat in Vietnam. Under tremendous, effective, coordinated lobbying pressure from the peace movement, Congress held fast. No more funds were forthcoming, and the war ended on April 30, 1975, with the victory of the liberation forces. While the public visibility of the movement may have faded with the end of the mass demonstrations, the life had surely not gone out of the movement. Far from being in disarray, the peace movement was surely at its most organized and perhaps at its most effective. Far from being discredited and marginalized as radicals and hippies, the peace movement worked more closely and more successfully during this period than ever before with mainline churches.

The singular effectiveness of the peace movement during this period was powerfully attested to shortly after the war ended by a most unexpected source. On January 27, 1976, the last U.S. Ambassador to Saigon, Graham Martin, testified before the House Committee on International Relations. In describing the reason for the American defeat in April 1975, Ambassador Martin said: "Military assistance for fiscal year 1975 had been reduced [by Congress] from the $1.6 billion original request to $1 billion in the fiscal year 1975 authorization . . . to $700 million in the final appropriation." Speaking of the effects of the peace movement during the period of the Tiger Cage Project and Week of Concern, Martin said, "In the United States the erosion of public support [for the war] was a progressive, palpable, almost measurable phenomena [sic] in the late summer and fall of 1974." Martin spoke of "the mounting crescendo of organized campaign" that came "to a focus with the December 'pastoral letter' convoking on January 29, 1975, [sic] in Washington the celebration of the second anniversary of the 1973 [Paris] accords."

Ambassador Martin went on to say that the decision of Congress to cut funds for the war "was made inevitable by one of the best propoaganda and pressure organizations the world has ever seen . . . The main organization I think is the Indochina Resources Center [sic], and I really think that another principal element would be the multifaceted activities of Mr. Don Luce . . . It's the constancy of the drumming in day after day after day of particular themes." Then the following exchange took place between Congressman Hamilton and Ambassador Martin:

> Mr. Hamilton. You impressed me with the great compliment you pay these people [peace activists], they have the resources to sway the whole country, 220 million Americans and the U.S. Congress.
>
> Ambassador Martin. I would fully concur with your statement that I am paying these people an enormous compliment. I mean it to be that. They deserve it . . . This is an enormously effective organization and I do think that they deserve the compliment I have paid them.

We pacifists—perhaps more than others in the peace movement, and probably more than the historians and scholars who study the peace movement—take a long-term view of social change. Doing so reveals important additional ways in which the Vietnam peace movement in the United States was effective.

When people asked Igal Roodenko what he had done during World War II, he often answered, "I fought in the war against war." His point was that his goal as an imprisoned pacifist war resister was not a short-term goal that focused on the immediate world situation right then. His goal was the long-term goal of making war itself an obsolete institution. My friend Jim Peck, who, like Igal, had been a World War II resister, expressed a similar sentiment in his prison memoir, *We Who Would Not Kill* (1958):

> I was convinced that a second world war was coming and I knew that when it did, I would refuse to kill and would be imprisoned as a result. I knew that my action and that of other COs would not stop the war. Yet I thought that setting an example was worthwhile. Some day the mass murder committed during wartime will be outlawed in the same way that individual murder is outlawed. It was time to make a start at bringing this about.

Igal and Jim had an important point. As a pacifist war resister during the Vietnam War, part of my goal was not just to affect U.S. policy in Vietnam in the short term. I wanted to continue the struggle that Igal, Jim, and others had participated in a generation earlier, the struggle to make war itself unthinkable. If nothing else, that struggle is surely a long-term one. An analogy may be seen in the struggle throughout the twentieth century for recognition of the right to be a conscientious objector.

During World War I, the only provision for COs was that members of traditional peace churches could go into the Army and serve in non-combatant roles. Seventeen unrecognized COs received death sentences. One hundred forty-two others were sentenced to life imprisonment, while still others received sentences as long as fifty years. No COs were actually executed, and all the COs still in jail in 1933 were pardoned. As a direct result of the World War I experiences of COs (and the lobbying by pacifists in 1940), the World War II draft law had more liberal provisions for COs in two important respects. First, conscientious objection was broadened to include all religious objectors, not just members of the historic peace churches. Second, in addition to noncombatant military service, provision was made for civilian alternative service. True, the Civilian Public Service (CPS) camps were under the control of an Army General, Louis Hershey (who was still head of Selective Service during the Vietnam War!) but many of the CPS camps were actually administered during the war by AFSC! During the Vietnam War, the provisions for COs were expanded again, this time by the Supreme Court, when it ruled in 1967 that a man need not believe in God to qualify as a conscientious objector (*Seeger*, 380 U.S. 163), and again in 1970 when the Court held that, the Selective Service Act's language to the contrary notwithstanding, nonreligious, purely ethical belief could qualify a man for CO status (*Welsh*, 398 U.S. 333).

Similar stories of progress over time can be seen with other social change movements. Eleanor Flexner, in her book *Century of Struggle* (1959), describes the 100 years of small and large protests that all contributed to the women's suffrage movement. Each separate demonstration may have been frustrating for the participants and without apparent effect on the American body politic, but the net result of all of them together was the passage of the Nineteenth Amendment. In the long struggle of the labor movement in the United States, each individual strike or union organizing effort may have arguably been futile or unsuccessful, but again, the net result of decades of labor struggle was a sea change in labor relations—minimum wage laws, maximum work weeks, worker safety standards, and so forth.

The lesson that I draw from this history is that much of the change that we pacifists are working toward is long-term in nature, and that in order to gauge properly our effectiveness, one needs to take a long view. In this context, the Vietnam peace movement clearly *was* effective in a variety of ways.

One way we were effective was by making nonviolent direct action, including civil disobedience, a widely used and respected tactic on the wider American scene. I organized participants for the April 1977 nonviolent occupation of Seabrook, and I know from firsthand experience that many of the participants, and nearly all the key organizers, were veterans of the Vietnam peace movement. As Professor Wittner put it, by shortly after the end of the war, "non-violent resistance had moved out of the category of Indian esoterica into the forefront of the American struggle against war and oppression."

Wittner, by his reference to "Indian esoteria"—that is, Gandhi—raises an important point about how movements build. It has often been said that the nonviolent peace movement of the 1960s owed a large debt to the civil rights movement's use of nonviolence and civil disobedience in the 1950s. But the civil rights movement of the 1950s surely owed much to the pacifist resisters to World War II. For example, the organizers of and participants in the first Freedom Ride in April 1947, called the Journey of Reconciliation, were in significant part a group of recently-released pacifist draft resisters from World War II—Wally Nelson, George Houser, Jim Peck, Igal Roodenko, and Bayard Rustin (as well as Ernest Bromley, a pacifist war tax resister who went to jail during World War II for nonpayment of war taxes). The efforts to desegregate lunch counters throughout the South in the late 1950s and early 1960s owed much to the efforts of Jim Peck and other imprisoned resisters to desegregate the mess halls of Danbury and other federal prisons during World War II. In a very real and direct way, the World War II witness of these pacifists showed the way for the nascent civil rights movement; the civil rights movement, in turn, showed the way for the Vietnam peace movement; and the Vietnam peace movement showed the way for movements that followed, including the anti-nuclear-power movement. Martin Luther King Jr., the American apostle of nonviolence, attributed his interest in civil disobedience to the Indian, Gandhi; but Gandhi, in his turn, credited the writings of an American, Henry David Thoreau.

Taking a long-term view of social change shows another way in which the Vietnam peace movement was effective—we helped to create a paradigm shift in the way many Americans view war in general. So widely recognized is this paradigm shift that conservatives even have a name for it; they call it the "Vietnam Syndrome," the hesitancy to send troops abroad on imperial adventures. A clear example of the paradigm shift I am describing can be seen in the events of February 1998.

In early February 1998, the Clinton administration was gearing up for a major attack on Iraq. The issue then, as later—was Saddam Hussein's possible possession of weapons of mass destruction and his refusal to allow international inspections. For weeks, the Clinton administration carefully prepared the public for the U.S. military action against Iraq. So foregone a conclusion was a U.S. attack on Iraq that, on February 16, the *New York Times* ran a front-page analysis by Steven Erlanger discussing the different factors that would influence the precise *timing* of the forthcoming attack: Ramadan, the winter Olympics, parents' weekend at Stanford (where Chelsea Clinton was in college), the time of the new moon. On the same day, at a news conference at the Pentagon, President Clinton laid out the U.S. goals for the upcoming attack.

The next day, as part of the administration's public relations blitz, Secretary of State Madeleine Albright, Defense Secretary William Cohen, and National Security Advisor Samuel Berger were dispatched to Ohio State University in Columbus to attend a carefully staged pro-war rally before a prescreened audience. To their shock and amazement, the administration's spokespeople met with strong and outspoken opposition. The confrontation between the students and the cabinet secretaries, during which the cabinet secretaries were seen to be unable to articulate a coherent story as to why we needed to go to war, was carried live worldwide on CNN. There was an overnight sea change in public understanding of what was happening. At the eleventh hour, war was averted.

The anti-war protest activities at Ohio State on February 17, 1998, were a direct result of the work done by Vietnam peace activists between 1965 and 1975. The fact that those student protesters confronted the administration officials with their anti-war message *before* the war started and without American lives in jeopardy showed that at least *some* of the lessons that the Vietnam peace movement had tried to teach had gotten through.

12

There Is No Way to Peace; Peace Is the Way

THERE ARE MYRIAD TACTICS AVAILABLE to the nonviolent activist. In addition to the four broader categories of tactics treated more fully below, I have in this volume mentioned or discussed petitions, letter-writing campaigns, silent vigils, walks, student strikes, mass legal demonstrations, voter initiatives, fasts, noncooperation with conscription, occupations, and sit-ins. I must emphasize, however, that for every type of nonviolent action I have discussed, there are at least a dozen that I have not discussed, including, among many others, teach-ins, guerilla theatre, picketing, work slowdowns, work stoppages, general strikes, tax resistance, and lysistratic resistance. This book is, after all, not meant to be an encyclopædic treatise—for that, the reader is referred to Gene Sharp's three-volume *The Politics of Nonviolent Action* (1973)—but rather a memoir. I intend in this chapter to compare and contrast some salient features of violence and nonviolence as a social change tool, but first let us review briefly four categories of nonviolent action techniques I have discussed in this volume: personal witness, legal direct action, noncooperation, and nonviolent destruction of property.

First, I discussed individual, *personal witness*. When I was in ninth grade and wore my big, blue "Peace in Vietnam" button to school, and got into trouble with Mr. Ranhoeffer, I did not seriously think that my small, individual act of wearing a peace button to class would have any effect at all on the war. I nevertheless wore my button because sometimes, when one sees something very bad happening, there is a need to witness against it, even where there is no hope of being effective.

In 2002, when the United States was gearing up to invade Afghanistan, my friend Joyce Katzberg stood during her lunch hour every day for weeks in a park across the street from the courthouse in Providence bearing a sign that said simply, "No War in Afghanistan." Joyce surely knew that her action did not prevent one bomb from falling, did not save the life of a single Afghani civilian or American GI. Joyce simply felt the personal necessity to speak against the violence she deplored, despite the almost certain knowledge that her action was, by most conventional standards, useless.

During World War II, there was a pious Catholic Austrian peasant, Franz Jägerstetter, who believed that what the Nazis were doing was incompatible with his faith as a Christian. He refused induction into the Nazi Army, and he denounced Hitler and the Gestapo. Not surprisingly, Jägerstetter was arrested. But he was no Jew, and the Nazis offered to release Jägerstetter if only he would recant. The local bishop pleaded with Jägerstetter, emphasizing the impossibility of his witness having any influence on policies emanating from Berlin. The Gestapo brought letters to the prisoner from his three young children pleading with him to come home. But Jägerstetter was firm; because of the biblical command to love your neighbor, he found it religiously impossible to support Hitler. On August 9, 1943, Franz Jägerstetter was beheaded.

It would be fatuous of me to compare my action of wearing a peace button to school in Great Neck in 1965 to Jägerstetter's witness, and I am certainly not doing so. But in high school, I read Gordon Zahn's biography of Jägerstetter, *In Solitary Witness* (1966), and was deeply moved. The lesson that I came away from that book with is that, when a person is confronted by a very great evil, there may be a moral obligation to witness against the evil, even if one has little or no hope of being effective.

To put it another way, the personal, perhaps quixotic, individual witness—the simple, existential statement of belief—has a place in the arsenal of the nonviolent activist.

At the same time, I am reminded of what Dave McReynolds said in that speech on Tuesday evening, December 6, 1966, that I described in chapter 2, about how difficult it is to know in advance when our small, personal witnesses will or will not be effective in changing society. In that speech, McReynolds spoke of the Montgomery bus boycott:

> Rosa Parks did not sit down in the front of that bus in 1956 because some central planning committee had decided that the strategic mo-

ment for integration had finally arrived and that her act would spark a revolution. Rosa Parks sat down in the front of the bus because she was tired, and she was angry, and she was tired of being angry, and she didn't care if she was arrested just for being human. And yet, her single action, her individual witness, *did* spark a revolution.

Much the same can be said for David Miller burning his draft card at the Whitehall induction center on October 15, 1965, in the immediate aftermath of the new law that made draft card burning a felony punishable by five years' imprisonment. Miller was arrested two days later and sentenced to two and a half years. On October 17, handcuffed and confronting a long prison sentence, Miller had no way of knowing whether his action had been a useless, quixotic personal witness or the beginning of a nationwide movement that succeeded in filling the prisons, swamping the courts, and eventually ending the draft.

Similarly, on October 27, 1967, when Phil Berrigan poured blood on those draft files in Baltimore, no one knew whether, in hubris and great folly, he would go to prison for twenty-three years and there be forgotten to all but a few movement faithful, or whether his Action would be a model for scores of people taking out hundreds of draft boards from coast to coast for years to come. With our 20–20 hindsight, we now know that the latter occurred, but it is important to keep in mind that, in October 1967, it was by no means certain that this would be the case.

The second type of nonviolent action I discussed in this book is *legal direct action*. The Tiger Cage Vigil and Fast is a good example, for fasting and public vigils and demonstrations are classic forms of legal direct action. Our grassroots organizing work in 1982 in support of the nuclear Freeze referendum question on the Rhode Island ballot is another good example of legal direct action. I recently spoke with a friend of mine who had been heavily involved in the referendum campaign. She commented that she had never considered that effort to be an example of legal, nonviolent direct action. (I was reminded of the college student who was surprised to learn, upon taking her freshman English course, that she had been speaking in prose her entire life, and hadn't even been aware of the fact.) The ostensible focus of the referendum campaign was the ballot question, and having the Freeze win in nine states out of ten in the largest national referendum in American history was certainly important. Nevertheless, the real purpose in our referendum campaign was that it gave us the opportunity to go door to door to almost every house in Rhode Island, speaking to people about the dangers of the nuclear arms race and about actions everyone could take to oppose the arms race. This is classic nonviolent action.

The third type of nonviolent action I have discussed here is *noncooperation*. My refusal to take shelter during the air raid drill in high school was an example of noncooperation, as was my public refusal to register for the draft in August 1969.

Noncooperation is, without a doubt, one of the most important weapons in the pacifist's arsenal. For centuries, the history of revolution has been the story of strong central governments falling when those governments lost the support of their own people. This was true of the French revolution, the American revolution, the Cuban revolution.

My personal experience has persuaded me of the effectiveness of noncooperation as a means for effecting social change. In high school, we petitioned against air raid drills, held forums on the issue, and sought exemption for individuals who were conscientiously opposed to participation in the drills. None of this worked. Then on Friday, December 20, 1968, about three dozen students simply refused to take part in a shelter drill. The school did not know what to do with this noncooperation. Two of us were suspended from school, but, at the same time, that was the last air raid drill that the school ever had.

In the case of a government that wants to wage war, the situation is particularly stark. In World War II, Hitler wanted to invade Czechoslovakia (then Poland, then France, then Russia. . . .), but Hitler was not about to go to the front lines himself to fight. In the case of Vietnam, Presidents Johnson and Nixon wanted to make war on Vietnam (and Laos, and Cambodia), but, although I looked for this carefully, I never saw either president with helmet on head and rifle in hand lying in a foxhole at Khe Sanh getting shelled. Johnson and Nixon understood, quite correctly, that doing that would have been *dangerous*; they could have been seriously hurt. Johnson and Nixon wanted to make a war in Vietnam, but they wanted *me* to fight it for them. When I, and millions of other young men refused to go in a myriad of ways—leaving the country, feigning illness, registering as conscientious objectors, "forgetting" to register but doing it quietly, or resisting publicly—both the war and the draft ended. And all of these methods are variations on the theme of noncooperation.

Finally, I have discussed carefully planned, public, *nonviolent destruction of property*. As I said earlier, the draft-board Actions were effective on two different levels. In the narrowest, most immediate sense, we stopped literally hundreds of draft boards from functioning. In the context of all the other anti-draft activity at the time, the government found it impossible to redistribute quotas from draft boards that had been raided to other draft boards. Put plainly, we saved lives, and that is not a small matter. In the wider sense, the draft-board Actions raised the cost to the government of prosecuting the war in much the same way that the 1968 prosecution of Dr. Spock and Rev. Coffin raised the cost of the war. All of these—like the acts of individual draft resisters—put the government on the horns of an exquisite dilemma. The government could prosecute and jail us by the hundreds or thousands, thereby creating martyrs for the movement, casting the government in a highly unfavorable light, and providing priceless favorable publicity for the movement. Or the government could *not* prosecute us, thereby sending out the unmistakable signal that you could resist the draft or destroy draft files with impunity. Whichever tack the government took, it would be bad for the government and good for the movement.

Considering these various forms of nonviolent action together, several themes emerge.

First, nonviolent direct action is not synonymous with civil disobedience. Many people believe that "nonviolent direct action" is simply a euphemism for "civil disobedience." That is not true. The eight-week Tiger Cage Vigil and Fast at the U.S. Capitol in 1974 was one of the most effective direct action efforts I have ever been involved with. All three components of the project—the fast, the vigil, and the visits to members of Congress—were entirely legal.

Second, the cumulative effects of different forms of nonviolent direct action are synergistic. In order to stand a reasonable chance of success, a nonviolent action campaign usually must embrace a variety of different methods or techniques. These individual methods or techniques may make little or no sense when viewed separately, and only seem sensible or reasonable when viewed within the broader context of the overall campaign. A few examples will illustrate this point.

The tactic of destruction of draft files was very effective in stopping the draft by rendering hundreds of draft boards inoperable. But some of that effectiveness depended on the wider context of many other, far less radical anti-draft actions at the time, including men registering as conscientious objectors, fleeing to Canada, feigning disabilities to obtain deferments or exemptions, and quietly refusing the register. The men who feigned disabilities or quietly "forgot" to register were not engaged in classic civil disobedience because they were not publicly announcing their noncooperation and accepting the consequences. Nevertheless, all these men provided the crucial, indispensable context that made our draft-board Actions effective, because it was the cumulative effect of the actions of all these men that created the situation that most local draft boards were not even meeting their own draft quotas before our Actions. Thus, when we hit certain draft boards and Selective Service tried to redistribute quotas from those boards to other draft boards, that effort was doomed to failure.

Civil disobedience should never (or almost never) be the first tactic used by social change activists when addressing a particular issue, because without the other, legal methods of protest and movement-building—most especially community outreach and public education—civil disobedience lacks context and will not be readily understood by the public. By the same token, once a movement has laid a firm foundation of outreach and education on an issue, civil disobedience can add a depth and dimension and urgency to our work that nothing else matches. In his classic *Letter From a Birmingham Jail* (1963), Martin Luther King Jr. wrote: "In any nonviolent campaign, there are four basic steps: collection of the facts to determine whether injustices exist, negotiation, self-purification, and direct action." (It is clear from the context of the *Letter* that King, in discussing direct action, was referring to both legal demonstrations and nonviolent civil disobedience.)

The same thing is true about lobbying efforts aimed specifically at Congress. In the previous chapter I discussed the tremendous success after 1972 of the Coalition to Stop Funding the War and how, for the first time since the war began, peace activists nationwide began devoting a large part of their efforts to lobbying Congress. Our efforts were successful; U.S. financial support for the war declined precipitously, and the war ended the following spring when liberation forces captured Saigon and the U.S. and its puppet were unable to respond. Peace activists nationwide, buoyed by our obviously swift success in ending the war by means of using what we called our "congressional strategy," tried to apply our newly learned lesson to other issues. Just one example of this was AFSC's nationwide campaign to stop deployment of the B-1 bomber during the late 1970s. For the most part, these efforts to apply our wonderful congressional strategy to other issues failed badly. This was because the movement had taken the wrong lesson from our quick success ending the war by means of lobbying Congress. The *wrong* lesson for the movement to learn was that lobbying Congress was the correct tactic that worked to end the war, and was far more successful than the public vigils, teach-ins, legal demonstrations, draft resistance, and draft-board Actions. The *right* lesson was that the focus on Congress worked so quickly in 1974 and 1975 *because* it had been preceded by a decade of public vigils, teach-ins, legal demonstrations, draft resistance, and draft-board Actions. It is almost always the wrong question to ask which is the one right tactic to use to effect social change; in order to be strong and successful, a movement must use a variety of tactics, from public education to legal direct action to civil disobedience.

A third theme emerges from my discussion of nonviolent action techniques. Nonviolence does not mean inaction, and pacifists should never be passive. In 1969 and 1970, I raided and destroyed files at fourteen draft boards, rendering those boards inoperable. Then I traveled all over the Northeast using those Actions as a springboard to organize more draft resistance. In 1975, when the government denied AFSC licenses to ship humanitarian relief supplies to Vietnam, I initiated and helped organize 6,000 people in fifty-two cities nationwide to contribute money to the illegal shipments and then turn themselves in to the FBI with written confessions that they had violated the Trading with the Enemy Act. In one fell swoop we raised hundreds of thousands of dollars for the relief effort and forced the government to reverse its license denial. It is simply a false dichotomy to posit that one's only choices when confronting injustice are to accept the status quo or use violence to work for change.

When one compares and contrasts violence and nonviolence as techniques for effecting social change, there are both similarities and differences. As a committed pacifist, I will always argue that the differences (which I will discuss in a moment) are important. Nevertheless, there are tremendous similarities between the two types of tactics as well. These are similarities that pacifists are often reluctant to acknowledge, perhaps out of fear of somehow compromising the purity of their beliefs.

First, and perhaps most obviously, both violence and nonviolence can work as effective tools for social change. (Pacifists just naturally hate to acknowledge that violence works.) In 1959, in Cuba, the young lawyer Fidel Castro successfully used violence to overthrow Fulgencio Batista, a despotic and brutal dictator who did not hesitate to use torture and murder to stay in power. In 1986, in the Philippines, Corazon Aquino used nonviolence to overthrow Ferdinand Marcos, a despotic and brutal dictator who did not hesitate to use torture and murder to stay in power. I emphasize the despotic and brutal nature of the dictator overthrown in each case because one of the most frequently heard canards about nonviolence is that it can only work against "civilized" opponents, but not against brutal dictators who resort to murder in order to stay in power. This just isn't true.

One of the most revolutionary things about Gandhi was the irrefutable way in which he demonstrated that nonviolence can, in fact, be used to accomplish some of the same things that can be accomplished through the use of violence. In 1776, the American colonies staged a successful revolution against British colonial rule using violence as the chief tactic. In the twentieth century, the Indians staged a successful revolution against British colonial rule using nonviolence as the chief tactic. Anyone who thinks that Gandhi's effectiveness depended on the fact that his opponents were the "civilized" (read: white) British should reflect for a moment on, for example, the Amritsar Massacre on April 13, 1919, when British soldiers fired on a peaceful crowd of unarmed Indians who were protesting against British rule, killing hundreds and wounding well over 1,000 more.

There is an ironic symmetry in the baseless opinions held by many pacifists and by many nonpacifists about the effectiveness of *other* people's tactics. As I said, pacifists hate to acknowledge that violence works, but of course it sometimes does. Nonpacifists are equally reluctant to acknowledge that nonviolence works, but of course it often does, too.

The other side of the coin is that both violence and nonviolence can fail. When Fidel Castro's compatriot, the physician Chè Guevara, went to Bolivia to make the revolution there by force of arms he failed miserably. Guevara was caught by the Bolivian Army in 1967 and immediately shot; today, more than three decades later, there has still been no revolution in Bolivia. Nonviolence can fail, too. I have already described how peace activists in the United States conducted a nationwide effort in the 1970s to prevent deployment of the B-1 bomber. We, too, failed miserably. Today, the Air Force describes the B-1 as "the backbone of America's long-range bomber force." B-1s carry nuclear weapons, and have conventional capability as well, as we saw in the American bombing of Afghanistan in 2002 and Iraq in 2003.

Another similarity between violence and nonviolence is that using either one can impose the risk of suffering, injury, or death on the participant. Nonpacifists often view the sacrifices involved in nonviolent action as a major drawback: if I resist the draft, I will almost surely go to jail; if I sit in on the railroad tracks, I could be run over by a train. What sort of deranged masochist would actually *invite* risk and sacrifice needlessly?

To be sure, nonviolent action does entail risk. In 1987, Brian Willson, a Vietnam veteran, had his skull fractured and lost both his legs while trying to block a train carrying munitions bound for El Salvador and Nicaragua. Both the Navy and the train crew had been given advance notice of the fast and sit-in at the Naval Weapons Station in Concord, California, and yet the train actually accelerated when it approached the peaceful protesters on the railroad tracks. On March 16, 2003, American peace activist Rachel Corrie was killed in the Gaza Strip when she was run over by an Israeli bulldozer, as she nonviolently attempted to stop the demolition of the home of a Palestinian physician. Both the Israeli authorities and the driver of the bulldozer were well aware of the sit-in in advance, and Corrie was in plain view of the driver when she was killed.

Even leaving aside these relatively extreme examples, it is well known that participating in nonviolent action entails inconvenience and risk. Phil Berrigan spent eleven of the last thirty-five years of his life behind bars. When Carol Bragg fasted on the Capitol steps for sixty-two days in 1974, protesting the war, the experience was difficult and sometimes painful. Each and every one of the thousands of draft resisters prosecuted during the Vietnam War would probably have much preferred not spending months or years in prison.

Yet there is something hypocritical about the criticism of nonviolent action because of the risk it entails of suffering, inconvenience, or even death. It is universally acknowledged that violence and war entail serious risks. Every soldier in history who has served in wartime has known with absolute certainty that he might come home minus a few limbs or in a body bag. Yet, the certain knowledge of the potentially serious consequences associated with war—while it often leads individuals to try to *evade* service themselves—rarely leads people to declare that the institution itself of war is naïve and unrealistic or that the participants in war are unstable masochists. This knowledge, for instance, did not prevent young Americans from lining up outside recruiting offices in the aftermath of the Pearl Harbor attack.

The fact is that accomplishing something worthwhile in this world most frequently involves commitment, risk, and—yes—even sacrifice. In this sense, using violence and using nonviolence are quite alike.

Nevertheless, despite the many important similarities between violence and nonviolence as means for achieving social change, there are, I think, at least three salient differences between the two techniques.

First, the use of violence against other human beings is wrong and immoral, but the use of nonviolence is not. It is too late in the day to argue about whether violence is or is not immoral, and I do not intend to make any extended argument on that point here. In the statement I presented to "my" draft board when I refused to register, I said: "The Sixth Commandment says simply, 'Thou shalt not kill.' It does not say, 'Thou shalt not kill, except if he is a Communist, or except if he is a Nazi, or except if. . . .'" This is nothing more than a restatement of the lesson that most children learn in the schoolyard when they are in first grade: two wrongs don't make a right. As innumerable teachers have told innumerable students after innumerable schoolyard altercations, "I don't care if Billy hit you first; you are just not allowed to fight at school." Interestingly, all military generals in recent centuries (except perhaps for a few true sociopaths) agree that war and violence are regrettable and bad. The generals argue that, while war is a very, very bad thing, it is, sadly, sometimes necessary. The insight of the pacifist is that if war is bad and immoral, we just won't participate. The pacifist is not interested in listening to the excuses of the Nazi general invading Poland in September 1939 or the American general in Vietnam in 1969 or the Soviet general in Afghanistan in 1980 about why *this* war is different, why *this* war, while regrettable, is justified by lofty goals. The pacifist says that the orgy of killing and bloodletting that are the inevitable concomitant of war is just never morally acceptable, and that we will not participate in it under any guise or any ruse.

In short, the first difference between violence and nonviolence is the moral or ethical one: one is right and one is wrong.

The second difference between the use of violence and nonviolence by social change movements is that violence is rarely practical, effective, or sensible, and sometimes it is downright suicidal. One thing we know for sure about governments is that they are heavily armed and rarely hesitate to use violence to preserve their power when they perceive their authority to be threatened or undermined. When social change activists use violence against the government, they are meeting the government on its own terms, in an arena in which the government has undisputed and overwhelming superiority, military might. That is stupid.

Consider the Days of Rage in October 1969, organized by the Weatherman faction of SDS to "bring the war home," as they put it, by raising the domestic cost of prosecuting the war through street rioting in Chicago. Weatherman spent months organizing the event nationwide; organizers predicted that 10,000 urban youth would come to Chicago to participate. The main problem with the Days of Rage was not that only a couple hundred scruffy kids turned up wearing helmets and armed with steel pipes to riot in the streets, attack police officers and trash buildings and cars. The main problem with the Days of Rage was that, regardless of how many kids turned up, the police, the FBI, and the military would *always* have the demonstrators outgunned. The Weatherman faction of SDS against the entire armed might of the United States? What a joke! Armed confrontation with the United States government was just not going to work. (The pathetic turnout despite months of arduous organizing probably does say something about the ability of violence as a tactic to attract a truly mass movement, especially when viewed in light of what else was happening in the country that autumn, including the massive Moratorium Day demonstrations that attracted millions of participants nationwide in October and November 1969.)

The genius of nonviolent action is that it does not meet the government in the arena, military might, in which the government has undisputed and overwhelming superiority. Instead, the use of nonviolence changes the rules of the game, switching the arena of battle to an arena where the movement can properly claim superiority, the arena of what is right and just. Consider the pro-independence demonstrators in India who were gunned down in the Amritsar massacre. No amount of armed resistance would have benefited the demonstrators, for the British forces had overwhelming firepower. But by using nonviolence as their weapon, the pro-independence demonstrators accomplished something they could never have accomplished by force of arms. They gave an irresistible push to the independence struggle. Today, historians point to the Amritsar Massacre as the crucial turning point in the Indian fight for independence; indeed, British historian Alfred Draper's book on the event is subtitled "The Massacre That Ended the British Raj." Gandhi launched his *satyagraha* campaign for independence in the immediate aftermath of the massacre, and the rest is history.

Much the same thing is true about the events in Birmingham, Alabama, in May 1963, at the height of the civil rights struggle, events that gave rise to Dr. King's *Letter,* which I quoted earlier. King and the Reverend Fred Shuttlesworth led a series of peaceful civil rights demonstrations (involving both legal demonstrations and civil disobedience) in what Dr. King referred to at the time as "probably the most thoroughly segregated city in the United States." Birmingham's police chief, Bull Connor, turned attack dogs and fire hoses on the peaceful demonstrators. The photographs of these events electrified the nation. King and Shuttlesworth knew they could never win a violent confrontation, for they were outgunned. But in this direct confrontation between overwhelming armed might and the power of nonviolence, the power of nonviolence won an unequivocal and long-term victory. As President Kennedy commented at the time, no one since President Lincoln had done more to advance the cause of civil rights than Bull Connor.

My discussion of the peaceful civil rights demonstrations in Birmingham in 1963 and Weatherman's violent Days of Rage in Chicago six years later raises an interesting issue. Both violent action and even the most carefully planned nonviolent civil disobedience can be off-putting to many people. In the case of Birmingham, the very occasion for Dr. King's *Letter* was a statement published by eight Alabama clergymen, including three bishops, criticizing the civil rights demonstrators for acting too precipitously and for breaking the law. In the case of the Days of Rage, ordinary Americans were so repulsed by the rioting that even some peace activists at the time wondered whether the event had been organized by Nixon's *agents provocateurs*. Yet the nonviolent activist, with her quiet dignity, combined with both the willingness to accept suffering herself and the unwillingness to inflict it on others through violence, stands a far better chance in the end of winning over the skeptics than does the rowdy violent activist. It is not an accident or a coincidence that today we have a national holiday commemorating the birth of Dr. King, while even many of the former members of Weatherman have come to see that their experiments with what they called at the time revolutionary violence were a mistake. Pacifists like me argue that the issue of nonviolence's *moral* superiority over violence is directly linked to the fact of its *tactical* superiority, but one need not be an absolute pacifist to recognize the tactical advantages of nonviolence in most situations.

There is also a third, and crucial, difference between violence and nonviolence. On July 16, 1945, the world entered the nuclear-weapons age when the United States exploded a test atomic bomb in the desert outside Alamogordo, New Mexico. By the 1950s, the United States and the Soviet Union had enough nuclear weapons to end all life on the planet. By the 1970s, the two superpowers had enough nuclear weapons to kill every man, woman and child on earth about twenty-four times over. Today, there are nine declared nuclear-weapons states (United States, Russia, United Kingdom, France, China, Israel, India, Pakistan and North Korea), and a score of additional states that could develop nuclear-weapons capability within a short time if they decided to do so. The nuclear-weapons arsenal and nuclear-fuel stockpile of the former Soviet Union are not secure, and there is widespread concern about international trafficking in bomb-grade nuclear fuel, and the danger this poses of atomic bombs getting into the hands of private terrorist organizations. (I use the term "private terrorist organizations" advisedly because governments—including the United States government—are engaging in terrorism of their own, having held the people of the world as nuclear hostages for years and decades.) The world has repeatedly come to the brink of nuclear war, either as a result of deliberate government policy (as in the Cuban Missile Crisis of 1962) or because of an accident (as when a 52¢ computer chip at NORAD failed in 1982, falsely showing that the United States was under attack by the Soviet Union, and we came within a few minutes of launching an all-out "retaliatory" strike against the USSR).

What is unique and different about nuclear weapons is that they threaten to end all life on the planet. The world emerged from the Crusades of the Middle Ages (though not without consequences that still plague us today; events do have consequences), but the Crusades, grim as they were, did not threaten to end life on the planet. Between 1348 and 1350, a third of the population of Europe was lost to plague, yet there was no threat to life on the planet. Today, for the first time, we are threatening not merely the extinction of our species, but the extinction of all species. This is something quite new in the history of the world.

In the aftermath of Hiroshima, Albert Einstein said, "The unleashed power of the atom has changed everything save our modes of thinking, and we thus drift toward unparalleled catastrophe." Humankind's traditional mode of thinking—an eye for an eye; defend yourself against violence by using superior violence—may always have been maladaptive and stupid, but never until now did this traditional way of thinking threaten extinction of all life on earth. Today even regional wars and other smaller conflicts threaten to escalate and become an unprecedented holocaust. In this context, even those who might have supported, say, the Revolutionary War in 1776 or the American Civil War or World War I might have pause about supporting war today when the result may be the end of life on earth.

13
Neither Fish nor Fowl

THROUGHOUT MY LIFE I HAVE HAD A FEELING of not really fitting in, of somehow being neither fish nor fowl.

An early influence on me was the writings of Bertrand Russell. When I was in junior high school I found his slim volume, *Essays In Skepticism* (1950), on my father's bookshelf. It is no coincidence that the book was also published under the title *Unpopular Essays*. In this wonderful little book, Russell inveighs against religious and other superstition, racism and other prejudices, retrograde sexual mores, and jingoism. I loved Russell's plain, direct style and his simple but brilliant exposition. In later years, I read many other works by Russell, but at this earlier time I was especially impressed with the meaning of the twin titles of this one. If a person thinks skeptically or independently, he is bound to be unpopular. The two alternative titles almost sent the message that the skeptic is unpopular.

When I joined WRL's staff in New York in 1969, all of my co-workers —Jim Peck, Dave McReynolds, Ralph DiGia, Igal Roodenko, even the secretary, Liz Aberman—had worked at WRL together for years. In fact, except for Dave, who had only been there for a decade or so, they had all worked there since before I was born. I felt like an outsider thrown in with a group of old friends. Although in some ways I fit in ideologically, I was almost alone in the office in my support of draft-file destruction. Also, I was a full generation younger than most of the staff. Jim, for example, had two sons who were about my age. At about the same time as my father had been drafted to serve in World War II, Ralph, Jim, and Igal had all been drafted too, but they had gone to prison as draft resisters. The reason these men seemed old enough to be my father is that they were.

The differences between me and those in the Catholic Left need hardly be belabored. The Berrigans, Dougherties, O'Rourkes, and Melvilles were, in many respects, religious Catholics. They were priests for whom the words of Jesus and the Apostles stood at the center of their political motivation; the parish and seminary stood at the center of their social world. It is not to be wondered at that a boisterous eighteen-year-old Jewish kid from the New York suburbs might feel a bit at sea among these middle-aged Irish Catholic priests.

At the retreats leading up to the Boston Eight Action, I felt that I was neither fish nor fowl. I agreed with the Catholic Left that civil disobedience, specifically destroying draft files, was a correct and important way to oppose the war. On the other hand, I did not really fit in with the Catholic Left either. At the cultural level, I was unable to join in the dinner-table discussions with anecdotes about the funny things my sixth-grade catechism teacher had done, and the teachings of our Lord Jesus were not what animated my resistance activities.

At the political level, too, I split with the group because when they said that going to prison was part of the *purpose* of their Action because suffering is itself redemptive, I had to say, "No, thank you."

AFSC of the 1970s was a very WASPy organization. Quakers are not merely Anglo-Saxon Protestants; their form of worship is *silence*. Every other Jewish AFSC staff person I ever discussed this with during the years I was on the staff shared my feeling of being a bit of an outsider in a very gentile organization. The way I was regarded by some AFSC staff and committee members put me in mind of the scene in *Annie Hall* in which Woody Allen imagines Annie Hall's midwestern gentile family viewing him as a Chasid with beard and *peyis*.

I am not trying to assign blame here; indeed, if anyone in this situation is to "blame" at all it is I. No one told me to seek out Phil Berrigan in 1969 and hang out with the Catholic Left. I did that as a result of carefully thought-out decisions, for reasons that at the time seemed good and which since then I have never come to doubt or regret. Yet, the feeling is nevertheless inescapable that I did not fully fit in with that crowd. Much the same can be said about my years in AFSC. My many years with that organization were not a result of mistake, accident, or coincidence. I chose to become affiliated with AFSC; I chose to maintain that connection for many years; and I do not regret a nanosecond of that association. Yet, the fact remains that I did not fully fit in.

In law school, the factors that set me apart were legion. I was the only convicted felon in Harvard Law School's class of 1990. When my criminal law professor described certain procedures that occur following a criminal arrest, I raised my hand and said, "In my experience, the process is somewhat different." When the same class studied the federal aiding and abetting statute, Title 18 U.S. Code Section 2, the professor asked me to bring my indictment from the RIPOFF Action to class to discuss with the students.

I was nearly a generation older than most of the students in law school, and was older than some of the professors. My classmates, who were amazingly and wonderfully diverse—racially, geographically, and politically—were all of a kind academically. Whatever college or university they had come from—small or large, private or state—they were all academic superstars. I alone had a long record from high school of flunking courses and getting frequent Cs and Ds when I had not flunked.

My first job out of law school was at a medium-sized firm (thirty-five lawyers) in Providence. I was as old as the partners but merely a first-year associate. The other associates were mostly single and without family obligations. They would occasionally go out for a beer after work and sometimes invited me to join them, but by then I was a single parent and had to pick my son Jonathan up from school, go home and put dinner on the table, and then read him a bedtime story. Neither fish nor fowl.

In my present firm, where we are five lawyers, the attorneys and staff all get together once a week on Fridays to have lunch together. People talk about sports—the Red Sox, the Super Bowl, the basketball playoffs—but I don't follow sports and cannot join in. People talk about favorite television programs but I don't have a television. A favorite recurring jest at these luncheons is for someone to ask me pointedly how I liked last night's episode of one show or another. I know perfectly well that these jibes are not hostile, that this is only good-natured ribbing. Yet the jokes do highlight how different I am from my colleagues.

My old friends from the peace movement view me as a corporate lawyer. My law partners view me as a peace activist. In the peace movement, I was viewed as being extremely entrepreneurial. I started an AFSC office and under my management it expanded rapidly. I was concerned with fundraising for the office, had grand plans for raising money, and consistently met or exceeded fundraising goals. While so many peace activists either loathe fundraising or do it poorly (or both; the two phenomena are doubtlessly linked), I raised money with gusto. Yet, in the world of corporate law practice, I am viewed as hopelessly unentrepreneurial. I have no ability at marketing and less than no interest in it. I do lots of *pro bono* work for peace and civil liberties groups, but have never brought in a paying client. I am everybody's first choice for researching and writing cerebral briefs on arcane or obscure points of law, but am also viewed as having little sense about the practicalities and finances of running a law firm.

Miss Ely taught me to view things skeptically, to question everything. I took that lesson to heart, and it has made for a somewhat contentious life. On the first day of sixth grade, when Miss Kozlarek lied to her class and said that we would plan our schedule together but meant no such thing, I was immediately on to her and let her know. Twenty-five years later, when a bookkeeper embezzled money and AFSC thought that the right way to remedy centuries of racial injustice was to look the other way because he was black, I just couldn't swallow it. By contrast, Communist Party members and all those who slavishly follow a party line, of whatever party or ideology, have it relatively easier. Even if they are out of step with mainstream culture, at least they fit in well with their own organization, even if that group is a tiny minority.

They may not be fish, but at least they are fowl. I have often felt that I am neither.

Afterword

ANNIVERSARIES ARE IMPORTANT. Every year on June 19 I return to Burnside Park in downtown Providence to spend a few minutes where Bug and I surfaced for the RIPOFF Action on that date in 1970. I see the hill where we stood at our press conference and, in my mind's eye, I picture Bug (age nineteen) and me (age eighteen) standing on that hill with a hand-held microphone, holding our press conference. I am wearing a white turtleneck and beads. I see the lines of plainclothes police officers and FBI agents watching us, with United States Attorney Linc Almond towering over everyone else. I see the TV cameras and newspaper reporters.

My visit doesn't take long—my office is downtown, just a few blocks from the park—but it is important to me to go every year. Visiting Burnside Park on June 19 is a way of honoring what I did, and remembering why I did it, and reflecting on how glad I shall always be that I somehow found the courage to do it. It is like remembering my Oma Elmer each year on her birthday, November 24, by making a special dinner, maybe *Wiener Schnitzel* or *Kastanienreis*.

I was a third-year law student on November 7, 1989, the twentieth anniversary of the Boston Eight Action. In 1989, there was a Thai restaurant on the ground floor of the building at 25 Huntington Avenue, the building that twenty years earlier had housed the Copley Square draft boards—the building in which I had spent the long, drizzly night of November 7, 1969, eating hero sandwiches, drinking ginger ale, and destroying draft files. I observed the twentieth anniversary of the Boston Eight Action by having dinner at the Thai restaurant. I also took a quick look through the building—its floor plan is indelibly set in my mind—and saw the back stairwell where I had hidden and the office now occupying Room 510.

In June 1990, I graduated *cum laude* from Harvard Law School on the twentieth anniversary of the RIPOFF Action.

That same spring, I applied for a license to practice law in Rhode Island. Naturally, one of the questions on the bar application is whether I had ever been convicted of a felony. I knew that, because my answer was yes, my application would receive special scrutiny.

It is the Character and Fitness Committee of the bar association that screens applicants to see if they are decent and moral enough to become practicing attorneys. In nearly all cases, the applicant has an extremely brief, perfunctory meeting with a member of the committee, and is then approved. I would not have been surprised, of course, if my meeting with the Committee had not been perfunctory. On the day of my interview, I was a bit nervous. I did not for a moment regret my participation in the RIPOFF Action, but I was also acutely conscious of the fact that I might not be allowed to practice law because of my criminal record. My interviewer, however, was far more nervous than I was. He dithered around a bit, seemingly tongue-tied. Then he said what was on his mind.

"So, you're the guy who destroyed all those draft files in 1970?"

"Yes, I am," I said. I was just getting ready to start in on my *spiel* about nonviolence, Thoreau, Gandhi, and Martin Luther King Jr., when my interviewer spoke again.

"My brother was classified 1-A when you did that. You probably saved his life. I've been waiting twenty years to thank you. You're approved."

That was the end of the interview.

Rhode Island has a separate bar membership for the Federal Court for the District of Rhode Island. After practicing law for about a year, I completed the requirements for the federal bar. In November 1991, I was sworn in as a member of the federal bar in the very same courtroom where Judge Day had sentenced Bug and me exactly twenty years earlier.

Index